Brief Histories

General Editor: Jeremy Black

Eastern Europe 1939–2000

Mark Pittaway

A member of the Hodder Headline Group
LONDON
Distributed in the United States of America by
Oxford University Press Inc., New York

First published in Great Britain in 2004 by
Arnold, a member of the Hodder Headline Group,
338 Euston Road, London NW1 3BH

http://www.arnoldpublishers.com

Distributed in the United States of America by
Oxford University Press Inc.
198 Madison Avenue, New York, NY10016

The advice and information in this book are believed to be true and
accurate at the date of going to press, but neither the author nor the publisher
can accept any legal responsibility or liability for any errors or omissions.

British Library Cataloguing in Publication Data
A catalogue record for this book is available from the British Library

Library of Congress Cataloging-in-Publication Data
A catalog record for this book is available from the Library of Congress

ISBN 0 340 76220 9 (hb)
ISBN 0 340 76219 5 (pb)

1 2 3 4 5 6 7 8 9 10

Typeset in 10 on 13 pt Utopia by Phoenix Photosetting, Chatham, Kent
Printed and bound in Malta

What do you think about this book? Or any other Arnold title?
Please send your comments to feedback.arnold@hodder.co.uk

Contents

Preface

This brief history of the origins, nature and aftermath of the socialist dictatorships that governed 'the lands between' Germany and the Soviet Union for much of the post-war period serves two purposes. First, it is intended as a thematic survey of the history of the Eastern European region during the second part of the twentieth century, a survey that concentrates on the everyday experience of the inhabitants of the states of the region and its relationship to multiple political upheavals. Second, it forms an extended interpretative essay, which aims to sketch the contours of a 'new' history of the region, a new history that has been made possible by the political developments of the last two decades. Crucially, however, this book is written at a time when historians are only starting to lay the foundations of that new history. Thus it is very much a first word, and is intended more to stimulate new thinking about aspects of the history, particularly the social history, of post-war Eastern Europe, than to present a definitive synthesis.

The political changes of the late 1980s and early 1990s created almost unparalleled opportunities for prospective historians of the region. Access to archival sources that relate to the wartime and post-war period have improved enormously, though somewhat unevenly. The ending of socialist dictatorship marked its passing into history by opening up public space for historical debate. Political taboos that constrained research before have been lifted – even if new political actors in some states of the region have sought to enact new ones. Political, economic, social and cultural transformations across the region have had an impact. These range from the tragic wars of succession in the states of the former Yugoslavia, to the imperfect consolidation of liberal democratic institutions in the states conventionally regarded as Central Europe – the Czech Republic, Hungary, Poland, Slovakia and Slovenia. Economic transformation has reshaped society, destroying many of the social institutions that shaped the fabric of everyday life under socialism, marginalizing social groups – like the industrial working class – previously believed to be hegemonic, and generating new social constituencies. The redrawing of boundaries and borders has reconstructed the identities of the inhabitants of the region as new states were carved out of Czechoslovakia and Yugoslavia. Central European states, like Hungary, rediscovered their cultural links to western neighbours, while those consigned to the south-eastern periphery faced new patterns of exclusion. All these transformations have changed the way in which the past, and particularly the recent past, has been seen.

While historians have been quick to discover the mountains of new material previously hidden in Central and Eastern European archives, they have, with a few notable exceptions, been slow to think through the implications of the changes occurring around them for their own practice. This has been understandable given the bewildering speed of radical transformation and the lack of an adequate pre-existing literature that could provide pointers. Yet this rethinking of the recent history of the region is nevertheless an urgent task, because of the political and cultural issues to which that past is relevant in the region today. Sections of the population perceive that the disappearance of dictatorship has been accompanied by the removal of the basic material security they felt during its existence, and have come to invest in nostalgia for the past. At the same time, both new and not-so-new political élites have legitimized political programmes through recourse to mythologized versions of the recent past. At one extreme, in the former Yugoslavia, this has had especially tragic consequences. With the growing fluidity of borders, both within Eastern Europe and between it and the rest of the continent – a process likely to be accelerated as the consequences of the first wave of enlargement of the European Union in 2004 become apparent – concerns that could be identified previously as peculiar to the region are likely to become the concerns of Europe as a whole.

Understanding the recent past of the region and its inhabitants is vital, therefore, to both an understanding of its present and an ability to sketch its likely future. If this kind of understanding is to be achieved, however, it demands that histories of the region shift their thematic focus. The focus of most historical research into the recent past of the region has been and, to a considerable extent, continues to be on the processes of high politics and Eastern Europe's role in international relations. While traditional political and international history both have much to say about the processes of great power relations that determined the place and, to a large extent, the politics of the region in the post-war period, they shed no light on the issue of how socialism was experienced by the region's population. This brief history does not seek to deny the importance of international or political history in terms of understanding the region's recent past; indeed it would be difficult to envisage a history of the region in the second half of the twentieth century that denied either. Instead it concentrates on the relationships between the different political regimes and those who lived under them from 1939 to 2000, arguing that only when one grasps the contours of the relationship between state projects and social groups can the course of historical development in the region be adequately understood.

This book concentrates on the lands between Germany and the Soviet Union and therefore excludes the territories that were part of the Soviet Union until 1991; it also consciously excludes the former German Democratic Republic (East Germany) and does not consider Greece, part of the political West for the whole of the post-war period. Its focus is thematic and therefore it avoids concentrating on the history of individual countries, except where these are central to the argument presented. While the book attempts to provide balanced coverage of all of the countries of the region, it is based on a literature which is richer and more extensive for some countries than others. It also builds on the specialized research of its author. Like many other, but not all, historians of the region, I am a single-country specialist, and many of the arguments advanced here build on my specialized work that has examined the social history of industrial labour during the period of the creation of socialist dictatorship in Hungary. In part, the analysis and arguments presented in this book reflect my own attempts to situate specifically Hungarian circumstances into their comparative regional context. My interest in exploring this comparative regional context stems from something which became painfully apparent to me while working and living in Budapest during the mid-1990s. Although it has been understood that the experiences of different countries in the region during the second half of the twentieth century were as different from each other as those of Western European states, the nature of those differences was grasped relatively poorly. While I do not pretend that the arguments presented here are in any way definitive, this book will have served its purpose if it contributes to the necessary rethinking of the history of Eastern Europe in the post-war period.

In writing this book I have incurred many debts. The first is to my immediate colleagues in the History Department at the Open University for providing a stimulating and supportive working environment, and to the research committee of the Faculty of Arts for its generous funding of research trips. Outside the boundaries of my institution I belong to a community of historians and historically minded social scientists, which has provided me with a source of support and assistance over the years that I have been interested in the recent history of the region. Many of them and their ideas have influenced my own, though of course I take final responsibility for the arguments presented here. Of this group I am especially indebted to John Connelly, Ben Frommer, Peter Heumos, Padraic Kenney, Martha Lampland, Katherine Lebow and Nigel Swain. Finally there are the friends with whom I have either explored the region or discussed my work. Thanks here are due to Andy Bell, John Dobson, Olga Gomez, Gyöngyi Hegedűs, Kevin Quigley, Darryl Reed, Vesna Sarčević and András Tóth. In addition, my family, especially my parents, have supported me constantly, for which I am eternally grateful.

Mark Pittaway
December 2003

Introduction: The other Europe

On one level it seems strange to write a book on the history of Eastern Europe at all at the beginning of the twenty-first century, given the challenges that the concept faced during the last two decades of the twentieth. For most of the second half of the twentieth century, with the continent partitioned by the Iron Curtain, the fact of socialist, dictatorial rule defined Eastern Europe in the mental geographies of many Europeans. While in Western Europe many agreed with Winston Churchill's 1946 claim that 'an iron curtain has descended across the continent',[1] even on the western fringes of the region conventionally regarded as Eastern Europe, in socialist but non-Soviet Yugoslavia, 'Europe was where the Soviet Union was not'.[2] The western border of the Soviet bloc – the so-called Iron Curtain – came to symbolize, for those on both sides of the divide, Eastern Europe's apparent exclusion from the continental mainstream.

The illegal crossing of the Iron Curtain by the citizens of the GDR in 1989, beginning with several hundred East Germans, using a demonstration organized by anti-regime activists in the Hungarian border town of Sopron in August to force their way into Austria, sparked a chain of events that by Christmas had led to the ending of socialist dictatorship across the region.[3] Oppositional activity of the kind that had spread to sleepy, western Hungary by August 1989 had been sustained throughout the 1980s by networks of activists, who, though small in number, shared ideas and sustained each other's activities across national borders in the face of state repression. These activists challenged the bipolar divide of Europe into East and West by attempting to create a 'Central European' space of oppositional activity to undermine and eventually destroy socialist dictatorship.[4] This activism, given significance by the accelerating crisis of socialist regimes, was supported, in turn, by an intellectual rediscovery of longer-term historical and cultural roots in the westernmost countries of the Soviet bloc, which tied them to their neighbours on the other side of the cold-war divide. This rediscovery formed a key plank in the challenge to post-war mental geographies of Europe and, at the same time, threw down the gauntlet to the region's socialist regimes.[5]

The immediate consequences of the collapse of socialist regimes and the political transitions that followed seemed to confirm that notions of a unified Eastern European region were misplaced. Across the western parts of the former Soviet bloc, the relatively smooth consolidation of albeit imperfect political democracies reinforced the claims of those states to Central European status. Further afield, where transition was accompanied by political turbulence, states were excluded from this status. In the former Yugoslavia, with the outbreak of war over Croatia and Slovenia in 1991, and then Bosnia-Hercegovina in 1992, the spectre of ethnic nationalism and brutal conflict brought with it a revival in Western discourse of notions of 'the Balkans', a zone of internecine strife, characterized (in the words of the British prime minister at the time, John Major) by 'impersonal and inevitable forces beyond anyone's control'.[6] The fragmentation of Eastern Europe seemed to be confirmed by the deep-seated economic disparities that emerged once the first post-socialist recessions across the region had run their course. In 1993, gross domestic product per capita in Central Europe ranged between Slovenia's US $6,490 and Slovakia's US $1,950, while in the Balkans, Romania's stood at US $1,140, while Albania's was a lamentable US $340.[7] A decade later, after an influx of multinational capital, and with the promise of imminent accession to the European Union, the states of Central Europe had surged forward. Slovakia, the poorest of these states in 1993, enjoyed a forecast gross domestic product of US $4,900 per capita in 2003, while Romania lagged behind at US $2,380.[8] Though the enlargement of the European Union, beginning in 2004 on paper, promised 'to reunite the European continent and thus consolidate peace and democracy,'[9] the first wave of eastern enlargement – which postponed accession for Romania and Bulgaria until 2007 and excluded the Balkans entirely – seemed set to institutionalize the new fragmented mental geographies of the eastern half of Europe. Despite the apparent fragmentation of the region since 1989, and the enlargement of the European Union, all the countries of the region still suffer from being regarded as part of an Eastern Europe. For many, the sense of exclusion from the West is symbolized by state practices at the external borders of the European Union, as the Croatian-born writer, Dubravka Ugrešič has observed:

> At airports I stand in the queue for passport control. Signs over the booths behind which uniformed officials sit indicate my place. In some places it says *others*, in some there is merely an absence of the blue board with the ring of little yellow stars. My queue is long, it drags on slowly … We are different, our skin is often dark, our eyes dart suspiciously about or stare dully straight ahead …[10]

Furthermore, concerns about migration from Eastern Europe have formed the backdrop to heated debates about immigration and political asylum in Western societies, from the controversies over Albanian migration into Italy to the attempts of Slovak Roma to seek political asylum in the United Kingdom in 1997. The symbolic practices of exclusion on Western borders and Western European racism aside, suspicion of and discrimination against former socialist states continued to infuse policy practice. Such discrimination has shaped the rocky road of many Central European countries to membership of European Union; according to the Hungarian-born sociologist, József Böröcz, reluctance on the part of the European Union to embrace the former socialist states of Eastern Europe delayed admittance for those countries. Hungary's wait of 44 months, between the submission of its initial application in 1994 and the European Union's decision to begin negotiations, represented 'the longest waiting time in the history of either the European Union, or its predecessor, the European Communities'.[11] What lay behind this was the persistence of notions of Eastern Europe among Brussels policy-makers; for them, 'the mental map of geographical Europe becomes a downward slope towards the east'.[12]

Notions of Eastern Europe as a region that was distinct from Europe, and seen in the Western European mind as 'backward' and 'inferior' did not only post-date, but also pre-dated the cold war. The writer Edith Pargeter, in her account of a visit to Czechoslovakia in spring 1948, remarked that the Prague *coup* of February 1948 that marked the beginning of single-party dictatorship in the country, had resulted in a situation where the country 'by some mental trick had been expelled by most English people to a limbo many thousands of miles removed from civilization'.[13] If ideas of the internal geography of Europe that sought to exclude the eastern half of the continent from full membership of European civilization were in operation at the dawn of the cold war, so were counter-claims about the Central European nature of the westernmost members of the Soviet bloc. The Communist Party newspaper in the industrial, western Hungarian county of Komárom-Esztergom, surprisingly proclaimed in 1948 that new housing to be built for mineworkers in the local industrial centre of Tatabánya would be the 'most advanced' housing in 'central Europe'.[14]

Debates about the broader regional affiliation of states in the East European region reach back beyond the cold war, with the alignment of geopolitical realities and Western designations of the East as backward.[15] These regional designations have reflected disputed notions of identity in the eastern half of the continent that date back to the crystallization of modern notions of Europe during the late eighteenth and early nineteenth centuries, as the continent was racked by the upheavals of the French Revolution and the Napoleonic wars. This crystallization was reflected in the demarcation of mental borders between the European and non-European world, borders that 'assumed a symbolic importance for human identity greater than their practical reality'.[16] In this process of demarcation, Eastern Europe lay on the perceived borderland between the European and non-European world; the south-east of the continent lay under the control of Ottoman Turkey, regarded as an emphatically non-European power by many of those thinkers who established the mental boundaries of Europe.[17] Russia was seen as existing in an ambiguous relationship to the rest of the continent.[18] These perceptions coexisted with a shift in cultural and economic power in the continent, which came to be concentrated increasingly in its north-western urban centres, particularly Amsterdam, London and Paris.[19]

Notions of Eastern Europe as a backward, 'different' region of the continent, which took shape with the development of modern notions of Europe, were strengthened by the transformations of the nineteenth century. Wealth was increasingly concentrated in the north-west of the continent as a result of its rapid industrialization. While industrialization was replicated on a significant scale in the Eastern European region itself during the dying decades of the century, outside the industrialized Czech lands, then under the Austrian monarchy, agriculture remained predominant, with the economy weak across the region relative to the rest of the continent.[20] The societies of the region remained largely excluded from the major political process of the century, the consolidation and spread of national, territorial and centralized states across the western half of the continent.[21] In the East, ruled largely by multinational empires, the impact of ideas of the 'nation' was deeply uneven. Given the centrality of ideas of the nation and industry to nineteenth-century notions of progress that dominated Western European societies, such as that of the United Kingdom,[22] such patterns of divergence reinforced beliefs in the backwardness of the eastern parts of the continent.

As Eastern Europe was being defined as a peripheral and backward region, ironically, it was becoming increasingly central to the great power politics of the continent as a whole. The example of Western European nationalism fascinated the intellectuals of Central and East European states and, consequently, they sought to establish the bases of national languages, literatures, cultures and, later, political movements among their own peoples.[23] Given the multinational nature of the states they inhabited, the progress of such national movements was uneven, and they generated increasing political stress. This was the case especially in south-eastern Europe, where tension between local and largely Slavic nationalism and the Ottoman rulers of the region generated frequent political instability throughout the nineteenth century, and the eventual collapse of the empire in Europe at the beginning of the twentieth.[24] The tensions generated by the rise of political and cultural nationalism shook the other dominant multinational empire in the region, Austria-Hungary. However, it was not so much the local conflicts around nationality themselves that heralded the eastern part of the continent's entrance into the mainstream of European politics; rather it was the combination of some of these local conflicts with intensifying rivalries between the great powers of the west of the continent that made them so explosive for continental stability. It was this combination of factors, following the crisis generated by the assassination of Archduke Franz Ferdinand in Sarajevo in June 1914, that triggered world war.

If world war demonstrated the centrality of political conflict in Eastern Europe to the political stability of the continent as a whole, it did not lead to Western Europeans revising their views of the region as backward and different. Instead, parts of the region came to be defined in pejorative terms as dangerous to the welfare of the rest of the continent. The south-east of the continent, in particular, was seen as an area of internecine conflict; indeed the writer Rebecca West admitted, prior to her first visit to Yugoslavia in 1936, that 'violence was, indeed, all I knew of the Balkans.[25] The world war had laid the foundation of a profound crisis in the region, which all but assured that local upheavals would threaten the stability of the rest of the European continent. At first sight, the war, and the treaties of Versailles, St Germain, Trianon, Neuilly and Sèvres that followed it, remade the political geography of the region, replacing multinational empires with nation states. In the entirely new states of Czechoslovakia and Yugoslavia, multi-ethnic Poland and expanded Romania, nation-building élites sought to build unified nations in a multi-ethnic context. Furthermore, the wars and their subsequent treaties divided the region into winners and losers, defenders and opponents of the post-war Eastern European order. This geopolitical tension, combined with economic weakness and social division in the new states that hampered nation-building, would prove explosive and had geopolitical consequences across the continent.

As chapter 1 of this book shows, Nazi Germany's attempts to revise the post-war settlement in the western part of the region met with support from other states on the losing side of the Versailles process. Hitler's violent attempts to transform the politics, economics and society of the region, which were implemented against the background of war, left a profound social and political legacy that shaped the social bases of the regimes that came after. Chapter 2 focuses on how, across Central and Eastern Europe in 1944 and 1945, the invading Red Army, together with the Communist parties of the countries of the region, began to build 'new' states that would be pliant to the Soviet Union. Across the region, societies were bitterly divided, not only along political lines, but also in terms of class and nationality. The second half of the 1940s was marked by intense conflict, in which the interests of international power politics interacted with more local struggles over the future of the countries of the region. The result was socialist dictatorship in Eastern Europe.

While in much of Western Europe the post-war political order had been largely consolidated by 1949, the effective consolidation of the dictatorial post-war settlement east of Churchill's Iron Curtain was a more conflict-ridden process. In contrast to much of the literature that has argued for the dictatorial and totalitarian nature of rule during the early years of socialist dictatorship, asserting that the repressive 1950s were followed by decades of thaw,[26] the second half of chapter 2 and chapter 3 advance an alternative interpretation. While the early years of socialist dictatorship were repressive, characterized by the show trials, the elimination of civil society, the expansion of prisons and political police forces, and violent attempts to institute revolutionary social transformation, the dictatorships were unable to guarantee stability. Chapter 2 argues that their social and economic transformations were undermined by a lack of political support and by large-scale infra-political or submerged resistance in factories, farms, offices and homes across the region. This led to the near complete collapse of industrialization and collectivization drives by the mid-1950s, and in some cases, most spectacularly in Hungary, to the outright collapse of the regime, thus forcing the dictatorship to rely on Red Army troops for its survival. Yet by the mid-1960s, though the post-war settlement would be challenged by both reform movements inside the party in Czechoslovakia and worker unrest in Poland's Baltic ports, across the region as a whole, socialist dictatorship rested on stronger social foundations than it had done a decade before. Chapter 3 outlines the process of consolidation that underpinned this shift, arguing that the change in the nature of socialist regimes to accommodate domestic political circumstances strengthened them immeasurably. Yet while the mid-1960s were the years in which Eastern Europe's socialist post-war political settlement was at its strongest, this settlement still rested on fragile foundations, which were tested across the bloc at the end of the decade.

This book argues that politically, therefore, socialist dictatorships did not simply represent the conquest of Eastern Europe by Soviet models (though the hegemony of the Soviet Union set the parameters of politics); instead they represented a distinctively socialist, Eastern European post-war settlement by the middle of the 1960s. Dictatorships had to adapt to domestic political constraints as well as international ones in order to survive the 1950s. Yet the dictatorships did not simply adapt to a static society; they also profoundly transformed it. The nationalizations and expropriations of the second half of the 1940s effectively eliminated the semi-peripheral capitalisms of the region. Industrialization drives changed employment structures decisively between 1950 and 1960, leading to radical reductions in the proportion of the population working in agriculture in all Eastern European states and an explosion in the numbers working in industry.[27] The successful conclusion of agricultural collectivization by 1962 (outside Poland and Yugoslavia, which permanently abandoned the policy in the mid-1950s), led to profound transformation in the experience and everyday life of the rural population. The spread of social welfare and the uneven development of 'socialist consumerism' during the 1960s further transformed society. Mass communication, urbanization and proletarianization under socialist conditions reconfigured those collective identities based on class, gender, nation, ethnicity and religion. In addition, socialist states did not fully control this process; social conflict – whether at work, at home, in the community or in the officially tolerated public sphere – placed severe constraints on the actions of socialist regimes. For this reason, political consolidation in the region was accompanied by a series of retreats from some of the early dreams of socialist transformation. Attempts to create egalitarian, work-based societies were modified, as regimes were forced to compromise, with established cultures of work reasserting themselves, along with traditional gender identities.

Chapters 4 to 6 examine these processes; therefore they represent a shift in focus in that they explore the nature and direction of the social changes that underpinned political consolidation by the mid-1960s and determined its limits. Each chapter concentrates on crucial dimensions of social change between the late 1940s and the late 1960s. Chapter 4 examines the social process that was probably the most central to the socialist project of the regimes in the region, namely the attempts across the region to integrate social groups into one society through the performance of productive labour in the socialist sector of the economy. It focuses on the intersection between politics, social policy and the everyday experience of work, concentrating on the attempts at transforming industrial, agricultural and intellectual labour in socialist societies. It also examines how many of these transformations were accompanied by the reproduction of pre-socialist cultures of work in a socialist context. Chapter 5 considers the impact of socialist transformation on the private sphere. It argues that changing state attempts and the meanings that socialist citizens gave to the private sphere were fundamental to understanding the direction of the social changes of the post-war decades. The state sought to reform housing and social policy and aimed at a radical shift in gender relations both inside and outside the household. At the same time, the shortages generated by the failures of state policy to satisfy perceived needs led East Europeans to see the private sphere as a site where those needs could be satisfied and as a space for resistance. Regimes accommodated these shifts by reorganizing their policies around the satisfaction of the material needs of households. These shifts, in turn, modified regime attitudes towards gender. Outside the home, as socialist rule was consolidated and the institutions of dictatorship gradually began to mesh with society, the boundaries of the state became blurred. By the mid-1960s a socialist public sphere had been created, which, to some extent, reflected the tensions and conflicts that had emerged within society. Many of these tensions drove social pressure for reform by the end of decade. These processes are the subject of chapter 6.

The argument that runs through these three chapters is about the nature of and limits to state intervention in the social realm. The state in the early 1950s was intent on remaking society as one that was egalitarian, productivist and work-based. This programme rested on the wholesale transformation of identities in the workplace, the home and the political sphere. In its egalitarianism and its stress on work, it advanced a distinctively socialist view of modernity. Socialist drives to remake work relations were infused with attempts to rationalize the workplace, importing practices derived from scientific methods of work organization into the factory, the farm and the office. In the community, the socialist regimes sought to reform behaviour both in the public and private realms, in line with what they saw as modern, socialist norms. Yet state drives to rationalize social behaviour met with widespread resistance, which often involved ordinary East Europeans articulating identities that rested on marked continuities with the past. In the workplace, drives to rationalize through the introduction of new wage systems, production lines or labour competitions were often resisted by those who attempted to preserve pre-existing cultures of work or occupational identities. Sections of the population invested in identities, like those of a religious nature, that anticlerical regimes often believed had been consigned to the dustbin of history. The combination of state policies and resistance based on identities inherited from the pre-socialist period created a situation in which older identities reproduced themselves in the circumstances of socialist Eastern Europe. The patterns of social behaviour that arose as a result of this process were often accommodated by the dictatorships; where they were not, they generated enormous social and political tensions.

By the end of the 1960s, 'the limits of dictatorship'[28] had become apparent across the region. The East European dictatorships were limited by the dynamics of the post-war settlement, whose emergence in each of the countries had allowed them to consolidate their rule. However, they were also constrained by the patterns of social behaviour and expectation that had been generated by the process of socialist transformation, which had occurred in parallel with the generation of the post-war settlement, often generating pressure for political reform. This coexisted with an economic base, which had expanded substantially during the post-war period, but nevertheless remained too weak to provide a sustainable base for the social settlement that had emerged across the region. This was to produce parallel pressure for the reform of the structures of central economic planning that had become hegemonic during the early 1950s. Finally, the events in Czechoslovakia in 1968 demonstrated the international constraints on a state that sought fundamental political reform and (as the retreats in neighbouring countries showed) economic reform to change the nature of their social settlements. The closing of the door to radical political reform after the suppression of the Prague Spring was a turning point in that it marked the beginning of the end of Eastern Europe's dictatorial, post-war settlement. As the international economic climate worsened throughout the 1970s and 1980s, the regimes paid for their failure to reform themselves politically and economically, as the post-war settlement across Eastern Europe unravelled – a process that is documented in chapter 7.

The circumstances in which Eastern Europe's post-war settlement fell apart differed from country to country, as regimes faced different pressures and adopted diverse routes to manage them. Hungary, under János Kádár, suspended and then accelerated economic reform; Poland and Yugoslavia lurched from crisis to crisis in the 1980s; while in Romania, Nicolae Ceauşescu imposed austerity backed by repression. Chapter 8 examines the end of socialist dictatorship in the region and concentrates on the different patterns of political change that occurred, focusing on the relationship between these and the routes that the unravelling of the post-war political settlement took in each state. It will be argued that the experience of states as socialism unravelled explains the trajectory of post-socialist politics across the region, as populations confronted the twin challenge of constructing post-socialist political orders and coping with the social strains imposed by the development of peripheral capitalisms. This argument is developed in the final chapter. Chapter 9 considers the continuing legacy of socialist dictatorship for the emerging and diverse post-socialist political settlements in the region. It argues that a focus on the recent past of all the states of Eastern Europe is fundamental to understanding its present, and possibly its future.

1 Crisis , war and occupation

Most histories of the socialist dictatorships of post-war Eastern Europe begin in 1945, with the end of the Second World War in Europe. Consequently they focus narrowly on how, in a climate of post-war devastation and reconstruction, Communist parties supported by the Red Army were able to seize power. These histories concentrate on the processes of high politics and neglect the social context in which the dictatorships were formed. To place the dictatorships in this social context, however, it is necessary to recognize, as Jan T. Gross has argued, that 'the Nazi-instigated war and the Communist-driven revolution in East Central Europe constituted one integral period'.[1] This broadening of focus entails setting both the wartime and the post-war periods in the context of an even longer period, in which the societies that came to be ruled as socialist dictatorships in the second half of the twentieth century constituted what the Hungarian-born economic historian Iván T. Berend has termed, 'the crisis zone of Europe'.[2]

The outcome of the First World War and the peace treaties that followed it remoulded the political map, ending the dominance of multinational empires like Austria-Hungary over the populations of the region, and replacing some with 'new' nation states, reconstructing others and strengthening some of those that had existed in the pre-war years. The new political map of Eastern Europe, however, conformed uneasily, at best, to the patterns of national, ethnic and linguistic identification across the region. The messiness of this settlement was thrown into sharp relief by the attempts of the nation-builders in the new, reinvented and expanded states to replicate the process of nation-building that had occurred further west during the nineteenth century. This tension was illustrated most starkly in a state like Poland, restored by the post-First World War settlement as an independent state for the first time since the partitions of 1772, 1793 and 1795. In 1921, while Poles, who made up 69.2 per cent of the total population in the restored state, were the dominant ethnic group, 14.3 per cent declared themselves to be Ukrainians, 7.8 per cent were Jewish, 3.9 per cent regarded themselves as Belorussian and a further 3.9 per cent were German. For many of those who advocated Polish independence, like the country's representative at the Paris Peace Conferences, Roman Dmowski, Polish nation-building involved ensuring the political, cultural and economic hegemony of the dominant Polish majority. In expanded Romania, the country's political élite found itself attempting to forge a new state by incorporating a number of diverse territories – previously Austrian-ruled Bukovina, Hungarian-ruled Transylvania and Russian-ruled Bessarabia – each with its own multi-ethnic populations. The radical cultural policies employed to do this placed Bucharest on a direct collision course with large sections of the population and with regional élites, who often identified with their former governors.[3]

Even the two new, formally multinational states in the region were riven by similar tensions. Czechoslovakia, probably the most successful inter-war state in the region, 'was riven by fault lines of ethnicity'.[4] The attempts of the Prague-based political élite to build a unitary state that rested on a firmly Czechoslovak identity were not only resisted by Slovakia, a junior partner in the project of creating a state for north Slavs, but also met with the simmering resentment of the country's 3.1 million Germans and its 750,000 Magyars. In Yugoslavia, the multinational state of the south Slavs, attempts to create a society based on an all-embracing pan-Yugoslav identity foundered on the persistence of national particularisms among the Croats, Serbs and Slovenes.[5]

The post-First World War settlement not only lay the foundations of internal political conflict around nationality in new states, but internationally it also led to the creation of losers who resented the settlement and frequently challenged its legitimacy. Many Germans, furious at the territorial losses mandated by Versailles, provided a social base for revisionist politics in post-war Germany and Austria. Magyars, who attached a notion of Hungary as a thousand-year-old kingdom in the heart of Europe, bitterly resented the Treaty of Trianion, which stripped the country of much of its pre-war territory – a resentment that was kept alive by the foreign and cultural policies of the nationalist-conservative inter-war regime.[6]

War not only transformed the political landscape of the region, but its impact within societies profoundly subverted hierarchies of class and ethnicity within its states.[7] Social disruption and the transformation of political authority produced a revolutionary wave across the region. In Hungary, the frustration of the industrial working class with wartime conditions and the political collapse of the ruling élite in the face of the fall of the Habsburgs and the Treaty of Trianon, produced a short-lived Soviet Republic, one which alienated the entire agrarian population and collapsed in the face of Romanian military intervention, to be replaced by the oligarchic conservative regime of Miklós Horthy. In Bulgaria, the war led to a revolutionary peasantist dictatorship that promised a 'third road' between traditional conservative politics and urban socialism. In Bulgaria, as in Hungary, revolution failed in 1923 in the face of a *coup d'état* mounted by the army with the backing of traditional élites.

While the revolutionary governments of Hungary and Bulgaria were exceptional, they were emblematic of a desire on the part of traditionally subordinate groups for greater participation in politics and an increased share of national wealth.[8] The region's economies were both disrupted by war and saddled with the consequences of uneven and peripheral economic development during the pre-war years.[9] The peripheral status of Eastern Europe within the European economy could be seen in the limited impact of industrialization on the economies and societies of the region. Bohemia and Moravia in the west of Czechoslovakia were the most industrialized parts of the region: 40 per cent of those employed worked in industry and trade in 1921, while 31.6 per cent worked in agriculture.[10] At the other extreme, some 80 per cent of the Albanian population depended on agriculture in 1930.[11] The weakness of the economies of the region was demonstrated during the depression that led to an intensification of the problems of poverty among the rural and, increasingly, much of the urban population.[12]

The tension generated by the clash between state-building projects, ethnic identities, subverted hierarchies of class and peripheral economic development formed the backdrop to the retreat of liberal democracy across the region and the apparently inexorable advance of authoritarianism. After the First World War, outside of Hungary, where Soviet revolution and violent counter-revolution had led to the creation of Miklós Horthy's conservative-nationalist regime, democratic political systems held sway across the region. By 1938, on the eve of Hitler's violent redrawing of the map of Eastern Europe, only Czechoslovakia successfully maintained a democratic system of government. While the retreat of democracy in the region began in the 1920s, with Józef Piłsudski's *coup* in Poland in May 1926, as well as the rise of royal dictatorships in Albania in 1928 and Yugoslavia in the following year, its extinction occurred during the 1930s.

The retreat of democracy and the rise of authoritarianism, however, was just one of the signs of mounting crisis in the region during the 1930s. The coming to power of the National Socialists in Germany in 1933 threatened to upset the delicate geopolitical balance between beneficiaries and losers of the post-First World War settlement. The consolidation and extension of Hitler's power within Germany was met with the politicization of German minorities within the region's states. This politicization was most marked in Czechoslovakia, where many of the country's 3.1 million Germans had never been reconciled fully to the state; the *Sudetendeutsche Partei* of Konrad Henlein, established with subsidies from Germany, was able to take three in every five German votes in 1935. The politicization and radicalization of German minorities, particularly when combined with active political and financial support from Berlin, threatened not only the fragile political balance of power in the region, but also the territorial integrity of some of its states. With Germany's armaments-based recovery after 1933 came increasing German economic penetration of the Eastern European region. Imports from Eastern Europe rose from 9.9 per cent of Germany's total in 1933 to 17.7 per cent by 1939; over the same period, exports to Eastern Europe increased from 10.7 per cent of the German total to 17.7 per cent.[13]

The growing influence of National Socialism also fuelled domestic fascism in the countries of Eastern Europe, though this took different forms in different states. In Romania, 'the precariousness and novelty of the democratic institutions, pandemic political corruption, democracy perceived as an urban phenomenon and therefore resented by the proponents of agrarian conservatism, and the beleaguered status of ethnic minorities'[14] shaped the social and cultural background of domestic fascism. In neighbouring Hungary, militant opposition to the post-First World War borders institutionalized at Trianon, the political and social marginalization of many public officials and growing frustration with the lack of social reform under Horthy generated similar pressures.[15] These contexts resulted in the formation of distinctive local fascisms. In Romania, domestic fascism was represented by the Iron Guard, which based its ideology on a mystical nationalism.[16] The Guard's political wing gained 15.58 per cent in the 1937 elections, posing a challenge to the established political system that was met by repression on the part of Romania's monarch.[17] In Hungary, the fragmented domestic national-socialist movement crystallized around Ferenc Szalási's Arrow Cross Party; this party would enjoy its finest hour in 1939, in the wake of Hitler's first major steps to remake the political order in Danubian Eastern Europe.[18]

This process began with Hitler's decision to annex Austria in March 1938, which heralded further expansion into Czechoslovakia, where the large German minority, politicized under the influence of both Berlin and the local *Sudetendeutsche Partei*, provided a suitable pretext. The German-speaking areas of the country, the so-called Sudetenland, were annexed in October 1938 in the immediate aftermath of the Munich conference, in which Britain and France had acceded to Hitler's demands that these territories be incorporated into Germany. Thrown into political crisis by both German intervention and the opportunistic decision of Poland to use Hitler's incursion as cover to seize Czechoslovakian Silesia, the multinational north Slav state survived until March 1939, when it was invaded by Hitler and partitioned.

The Czech parts of the state were transformed into a German protectorate. In the Protectorate of Bohemia and Moravia, as the new entity was known, Germans were given the status of full citizens of the Reich, while the Czechs became second-class citizens. Emil Hácha, president of the weakened post-Munich Czechoslovakia, retained a titular position, but real power was held by the Nazi protector, Konstantin von Neurath.[19] In Slovakia, members of the separatist Slovak People's Party, in cooperation with the Germans, proclaimed an independent Slovak state under the protection of the

Reich. Led by Jozef Tiso, the Slovak regime based itself on an authoritarian Catholic ideology that has led some to characterize the state as representing a 'clerico-fascism'. Its debt to National Socialism could be seen in the power of the paramilitary Hlinka Guard, which represented a centre of power within the new regime.[20] In the new Slovakia, anti-Czech and anti-Semitic sentiment fused in official propaganda.[21]

The impact of Hitler's annexation of Austria and destruction of Czechoslovakia was felt throughout Danubian Eastern Europe. While the dismemberment of Czechoslovakia allowed Hungary to regain territory in both Ruthenia and southern Slovakia (and thus to satisfy, to a limited degree, the domestic appetite for a revision of post-war borders), it created a climate in which the Arrow Cross Party was able to mount a serious challenge to the conservative-nationalist regime. The radical right mobilized substantial sections of the urban population in the May 1939 elections, on the basis of hunger for territorial revision and frustration with the lack of social reform inside the country.[22] To defuse the domestic challenge of the Arrow Cross, which increasingly sought to mobilize industrial workers, the Hungarian political élite pursued a policy of closer links with Germany as a means of gaining 'lost' territory to placate the radical right at home. As Romania, alarmed at its loss of Bessarabia to the Soviet Union in 1940, sought closer links with Germany, Hungary was able, with Hitler's support, to secure territorial revision in Transylvania. As a result of the second Vienna Awards, the territory was partitioned, with northern Transylvania transferred to Hungary. A large transfer of populations resulted, as 200,000 Hungarians left Romanian-ruled southern Transylvania and a similar number of Romanians departed the Hungarian-ruled territories.[23] The loss of Bessarabia, the enforced transfer of northern Transylvania and, to a lesser extent, that of southern Dobrudja demanded by Bulgaria with Hitler's support, created political crisis in Bucharest. This in turn led to the replacement of royal dictator-ship with that of General Ion Antonescu, whose desire to revise the partition of Transylvania led him to conclude that alliance with Germany was the only viable foreign policy course for Romania.

The consolidation of German political hegemony over Danubian Eastern Europe combined with economic hegemony. The advent of the Protectorate of Bohemia and Moravia allowed for the exploitation of the industrial plant of the Czech lands for armaments production, as the German administration of the protectorate integrated the local economy with that of the Reich.[24] Hungary had mandated its own programme for developing heavy industry, in large part to meet demand from Germany, as early as 1938, when it proclaimed the Győr programme that placed the development of armaments and armaments-related production at its heart.[25] The 1930s had seen increasing German economic penetration of Romania's economy, culminating in a 1939 trade agreement that effectively sealed the country's integration into a German-dominated economic space.[26] The growing hegemony of Germany could also be seen in the intensification of anti-Semitic legislation across Danubian Eastern Europe. Romania purged its civil service of Jews in 1940 as a prelude to further anti-Semitic legislation.[27] In Hungary, radical anti-Semitic legislation had been passed in 1938 and 1939, which severely restricted the political and economic rights of Hungarian Jewry and heralded further restrictive measures during the war years.[28]

The remaking of the political, economic and social orders of Danubian Eastern Europe was, however, only the beginning. Germany's invasion of Poland in September 1939 was the precursor of more radical attempts to reshape the societies of the region. The attack on Poland by the Germans was joined by the Red Army, incorporating eastern Poland into the Soviet Union,[29] while western and central Poland fell under Nazi occupation. In contrast to the earlier dismemberment of Czechoslovakia, as Hitler's most recent biographer, Ian Kershaw, has pointed out, the invasion of Poland 'was imperialist conquest, not revisionism'.[30] Poland was transformed into a laboratory for National Socialist attempts to shape what Hitler termed 'a new ethnographic order'[31] in the Eastern European region. A swathe of western Poland was incorporated into the Reich, extending the administrative border of Germany almost to Warsaw. The Nazi administrative units (*Gaue*) of the Wartheland and West Prussia-Danzig were carved out of this annexed territory. These territories were marked for 'Germanization', a euphemism for the mass expulsion of the Polish and Jewish populations in order to make way for the resettlement of ethnic Germans from the Baltic states and the south Tyrol.[32] While in West-Prussia-Danzig the authorities sought to achieve the goals of Germanization through actively seeking the incorporation of Poles into the assimilated German population, in the Wartheland, which centred on the industrial city of Łódź, the region's Nazi rulers pursued policies of discrimination and deportation towards Poles.[33] In the year following the invasion of Poland, it has been estimated that around 400,000 people were deported from the annexed western territories.[34] In the violent remaking of the ethnographic order in the Wartheland, the origins of later mass genocide can be discerned. The murder of psychiatric patients in Polish port cities in October 1939, to clear space to temporarily house German settlers, was both an extension of policies of euthanasia practised inside the Reich, and a precursor of the extensive genocide to follow.[35] The racist policies employed in the Wartheland towards the large, urban Jewish population, particularly in Łódź, culminated in the closure of the city's ghetto in April 1940, creating 'a sweatshop writ large'.[36]

While western Poland underwent Germanization, central Poland formed the area controlled by the 'Generalgouvernement', under its Nazi governor, Hans Frank. The population bore the brunt of the National Socialists' anti-Polish and anti-Jewish policies; as early as October 1939, Hitler warned that governing Poland would entail 'a hard ethnic struggle that will not permit any legal restrictions'.[37] The Nazis sought to destroy the cultural infrastructure of the Polish nation by targeting its intellectuals. This policy was heralded by the closure of Kraków's higher education institutions in November 1939 and the deportation of 183 of their staff to concentration camps.[38] Poland, minus its intelligentsia, was to be transformed into a source of cheap labour for the factories of the Reich. In October 1939, the authorities in the Generalgouvernement introduced the obligation to work for all Poles between the ages of 14 and 60 (and all Jews aged between 12 and 60). This measure underpinned plans to export large quantities of Polish labour to Germany; indeed, by 1944, between 1.3 and 1.5 million Poles, from a total population of 15 million, had gone to work in Germany.[39] In terms of economic policy, the Generalgouvernement's Nazi rulers envisaged its total de-industrialization; in 1940, Hans Frank stated that 'we shall take away from this land all the valuable machinery, dismantle all the valuable factories, destroy, if possible, all its valuable communication lines'.[40] However, due to the needs of the German war economy, this policy was never completely implemented, and following Barbarossa in June 1941, it was partially reversed. Nevertheless, German policies had an impact that was both immediate and catastrophic: it has been estimated that industrial production in the Generalgouvernement in 1940 stood at 30 per cent of its level prior to the war, and even though it recovered under the pressures generated by the war in the east, it never surpassed 80 per cent of its pre-war total.[41] Agriculture was to be bled dry, as Polish peasants faced the compulsory requisitioning of their production in the interest of feeding the Reich.[42]

The effect of Nazi rule on living standards within the Generalgouvernement was catastrophic. Unofficial estimates suggested that the real incomes of ordinary Poles stood at less than 40 per cent of their 1938 level in 1940–1.[43] Inadequate rations and low standards of living forced many urban residents to rely on a burgeoning and increasingly expensive black market; in the industrial town of Radom in November 1941, black market bread was 25 times the price that residents had paid in 1939.[44] A sharp increase in the level of repression combined with growing economic impoverishment.[45] The degree of violence against the population accelerated as the war progressed; in 1942 alone, according to one estimate, a total of 7,000 non-Jewish Poles were murdered by the Nazi authorities.[46] Poverty and repression engendered resistance, which in turn was fuelled by the fact that the occupation authorities completely ignored the need to legitimate their rule among the subject population. Resistance snowballed, shaping an 'underground' society able, to some extent, to circumvent the mechanisms of Nazi rule, developing an organization, a press and eventually a military arm in the form of the Home Army.[47]

Yet it was Poland's Jews who were the greatest victims of the policies the Nazis pursued in the Generalgouvernement. Poland was a laboratory for the radical anti-Jewish policies that culminated in the 'final solution'. The invasion of the country in 1939 led to an acceleration of the genocidal logic of the National Socialist regime, as Jews were deported *en masse* from the territories annexed by the Reich and attempts to create a 'reservation' for deported Jews in south-eastern Poland foundered. Many were expelled into the Generalgouvernement, and others were locked into closed ghettos across urban Poland in appalling conditions; 2.4 per cent of the area of the Polish capital came to house 30 per cent of its population.[48]

These measures were envisaged as temporary, as the Nazi leadership searched for a 'final solution' to its 'Jewish problem'. It took the launch of Barbarossa in 1941, and the marked radicalization of Nazi policies that war in the east brought in its train, to begin the extermination of the Jewish population that would take place largely on Polish soil.

The experience of shaping Hitler's new ethnographic order in Poland led to a radicalization of Nazi policy elsewhere. In the Protectorate of Bohemia and Moravia, Reinhard Heydrich was appointed acting Reich protector in September 1941, ostensibly with a brief to break Czech resistance to German rule. Heydrich had been a key figure in Nazi attempts to implement Hitler's new ethnographic order in Poland, and his appointment heralded a radicalization of Berlin's approach to the Czech lands. He tightened German political control over the protectorate, intensified repression against Czech resistance and moved to deport Jews.[49] Heydrich combined this with a drive to Germanize 50 per cent of the Czech population and deport the rest, linking this with broader policies to reshape the map of Eastern Europe: 'The future of the Reich after the war's end depends on the ability of the Reich and the ability of the people of Reich to meld these newly acquired areas into the Reich'.[50] Heydrich's own rule was short-lived: he was assassinated by Czechs flown in from London by the Special Operations Executive in May 1942. Reprisals were ruthless: the villages of Lidice and Ležáky were destroyed in retaliation, thus fuelling opposition to Nazi rule among the Czech population. Yet while Heydrich's policies bore the influence of the drive to shape a new ethnographic order that had been pioneered in Poland, Nazi rule in Bohemia and Moravia was immeasurably less destructive than further north. Hans Frank, Governor of the Generalgouvernement, had commented on this while on a visit to Prague in 1940: 'There were large red posters in Prague announcing that today seven Czechs had been shot. I said to myself: if I wanted to hang a poster for every seven Poles that were shot, then all the forests of Poland would not suffice in order to produce the paper necessary for such posters.'[51] Repression and arbitrary violence never reached the levels experienced in the Generalgouvernement, even after Heydrich's assassination. Furthermore, the Nazi authorities in the protectorate did not seek to pursue the kind of scorched earth policies against Czech industry that were envisaged, if not fully implemented, in Poland. Industry was central to armaments production; after the creation of the protectorate, the sector was rationalized and the two major arms companies, Československá Zbrojova Brno, the Škoda works and its subsidiaries were incorporated into the Herman Göring Werke and forced to reorient their production to meet the demands of the German military.[52] The centrality of industry in the protectorate to the German war effort ensured that the living standards of Czech workers were protected for the first half of the war, despite large increases in the cost of living.[53]

German incursion into south-eastern Europe came on the eve of Barbarossa, brought about by a *coup* in Yugoslavia in March 1941, launched by officers in the army and the air force who were concerned about the country's drift into the arms of Germany. Hitler's reaction was swift, launching a brutal air assault on Belgrade on 6 April in which up to 20,000 of the city's residents died. Germany's lightning campaign smashed the country's armed forces, resulting in an unconditional surrender a mere 11 days after the first attack on Belgrade. Following their victory, the Germans set about dismembering the Yugoslav state.

Two-thirds of the territory of Slovenia was incorporated into the Reich and merged into the Nazi *Gaue* of Carinthia and Styria; Istria was awarded to Italy and a small corner of the north-east of the territory to Hungary. Within dismembered Slovenia, the Germans pursued policies that were reminiscent of the attempts of the Nazis to create their new ethnographic order in Poland, by expelling Slovenes and replacing them with ethnic Germans transferred from Italian-occupied Slovenia and German-occupied Serbia.[54] The Italians were less harsh, at least prior to the outbreak of widespread partisan activity.[55] The extent of their conquest was not limited to Istria; most of the Dalmatian coast was incorporated into Italy and ruled, like Istria, in a manner which respected the distinctive nature of the region.[56] Montenegro became an Italian protectorate, extending the power base it had gained in south-eastern Europe two years before when it invaded Albania in April 1939. Italy deposed the country's monarch, King Zog, and replaced him with a pro-Italian regime. In December 1941, it tightened its control over the country when it forced Albania to accept the Italian king as its new head of state.[57]

The dismemberment of Yugoslavia brought Bulgaria directly into the war on the German side; for its cooperation it gained Macedonia, long disputed between Bulgaria and Yugoslavia and, prior to the existence of the multinational Slav state, with Serbia. Serbs and Bulgarians had fought over the ethnic identity of the inhabitants of Macedonia, each claiming that the population was either Serb or Bulgarian. Bulgaria ruled the state as an occupied territory, adopting a radical agenda of Bulgarianization, an agenda which would have important implications for defining Macedonia's place in the second Yugoslavia.[58] The annexation of Macedonia brought Bulgaria into direct military confrontation in Yugoslavia, generating internal political difficulties for the pro-German regime.

Croatia was divided into Italian and German zones of military influence, but the occupying authorities sponsored the establishment of an independent Croatian state – the *Nevazisna Država Hrvatska* (NDH) – under the leadership of the fascist Ustaša and its leader, Ante Pavelić. A violent and extreme nationalist organization, the Ustaša had suffered from political persecution under the royal dictatorship of the 1930s; while its leaders had spent the period in exile in Italy, many of its activists filled Yugoslavia's jails.[59] The installation of Pavelić led to the creation of a violent dictatorship that ruled deploying an ideology that was an extreme variant of National Socialism. The new regime crushed political opposition and rounded on perceived enemies by mandating the death penalty for infractions committed 'against the honour and interests of the Croatian nation'.[60] Despite the dictatorial nature of the new regime, it was greeted with enthusiasm by many Croats, and received support from large sections of the local Catholic clergy, if not from the Vatican. The Archbishop of Zagreb, Alojzije Stepinac, proclaimed at the beginning of Pavelić's rule, that 'we are convinced and expect, that the Church in the resurrected state of Croatia will be able to proclaim in complete freedom the incontestable principles of truth and justice'.[61]

Such support was unfortunate, especially given the genocidal nature of the Ustaša regime. The dictatorship moved quickly and enthusiastically against the Jewish population on its territory, passing anti-Semitic legislation on the day after the unconditional surrender of the Yugoslav army, and began to intern Jews in June 1941.[62] Yet it was because of its attempts to shape its own local version of Hitler's new ethnographic order, in the territory of Croatia and Bosnia that it ruled, that the Pavelić regime gained a distinctive reputation for brutality. The territory of the NDH was a multi-ethnic patchwork; of a total population of 6.3 million, 1.9 million were Serbs. The Serbian population of the NDH was targeted by Ustaša attempts to transform the territory into a 'pure Croatian nation'; in the words of one leading Ustaša figure, 'there is no method we would hesitate to use in order to make it truly Croatian and cleanse it of Serbs'.[63] The aim of eliminating the Serb population of the NDH was pursued through a variety of means. Zagreb concluded an agreement (which was later suspended) with the German occupation authorities to deport Serbs living in the NDH to Serbia; around 300,000 had either been deported or had fled Ustaša rule by 1945.[64] The regime initiated a campaign to ensure the mass conversion of Serbs to Catholicism in order to integrate them into 'the Croatian nation'; this campaign was violent and was frequently accompanied by atrocities. Furthermore, the regime and its supporters relied on terrorist methods against the Serb population, mobilizing Ustaša militants to attack Serb villages, massacring the population and then destroying the village.[65] Others were rounded up and interned in the network of Ustaša concentration camps, the most notorious of which was at Jasenovac, south-east of Zagreb. Attempts to estimate the extent of Ustaša genocide have been mired in historical controversy, generated both by the lack of documentation – in itself a legacy of its extreme and random nature – and by the subsequent politicization of the subject.

The vast majority of Serbia fell under German occupation, and was placed for the first few months of that occupation under direct military administration. The collaborationist administration, established in August 1941 and led by a former Yugoslav army general, Milan Nedić, was weak. Its own internal security forces, the State Guard, made up of a small number of former gendarmes, was supplemented by a paramilitary organization recruited from among Serb fascists.[66]

While like Poland, Yugoslav society engaged in broad resistance to the new political order imposed on it, what made the south Slav territories unique was the breadth of partisan activity in the face of the collapse of the inter-war political order. Partisan activity was triggered initially by the rapidity of the Yugoslav army's collapse as many soldiers abandoned their arms, deserted or simply made for the hills in the face of the German advance across the country. Furthermore, the tenuous hold of the occupation authorities on rural areas created a power vacuum as the Yugoslav state collapsed. In Italian-occupied Istria, during the year after occupation, partisan activity in rural areas spread.[67] The moves by the Italian authorities to establish a puppet government in Montenegro provoked an uprising of the former army officers holed up in the mountainous countryside; Montenegro was to form a centre of partisan activity until Italy's withdrawal in 1943. Partisan conflict in the areas annexed by Italy provoked a draconian response, as the Italians interned adult males across their territories in camps like Rab on the Adriatic coast. According to some estimates, by 1943, internment camps held around 50,000 inmates.[68] The severity of this response only served to increase the intensity of partisan activity along the Adriatic coast. Across Croatia, Hercegovina and Bosnia, the genocidal policies of the Ustaša regime in Zagreb fuelled partisan activity among Serbs; in Bosnia it frequently led to violence between Serbs, Croats and the Bosnian Muslims, whose position *vis-à-vis* the NDH was ambiguous.[69] In other ethnically mixed regions, such as the Sandžak region of southern Serbia, partisan activity degenerated into internecine ethnic strife, between Serbs and the local Muslim population.[70]

Principal partisan activity was directed by the Communists, under Josip Broz Tito, and the Serbian non-Communist resistance, known as Četniks, under the former Yugoslav army officer, Draža Mihailović. Partisan activity by both groups was at its strongest in western Serbia under German occupation, resulting in ferocious reprisals from the occupying forces. Nevertheless, the Communists were the more militant of the two groups, and little love was lost between them. The Communists were driven out of Serbia in early 1942, re-establishing their headquarters in the Bosnian town of Foča soon afterwards. Embroiled in a three-cornered conflict with local Serbs and the Ustaša in Bosnia, the Communists profited, gaining a huge swathe of territory in the region due to the effectiveness of their organization, their advocacy of ethnic coexistence to a population tired of internecine strife and the desperate opposition of local Serbs to Croatian genocide. These gains were temporary as the partisans fought a cat-and-mouse game with the Italian and

German occupation forces. The eventual withdrawal of the Italians from the war in September 1943 led to German occupation of the whole territory; it also immeasurably strengthened the influence of Tito's partisans across Bosnia, Croatia and Slovenia. In Serbia, Mihailović and his supporters dominated the armed opposition – a situation that would remain until the Red Army advanced into the region a year later.

The political fate of the whole of the region would be decided by the outcome of Hitler's war with the Soviet Union. As German troops swept eastwards, the impact of war was felt by the societies of those parts of the region directly occupied by the Reich, through the deportation and mass extermination of their Jewish populations, as Poland's ghettos were liquidated during 1942 and 1943. In Bohemia and Moravia, measures to force Jews into ghettos as a prelude to their deportation and extermination began in 1942. Even those areas not directly occupied by Germany came under pressure to deport their Jewish populations in the interests of the Nazis' 'final solution'. In Slovakia, Jews were forcibly deported in 1942, leaving for the camps with an allowance of only 75 pounds of baggage per person.[71]

With the turn of the course of the war during 1942 and 1943, as Hitler's advance into the Soviet Union was checked and rebuffed, the strains of waging the war were felt in the societies of the region. In the protectorate of Bohemia and Moravia, policies towards labour became more despotic, with the lengthening of the working week and forced measures to expand the workforce.[72] In Hungary, industrial expansion had occurred in order to feed the demands of the Nazi war machine, and consequently, employment in industry rose from 330,048 in 1938 to 451,032 in 1942. As war rumbled on, policies in the workplace became increasingly despotic and labour shortages were filled with the increased use of forced labour.[73] War led to a burgeoning black market and high inflation, as the attempts of the state to supply the urban population with food through coercive measures failed.[74] In Bulgaria, these problems had led to spiralling inflation during the first half of the 1940s.[75]

The growing strains on living standards, combined with a growing realization among the population of eventual German defeat, produced both frustration and active opposition to Hitler's new order in the region. In the Protectorate of Bohemia and Moravia in 1944, according to one of the small minority who took part in active resistance, 'everyone is united in hatred of the Germans'.[76] While society was gripped by an intense nostalgia for the Czechoslovak state, few were prepared to engage in any more than small-scale individual acts of resistance.[77] Poland's own resistance movement was growing; in March 1943, the Home Army, the military wing of the underground, was estimated to have a membership of 300,200.[78]

Outside those areas formally occupied by Germany, in territories that were allied to Berlin, fear of the consequences of Soviet victory and weariness with the social impact of the war resulted in political mobilization against Germany by 1943. While the Tiso regime in Slovakia would not be shaken until the Slovak uprising of August 1944, limited partisan activity began in the country's mountainous regions early in 1943.[79] In Hungary, wartime industrialization, peasant and worker discontent and a growing feeling that the war was lost produced increased support for the labour movement and political parties, such as the Social Democrats and the Smallholders, that advocated a more democratic society.[80] For Romania, military disaster at the hands of the Soviets in the Crimea in 1943 likewise strengthened those political actors who had opposed the war.[81] Bulgaria's proximity to Yugoslavia, and to the approaching Red Army, stimulated partisan activity on its territory; according to some estimates, as many as 18,000 participated.[82]

The advance of the Red Army provoked panic among Hitler's East European allies, and some, most notably Romania and Hungary, sought to extricate themselves from the war. In the Romanian case, while General Antonescu's regime continued to fight on the German side, political groups opposed to the war conducted secret negotiations with the Allies to extricate the country from the conflict from the end of 1943. Antonescu's refusal to accept Allied terms, and the growing advances into Romanian territory made by the Soviets in 1944, provoked a growing political crisis. Opponents of the war, together with King Michael, mounted a royal *coup* in the face of imminent military defeat on 23 August, effectively pulling Romania out of the war.[83] Hungary's attempts to negotiate its way out of the war resulted in disaster, as Hitler launched a pre-emptive strike by occupying the country in March 1944 and installing Hungary's radical right-wing ambassador to Berlin, Döme Sztójay, as prime minister. Horthy was removed in October and replaced by a National Socialist puppet regime headed by the Arrow Cross and its leader, Ferenc Szalási. In the last nine months of 1944, an estimated 569,505 of Hungary's 700,000 Jews were murdered as the 'final solution' was implemented in the country. The rest of the population found the country plunged into destructive conflict, as Szalási and the German occupying forces chose to fight to the last.[84] In Slovakia, political upheaval elsewhere undermined support for the Tiso regime. This enabled the Slovak Communists and the non-Communist opposition to form an alliance with elements within the Slovak army. This formed the basis of a short-lived uprising led by partisans in August 1944, which led to the German occupation and reorganization of the Slovak state.[85]

To the north of Slovakia, the Red Army crossed the eastern border of inter-war Poland in July 1944. This was to lead to conflict not only with the country's German occupiers, but between the Red Army's domestic Communist clients, who had organized themselves into the Polish Workers' Party (*Polska Partia Robotnicza* or PPR) in January 1942, and the Home Army that sought the return of Poland's government-in-exile, based in London. With the 'liberation' of the city of Lublin, the PPR staked its claim to lead post-war Poland, setting up a Committee of National Liberation – an alternative Soviet-backed government.[86] Faced with the prospect of a Communist-dominated government in post-war Poland, rather than the return of the London-based government-in-exile, the Home Army attempted to seize the initiative. On 1 August, in the face of Red Army advance, the Home Army led an uprising in Warsaw, anticipating taking the capital as the Germans were beaten back by the Red Army. The uprising failed, the Red Army advance was stopped in its tracks by the Germans, while Stalin failed to provide air support or arms to the uprising, preferring that the London government take no credit for the 'liberation' of Poland. The uprising was brutally crushed by the Germans. Warsaw was finally 'liberated' by the Red Army on 12 January 1945, but this was not to end the bitter political contest over Poland's future.

In Bulgaria, Soviet advance and almost total Bulgarian capitulation brought swift political change, with a transfer of power to a Fatherland Front government in September 1944. The Red Army advances into Bulgaria and Romania strengthened Tito's partisans in Serbia, where they had been weak previously. As the Soviets swept through Hungary, installing a provisional government formed by the Hungarian Communist Party (*Magyar Kommunista Párt* or MKP) and other democratic parties, German rule in Yugoslavia collapsed, leaving the partisans to sweep away its remnants. Tito's influence ensured the victory of Communist partisans in Albania under Enver Hoxha. The Soviet advance led to the setting up of a new government for a reconstituted Czechoslovak state in the Slovak city of Košice. As the Americans entered Bohemia, Soviet troops swept westward, taking Prague in the midst of an uprising of the city's population against the Nazi occupiers.

The creation of a new political order to replace the defeated Nazi one was accompanied by enormous political violence across the region. This violence was committed both by retreating German troops and advancing Soviet ones. The most dramatic single German atrocity committed during their retreat was the manner in which they suppressed the Warsaw uprising in 1944. They executed 40,000 people, while 200,000 died in the battle in which the Germans reoccupied the city, which in turn destroyed 80 per cent of the city's buildings.[87] In the chaos of German-occupied, Arrow Cross-ruled Budapest, prior to the Red Army siege of the city in December 1944, the authorities massacred Jews, rounded up political opponents and sought to dismantle factories to carry them west in a dramatic scorched earth policy.[88] While Red Army atrocities towards the civilian population were less spectacular, brutality was nevertheless extensive. Rape was widely employed as a weapon of war right across the region by its new occupiers. Its extent in Budapest during the first months of 1945 has been particularly well documented.[89] The Soviets, fearful of guerilla resistance as they advanced, deported large numbers of male civilians. In Transylvania, their measures targeted the ethnic German population, whom they regarded as a potential fifth column; according to some estimates, almost 100,000 males were deported from Transylvania by the Soviets in early 1945, from a total ethnic German population of just over half a million.[90] In Hungary, measures to deport those 'with German names' resulted in the indiscriminate rounding up and deportation by the Red Army of thousands of male civilians in the first months of 1945.[91] Yugoslav partisans were also guilty of atrocities, not least when the remnants of the Croatian army, with a huge number of civilians in tow, attempted to cross into Austria at Bleiberg in May 1945. Turned back and handed over to the partisans, tens of thousands were simply massacred at the border.[92]

Yet violence was not merely perpetrated by military forces against a passive civilian population at the end of the war. Parts of that civilian population actively participated in widespread violence. This was particularly marked where Nazi policies had sought to remake the pre-existing ethnic composition of a territory to the advantage of Germans. In these areas, previously subject populations exacted retribution, directing their anger against ethnic Germans. In Poland, as the Red Army pushed west, Polish resistance groups began a process of 'wild expulsion' of the ethnic German population; fighters in the second Polish army determined to 'treat the Germans in the way that they have treated us'.[93] It was not just fighters who terrorized German populations, but in many cases ordinary Poles; in August 1945, according to local representatives of the Red Army, 'not only does the plundering of the Germans on the part of the Poles not stop, but it gets stronger all the time. There are more and more frequent cases of unprovoked murders of German inhabitants'.[94] This wild expulsion was replicated in the former Protectorate of Bohemia and Moravia, just as it was being reincorporated into a resurrected Czechoslovakia. Probably the most notorious incident in this process was the forced expulsion, on foot, of 20,000 Germans from the city of Brno by the new rulers of the Moravian capital.[95] In Istria, as early as 1943, when the Italians withdrew, the Yugoslav partisans pursued a policy of retribution against the Italian population, which heralded 11 years of sustained population transfer.[96] Even in areas like annexed Vardar Macedonia, where ethnic identities were more fluid and ambiguous than further north-west, reaction to the Bulgarianizing policies of the occupiers underpinned political violence against sections of the population perceived to be perpetrators, though far more unevenly than in Poland or Czechoslovakia.[97]

Retribution on the part of previously subject populations against those associated with the policies of former occupiers was one of the stimulants to enormous movements of people at the end of the Second World War. During late 1944 and 1945, millions of people were on the move across the region: the victims of wild transfer in Poland and Czechoslovakia fled west; those who had worked as foreign labour in Germany's industries returned home;

the inmates of camps, both Jewish survivors of the 'final solution' and prisoners of war, tried to return home.[98] Holocaust survivors invariably found themselves unwelcome in their former home towns; anti-Semitism across the region and the harsh post-war economic climate contributed to localized anti-Semitic violence, most notoriously at Kielce in Poland and Kunmadaras in Hungary in 1946.[99] Shifts of population were exacerbated by the flight of collaborators and traditional élites in the face of the Red Army advance. In the Hungarian town of Szolnok, one observer watched 'the whole of the lordly population of the lands east of the' river 'Tisza', queue to the cross the river at the bridge in the town to escape the Soviets in late 1944.[100] The flight of traditional élites resulted in a shift of power to previously subordinate groups. In Czechoslovakia, land seizures by the rural poor and the democratization of factory administration through the institutionalization of works' councils accompanied the Soviet advance, a pattern that was replicated in Hungary.[101]

The social revolution initiated by war took place against a background of almost complete economic penury across the region. War left the whole region economically devastated; agriculture, industry and infrastructure alike suffered tremendous damage. With cities like Warsaw flattened, and the industrial sector across the region ruined, the population was faced with a formidable task.[102] Poor agricultural production in Polish Lower Silesia contributed to desperate poverty, a burgeoning black market and galloping inflation; starvation was avoided in 1945 and 1946, but the situation resulted 'in widespread malnutrition'.[103] In post-'liberation' Budapest, one factory in the heavy engineering sector could only guarantee food of a calorific value of 35 per cent of what they estimated was needed by a manual worker.[104] In Romania, war and Red Army occupation had brought considerable destruction in agriculture, while the unstable political situation had led peasants to hoard grain. This led one American diplomat in Bucharest to indicate the existence of 'a critically short supply' of basic foodstuffs for the urban population in summer 1945.[105]

Alongside widespread violence, mass movements of population, the revolutionary subversion of pre-existing social hierarchies and economic devastation must be set the enormous human cost that was paid by the societies of the region as a result of the war.

According to estimates presented by the historian Bradley F. Abrams, Eastern Europe lost around 10 per cent of its population during the Second World War, ranging from the 6 million Polish and 1.5 million Yugoslav deaths at one extreme to the proportionately small losses of around 0.5 per cent in Bulgaria.[106] This enormous human tally shaped the societies of the region for decades to come. The social dynamics of war, occupation and 'liberation', furthermore, set the context for the politics of the region, defining the social background against which the region's new rulers sought to construct their new socialist political order.

2 Building socialism

War wrought economic and human devastation on an unprecedented scale, but it also acted as the midwife of political transformation across Eastern Europe. The nature and direction of this
transformation was not immediately clear; the new Soviet occupation forces and their Communist allies proclaimed something they
termed 'people's democracy' in 1944 and 1945. Until the late 1940s,
with the exception of Yugoslavia and Albania, the region found itself
in a state of political transition. For most of the region, single-party
socialist dictatorship did not emerge until the period between 1947
and 1949. Despite the deployment of considerable repression by the
state after 1949, the single-party dictatorships found it difficult to
generate circumstances of political stability, given the limited nature
of the legitimacy on which their ruled rested and considerable
economic failures, which had become painfully apparent by the
mid-1950s. While economic failure stemmed from the radical nature
of policies of forced industrialization and collectivization that
impoverished populations, limited legitimacy had different roots. It
stemmed from the way in which Eastern Europe's new rulers
attempted to govern post-war society.

The Soviets' initial policy of installing broad anti-fascist coalitions in power across the region, in which the local Communist
party was *primus inter pares*, was rooted in the approach of
Communist parties internationally to the threat of fascism. From the
mid-1930s onwards, Communist parties across the continent abandoned the strategies of revolutionary sectarianism that had pushed
them towards isolation. The shift in policy had been mandated by
the Comintern, the international organization of Communist parties
in Moscow, due to Stalin's increasing fear of fascism in general and

Germany's National Socialist regime in particular. This shift resulted in Communist parties adopting a 'popular front' approach of unity with all 'anti-fascist' parties; while during the 1930s this included only other left-wing parties, the ideological formula did not explicitly exclude cooperation with some groups on the bourgeois right. While this policy was temporarily abandoned in the face of the Molotov-Ribbentrop pact in 1939, it was renewed with a vengeance following Hitler's invasion of the Soviet Union in 1941. Communist parties were to subordinate revolutionary goals to those of defeating fascism, therefore collaborating with all anti-fascist forces in each country. Georgi Dimitrov, then the secretary-general of the executive committee of the Comintern, stated clearly what this shift would mean: 'In Czechoslovakia, we earlier classified Beneš [the pre-war president of Czechoslovakia] as an agent of English imperialism. Now the fire has to be directed against traitors like Hácha.'[1]

As the Red Army occupied Eastern Europe, this policy of cooperation had to be translated into an ideological formula which would enable Communist parties to govern in broad anti-fascist coalitions. For parties that had argued for the revolutionary trans-formation of the existing order, this was a difficult manoeuvre to effect. The concept worked out was that of the people's democracy – a state that rested on a definition of democracy that relied as much, if not more, on social equality, than more Western concepts of repre-sentative government or a state based on the rule of law. Dimitrov, installed as secretary of the Bulgarian Communist Party, argued in September 1946, that 'Bulgaria will not be a Soviet republic but a people's republic in which the functions of government will be per-formed by an enormous majority of the people – workers, peasants, craftsmen, and the people's intelligentsia. In this republic there will be no dictatorship of any kind'.[2] His Hungarian counterpart, Mátyás Rákosi, used the term 'new democracy' and defined it through the need to effect radical changes in the balance of class power in Hungarian society. In the villages, 'the acid test of the new democra-cy is the land question. He who does not want to see land given to the peasants, who wants to retain the system of great estates, is an enemy of Hungarian democracy.' For industrial communities, 'the basic demand of Hungarian democracy is the immediate abolition of any obstacle to the full economic and political realisation of the power of the working class'.[3] This tension between the need for a broad coalition on the one hand and social radicalism on the other would dog Communist parties in implementing popular-front policies in the region.

Popular-front policies based on notions of broad coalitions of all anti-fascist forces were unevenly implemented across the region. This approach was taken least seriously in south-eastern Europe, where Communists had taken power through military victory in partisan struggle. In Albania, the Communists governed through a Democratic Front, under Enver Hoxha, which maintained the pretence of unifying the Communists and other anti-fascist forces – at least until the Front's 93 per cent victory in the rigged elections of December 1945.[4] Likewise in Yugoslavia, the Communists acted through a Popular Front that was initially a coalition of separate parties; soon after elections in November 1945, it was transformed into a front organization for the Communists.[5]

Elsewhere the transition was not so immediate, for a variety of reasons. In Bulgaria, the Communists governed from September 1944 through the Fatherland Front, nominally a coalition, which was able to introduce quickly policies of radical nationalization and anti-fascist purges. The speedy collapse of the collaborationist government and the existence of domestic partisans aided the consolidation of the new regime's authority.[6] In Romania, following the royal *coup* in August 1944, a National Democratic Bloc government had been created, a coalition in which the Communists were represented. Over the course of the autumn, the country was sharply polarized by political conflict, between the Communists and socialists on the one hand, and the bourgeois National Liberal and National Peasants' parties on the other. Under growing pressure from the left on the streets and the country's Soviet occupiers, the king was forced to appoint a Communist-dominated government under Petru Groza in March 1945. Though nominally a popular-front government, the country's two bourgeois parties were excluded from it.[7] In Hungary, a popular-front provisional government was formed from four parties, including the conservative Smallholders and the trade unions; while technically a coalition, it was, at least until the November 1945 elections, dominated by the left.[8] In Poland, the road to coalition was a tortuous one and took place against a background of civil war between the Home Army and the Communists, supported by the Soviets. The coalition that emerged was contested by armed resistance in the countryside and, politically, by Stanislaw Mikołajczyk and his Peasants' Party (*Polskie Stronnictwo Ludowe* or PSL). At the end of 1945, Communist control in Poland seemed far from secure.[9] In Czechoslovakia, by virtue of their broad base of popular support, especially in Bohemia and Moravia, the Communists had considerable influence over a National Front coalition government, which included the pre-Munich political élite. The country's president was Edvard Beneš, who had headed the London-based government-in-exile, and whose new coalition government was based on an agreement brokered between the government-in-exile and Stalin in 1943.[10]

Behind the formal front of coalition, however, the Communists built parallel security states that they would be able to use against present and future opponents. In Czechoslovakia, the Communist Minister of the Interior, Václav Nosek, moved in 1945 to reorganize the country's police to form a State Security Guard, in which Communists were quickly promoted to positions of influence. Within this guard, the state security division (*Státni bezpečnost* or StB) was given the task of rooting out enemies of the republic and was given formal independence in 1946.[11] In Poland, the climate of civil war against the Home Army and political forces loyal to the government-in-exile in London was used as cover for the establishment of a parallel security state. The Security Office (*Urząd Bezpieczeństwa*, or UB) was established under the auspices of the Soviet NKVD in 1944. Alongside this, civil strife was used to justify draconian actions by the new Polish state, including the sentencing of between 40,000 and 50,000 people by military courts between 1944 and 1949.[12]

In those states which had fought on the side of Nazi Germany, namely Hungary, Romania and Bulgaria, the power of the Communists was bolstered by Allied Control Commissions. While these nominally represented the interests of the United Kingdom and the United States as well, in each of these countries they were dominated by the representatives of the Soviet Union. This afforded the Communists in each country some protection when building a parallel security state under their control. In Hungary, the task of creating a new political force was entrusted to Communist Gábor Péter, who recruited his new policemen from the ranks of left-wing activists, creating a political department, initially to round up 'fascists'.[13] In Romania, the Soviets infiltrated the pre-1944 state security services, the *Siguranţa*; with the advent of the Groza government in 1945, it was placed under the supervision of the Communist-controlled Ministry of the Interior and given the task of spearheading the new government's drive against 'fascists'.[14] In Bulgaria, the army was purged and reorganized, while Communist control of the security apparatus was assured through the creation of the People's Militia and People's Courts.[15]

In south-eastern Europe, where lip-service had been paid to the principle of popular-front coalition, the construction of a security state was closely linked to the overt attempts of local Communists to build a dictatorship over the societies they ruled. In Yugoslavia, the elimination of political opponents merged with the violence that surrounded the end of the war, as the remnants of Mihailović's non-Communist Četniks were destroyed militarily in 1945 and 1946. With the liberation of Belgrade, the Communists moved to construct a security apparatus that would serve their needs in peacetime. In 1944, Aleksandar Ranković, a senior partisan, began to create a security force that would aim at the liquidation of all those who, in Tito's words, did 'not like this kind of Yugoslavia'.[16] As the scope of the security service expanded, in 1946 becoming the State Security Administration (*Uprava državine bezbednosti* or UDBa), Ranković recruited in 'every block of flats, in every street, in every village and every barrack room'.[17]

In south-eastern Europe, the development of a police state went hand in hand with immediate action against political opponents of the Communists, whose retribution against former 'fascists' often dovetailed with the elimination of opponents. In February 1945, the new Albanian government introduced special courts for 'war criminals' right across the country, and ordered the confiscation of their property.[18] These measures were to herald a wave of generalized repression that led to an estimated 80,000 arrests of ordinary Albanians for political offences prior to 1956.[19] In Yugoslavia, retribution against those perceived to be fascists or believed to have been collaborators was severe. The country passed a law to punish 'offences against people and the state', which included provisions against those who had committed what were deemed to have been war crimes.[20] Among the most spectacular measures of retribution in the Yugoslav context was the trial and execution of Draža

Mihailović in summer 1946, for war crimes and collaboration with the country's Nazi occupiers. In a similar show trial in the autumn, Alojzije Stepinac, Archbishop of Zagreb, was tried and sentenced to imprisonment with hard labour for his collaboration with the Ustaša regime. The net was then drawn to attack non-Communist politicians guilty of minor forms of collaboration.[21]

In post-war Yugoslavia, retribution was not simply about a reckoning with the immediate past, nor was it only to do with providing a justification for the elimination of political opponents, though both these elements were present; it was also about constructing a basis of legitimacy for the new state. In the immediate post-war period, in party propaganda, 'fascist' and 'collaborator' came to be used synonymously for those who opposed the policies of the new regime.[22] The state based its legitimacy on the fact that it was the representative of 'the anti-fascist struggle' and promoted this through propaganda and patterns of commemoration. The commemoration of 'uprising days' in each of the Yugoslav republics – in other words, the days when, according to the regime, the partisan struggle began – played an important part of officially promoted commemoration into the post-war period.[23]

While Yugoslavia, with its partisan past, was in many ways unique, anti-fascist measures right across the region combined the three elements of retribution, measures to eliminate potential political opponents and attempts to legitimate the new political system. Because of differing patterns of social reaction to war and political identification, anti-fascist retribution played out in different ways in the varying national contexts across the region. In Bulgaria, where 10,987 were tried under retributive justice and 2,138 were executed between September 1944 and March 1945,[24] such measures were used to legitimate the extensive purges that accompanied the Fatherland Front government's consolidation of its power.[25] In Hungary, however, the numbers of those affected were far lower and the picture in terms of popular reaction was deeply ambiguous. From their establishment until mid-August 1945, Hungary's retributive courts had arrived at verdicts in 3,893 cases, of which 1,014 had resulted in acquittals and 64 in death sentences.[26] In addition, those deemed to be fascists were interned – 16,949 of them up to January 1946. 'Verification committees' were set up in factories to prevent those with 'fascist' pasts from returning to white-collar or managerial posts, and these continued to function throughout the late 1940s.[27] These measures proved to be a poisoned chalice for the regime – internment and verification alienated large sections of the urban middle class, who believed that the state had criminalized many for simply working under the inter-war Horthy regime. At the same time, in the climate of social tension and political division that gripped the country in the immediate post-war years, they also failed to satisfy the regime's working-class base, who wanted more radical purges, not only of those who had been involved in the brief Arrow Cross regime, but also of those who had undertaken anti-labour measures in the inter-war years.[28]

In Czechoslovakia, radical retribution against collaboration was backed by a broad political consensus that stretched from the Communists to the bourgeois parties, and included the non-Communist president, Edvard Beneš. This resulted in the passage of draconian legislation against former collaborators, with little political debate and an extensive process of retribution. In the Czech lands, until February 1948, 32,853 appeared before retributive courts, of whom 22,087 were convicted, while in Slovakia, 8,059 received convictions from a total of 20,561 tried, with more than 700 death sentences carried out.[29] While retribution received considerable support in the Czech lands, because of their occupied status during the war years, in Slovakia it was regarded with much more suspicion. The trial and execution in 1946 of Josef Tiso, the wartime leader of the Slovak state, provoked strong feelings among Catholic and nationalist opinion in Slovakia, which underlined political differences between the two component parts of the Czechoslovak state.[30] The politics of retribution in Czechoslovakia provided cover for the extension of undemocratic measures that supported the parallel security state constructed by the Communists. Paradoxically, in punishing patterns of behaviour that had sustained an illegitimate and repressive regime in the war years, they allowed those same patterns of behaviour to reproduce themselves in new post-war circumstances. According to the journalist Jiří Bilý, in 1947, 'the vice called denunciation, which was born on 15 March 1939, lives on'. For him, the witch-hunting climate promoted by retribution ensured that 'a new army of denouncers is already being born among us'.[31]

Retribution was often directed not just against individuals but against entire ethnic groups, particularly Eastern Europe's German population. Here the concerns of the region's new rulers combined with the strong desire for revenge on the part of those who had suffered from the plans of Nazis and their clients to shape a new ethnographic order. In newly liberated Czechoslovakia, the language of left-wing politicians fanned the flames of Czech anger, which manifested itself during the process of wild expulsion that accompanied liberation. In May 1945, Zdeněk Nejedlý, minister of education, proclaimed that the country's new rulers 'will purify Prague and the border districts [of Germans] and we are in a position to do so, because we have a great helper in doing this – the Red Army'.[32] The preparations for the organized expulsions, due to begin in January 1946, occurred against a background of continued wild transfer that was incited by representatives of the state. One publication in the Bohemian town of Ústí nad Labem warned local Czechs that ' "social relations" with Germans are also punishable; don't forget that there are still people who want not only to interact with Germans far more than is necessary, but who even want to marry German women'.[33] As a result of organized deportation, an estimated 2.5 million Germans left. Despite war losses, expulsion accounted for most of the 25.5 per cent drop in population in Bohemia, and the 21 per cent fall in Moravia and Silesia, between 1937 and 1947.[34] Deportation from Poland was more radical, as it was combined with the geographical shift as the country moved 150 miles west of its territory in 1939. In addition to the wild expulsion, the new Polish state began the transfer of millions of Germans westwards. In the chaos of the immediate post-war months, with Poland itself racked by near civil war, 'the transports of the settlers were sent over the borders in an unorganized and unplanned manner', a situation that began to improve in the second half of 1946.[35] However, organized transportation was carried out in a manner that increased the suffering of those expelled; at the assembly points in Poland at the turn of 1947, German 'women, the elderly, and children are in an exceptionally difficult predicament. They are literally half dead with hunger'.[36] The organized transfer of 2.2 million Germans from Poland was combined with an estimated 4 million who had left the western territories ceded to Poland during the period of wild expulsion.[37]

The post-war expulsion of Germans from Poland and Czechoslovakia was but the most spectacular act in a wave of population transfer and ethnic retribution which swept Eastern Europe in the late 1940s. In the former east of Poland, 2.1 million Poles found themselves forced from their homes as the territory was annexed by the Soviet Union.[38] Germans were expelled across the region, with an estimated half a million thrown out of countries other than Poland and Czechoslovakia.[39] In Vojvodina in northern Yugoslavia, the expulsion of Germans smoothed land reform policies in that their land swelled the land fund, which, in turn, was distributed to 'colonists', poor peasants from elsewhere in the federation, 71.97 per cent of whom were Serb, altering the ethnic balance of the local population.[40] In 1947, Czechoslovakia and Hungary agreed to an 'exchange of populations', in which substantial numbers of Magyars were expelled from southern Slovakia, while members of Hungary's Slovak minority were removed to make room for them.[41]

The profound ethnic conflicts of the 1940s demanded that the region's new rulers pay close attention to issues of nationality during reconstruction. This was at its most marked in those regions that had borne the brunt of post-war campaigns of expulsion. An official in the British Embassy in Prague commented on the impact of expulsion on the landscape of north-western Bohemia in striking terms in August 1948: 'A traveler entering Czechoslovakia by road from Germany is struck by the contrast between the rich and well-kept fields and busy villages through which he has just passed and the desolate weed-grown wastes and empty dwellings which are his first sight of Czechoslovakia.'[42] Policies of reconstruction had been pursued in this borderland for three years when the official made his observation. Under the auspices of a Resettlement Office set up by the state, the region was to be rebuilt as an industrial heartland, but one populated by Czech and Slovak settlers, not by Germans. Nation-building and industrial reconstruction went hand in hand.[43] Similar policies were pursued in western Poland, annexed from Germany, as Poland's Ministry for the Regained Territories bolstered ethnic homogeneity by resettling Poles in the areas vacated by Germans. While the total population in the post-war territories never matched the pre-war population, the influx of settlers created new Polish population centres. Wrocław, formerly Breslau, capital of Lower Silesia, saw its population increase from 170,700 in 1946 to 308,900 by 1948.[44] One settler in the city described the urban landscape he found in terms that would have been familiar to contemporary travellers in north-western Bohemia: 'Endless ruins, the stink of burning, countless huge flies, the clouded faces of occasionally encountered Germans, and most important, the emptiness of desolated streets'.[45]

The policies pursued in Poland and Czechoslovakia aimed at rebuilding the countries around the hegemony of dominant ethnic groups. In other states, new rulers pursued policies that were based on nation-building strategies. In Albania during the late 1940s, Enver Hoxha's regime pursued policies that combined the standardization of language and campaigns of repression, to advance a version of Albanian identity that rested on the culture of Tosks, who inhabited the south of the country, and aimed at the marginalization of the Ghegs, who inhabited the north.[46] Albania, however, was somewhat exceptional. Outside of Poland and Czechoslovakia, the most dramatic attempts to pursue policies of nation-building were in multi-ethnic Yugoslavia. Because of the bloodletting of the war years in the multinational south Slav state, and the appeal of its Communists to sections of the population tired of the violence that accompanied the politics of ethnic exclusivity, the remaking of both state and nations was essential to the survival of the regime. The Communists promoted a revival of Yugoslavia based on a 'supranational "universal" culture' that could exist together with the separate 'national' cultures of the constituent peoples of the state.[47] This pushed the country's new rulers down the road of a federalism based on 'the brotherhood and unity' of the state's constituent parts; as the first article of the 1946 constitution stated: 'The Federal People's Republic of Yugoslavia is … a community of peoples with equal rights'.[48] Six constituent republics were created by the constitution: Bosnia-Hercegovina, Croatia, Macedonia, Montenegro, Serbia and Slovenia. At the same time, five 'nations' were recognized – Croatians, Macedonians, Montenegrins, Serbs and Slovenes. Defined by culture, a citizen could be a member of any of these 'nations', regardless of the republic he or she lived in. This political formula allowed a Yugoslav identity to be promoted, based on (in the words of a statement of principles to be used to define the post-war school curriculum): 'the building of socialism in our homeland, fraternity among the Yugoslav peoples, pride in the achievements of the War of National Liberation'.[49] However, it enabled the republics to pursue cultural policies of nation-building, albeit within the political limits imposed by the regime, and of 'Yugoslavism'. This was at its most evident in Macedonia, where language and education were used to promote a Macedonian identity distinct from the Serb and Bulgarian identities that had been ascribed frequently to the populations of the territory.[50]

Reconstruction everywhere was accompanied by nationalist rhetoric, often appropriated by the Communist parties and their leaders. Hungary's Communists, for example, cast themselves as 'the heirs of Kossuth, Petőfi and Tánsics' in order to bolster their legitimacy.[51] In part, reconstruction was about 'national' reconstruction and recovery from the devastation of war, but it was also about radical change that would increase the role of previously subordinate groups in each national society. It was at its most radical in Yugoslavia and Albania, where the politics of reconstruction were virtually synonymous with those of socialist transformation, and at its least radical in Hungary, where a substantial private sector in commerce and industry was allowed to survive until 1948. Right across the region, the politics of reconstruction meant the expropriation of large landholdings and their distribution to peasantries and the rural poor, in many cases simply legalizing land seizures and occupations that had occurred as the Red Army advanced westward.

In the factories, the politics of reconstruction posed more acute problems for the region's rulers, because the industrial working class provided the most secure base of support for the popular-front regime, yet also demanded political change that was very different in nature – and often more radical – to that envisaged by governments. The factory committees and works' councils that sprang up in the face of the Red Army advance were quickly incorporated into the trade-union bureaucracies and given the task of ensuring a degree of control over enterprises; in the words of Czechoslovakia's trade union leader, Antonín Zápotocký, 'the aim of the control activity of the works' councils is to inspect production, trade and administration so that it is not abused against the interests of employees and the state'.[52] Workers were to maintain discipline in the interests of reconstruction, even if this meant cooperation with private owners; as far as Hungarian Communist theorist Aladár Mód was concerned, workers and their representatives should 'abandon the kind of behaviour that big capital expects of them'.[53] In the desperate post-war conditions of penury, shortage and hyperinflation, and believing in the promise of a better, more socially just future, workers struggled in the interests of reconstruction. In the Polish industrial city of Łódź, in the first post-war months, 'no-one asked about pay, but everyone s[tood] resolutely at his post'.[54] Yet frustration soon set in across the region. In Hungary, miserable living conditions created by hyperinflation, the failure to conduct extensive purges of managerial and supervisory personnel, and unpopular collective agreements all stoked sporadic labour conflict in the second half of the 1940s.[55] In post-war Łódź, working-class protest was often stimulated by management authoritarianism and labour policies, which were seen as a threat to traditional shop-floor cultures in the city's factories.[56]

Industrial workers provided an insecure base of support for the post-war regimes of the region, but there were many others who opposed popular-front rule. It was only in Czechoslovakia, where they won 38 per cent of the popular vote in elections in May 1946, that the Communists were able to legitimate their rule through fair elections. Even this result revealed the limited nature of the left's legitimacy, in that the Communists captured the Czech lands, winning 40.17 per cent in Bohemia and Moravia, but failed dismally in Slovakia.[57] Here, a large rural majority, attached to individual land-holding and thus suspicious of Communist egalitarianism, and the existence of a strongly Catholic political culture in the villages hampered the left's advance, creating a situation in which they were trounced by the centre-right Democratic Party (*Demokratická strana* or DS) which took 61.43 per cent of the Slovak vote to the 30.48 polled by the Communists.[58] The constellation of forces that emerged in Slovakia in 1946 replicated that which had appeared in Hungary the previous November. Beneficiaries of land reform attached to property, the prevalence of political Catholicism in the centre and west of the country, middle-class distrust of the new state, and the decision of the Allied Control Commission to ban other right-wing parties from contesting the election combined to hand the conservative Smallholders' Party a landslide victory in parliamentary elections, with 57.03 per cent of the vote. The Communists emerged with a mere 16.95 per cent. It was only through rallying a fragmented left, and using Soviet support to maintain a key position in the government that it was able to recover the situation, mobilizing its supporters and using its control over the security services to destroy the Smallholders' Party in 1946 and 1947. It recovered its position at the head of a popular-front coalition only through the semi-rigged elections of August 1947.[59] Nowhere else in the region were the elections in the mid-1940s as fair or as free as those held in Czechoslovakia or Hungary. Apart from Albania and Yugoslavia, which have already been discussed, Communist-dominated popular-front governments held power despite the considerable opposition of large sections of the societies they ruled. In Romania, where Petru Groza's government had ruled without the support of the country's non-socialist majority, elections in November 1946 were conducted against a background of intimidation, political tension and attacks on the non-Communist press. The landslide election victory of the Communist-dominated Bloc of Democratic Parties was produced, according to observers, through widespread electoral fraud.[60] In Bulgaria, while widely discredited elections had been held in November 1945, the real electoral contest between the Communist-dominated Fatherland Front and the opposition, led by Nikola Petkov, was held in October 1946; the Front's victory was the product of an ugly and polarized political climate.[61] In Poland, the government in Warsaw faced opposition from both the armed groups, formed from the Home Army, and the political opposition of the PSL around Stanislaw Mikołajczyk, which attempted to organize the anti-Communist majority in the country. This majority was underlined when, in a climate of generalized political polarization, the government held a referendum on 30 June 1946 on the issues of constitutional reform, nationalization and the new borders. Though the referendum resulted in 'yes' votes on all three counts, fraud disguised the degree of hostility among ordinary Poles towards the PPR. Consequently, the PSL judged that it could defeat the PPR and its Socialist allies in forthcoming elections, held in January 1947. The elections were far from free and fair: members of the PPR dominated electoral commissions and in much of the country there was no secret ballot. PSL scrutineers were denied access to the counting of the votes across the country. Officially, the Democratic Bloc, dominated by the PPR, won 80.1 per cent to the 10.3 per cent recorded for the PSL.[62]

Some commentators have regarded the post-war popular-front regimes as little more than a stage in the drive of Eastern Europe's

Communist parties for absolute power.[63] This understates the distinctiveness of the immediate post-war period, when the economies of the region were characterized by mixed forms of ownership and multi-party systems were permitted (save in Yugoslavia and Albania), even where elections were not free and fair. Yet to term the period a 'democratic interlude', as others have done,[64] is to overstate the case. The Soviets and their Communist allies ensured close control over politics, either through the Allied Control Commissions, in those states which had fought alongside Hitler, or through parallel security states. The manner in which Communists used policies of anti-fascist retribution to strengthen their position or their undemocratic tactics when their hold on power was threatened by election defeat attests to the limits of democracy in the post-war states. Popular-front rule was the Eastern European product of the wartime alliance between the Western powers and the Soviet Union. As the wartime alliance itself broke down, popular-front rule was destined to disappear with it.

The breaking of the wartime alliance was partly precipitated by tension generated by the undemocratic behaviour of the Soviets and their Communist allies in popular-front Eastern Europe. American concern about the 'communist threat' prompted the United States to offer Western European states Marshall Aid. The anti-communist nature of politics in post-war Western Europe was cemented with the expulsion of the powerful Communist parties of France and Italy from the coalition governments in those countries in 1947. The Soviets responded with the foundation of the Cominform, a new international organization of Communist parties, which heralded greater coordination. The founding meeting of the organization, held in the Polish town of Szklarska Poręba in September 1947, sounded the death knell not only of the wartime alliance, internationally, but also of popular-front policies, domestically.

This was underlined most dramatically in the months following Szklarska Poręba by events in Czechoslovakia. Prior to September 1947, the Czechoslovak Communist Party (*Komunistická Strana Čekoslovenska* or KSČ) had committed itself to an electoral road to socialism, in view of its success in the 1946 elections; its secretary, Klement Gottwald, had set the party the goal of winning 51 per cent in the next elections.[65] In an atmosphere of growing tension between the coalition parties over KSČ control of the police, Stalin's ban on the country applying for Marshall Aid and a deteriorating economic situation, popular support slipped away from the party in 1947.[66] Political crisis erupted as 12 non-Communist ministers walked out of the government over KSČ control of the security forces in February 1948. A majority of ministers stayed and Gottwald, bolstered by support from the unions, was able to force President Beneš to accept a single-party KSČ government. The security forces and KSČ supporters set to work, forming 'action committees', which took over the non-Communist parties, and established themselves in 'the civil service, in all large enterprises, in the professions, and in all towns and villages', to conduct purges and thus consolidate the party's power.[67]

The Prague *Coup*, as the Czechoslovak events became known, was only the most spectacular in a series of processes that characterized the region's slide into overt dictatorship. In Hungary, where Communist power over a popular-front government was only fully consolidated in August 1947, 1948 witnessed the liquidation of the non-socialist opposition, the enforced merger of the Communist and Social Democratic parties to form the Hungarian Workers' Party (*Magyar Dolgozók Pártja* or MDP) and the creation of the personal dictatorship of Mátyás Rákosi.[68] Where Communist power had been consolidated earlier, similar shifts from 'popular-front' to overt dictatorship were under way. In Poland, the PPR deployed increasingly radical class rhetoric throughout 1948, culminating in its merger with the Socialists in December to form the Polish United Workers' Party (*Polska Zjednoczona Partia Robotnicza* or PZPR), which established a political system in which one party enjoyed 'the leading role'.[69] In Romania, non-Communist political opposition had been all but eliminated by early 1948; the Communist Party swallowed the Social Democrats in September 1947 and then purged its membership, expelling around 340,000 between 1948 and 1950, thus laying the foundations of the personal dictatorship of Gheorghe Gheorgiu-Dej.[70]

In Yugoslavia, where socialist dictatorship had been institutionalized as early as 1946, the changes of 1948 initiated a new phase in the development of the state. Because of its roots in partisan warfare rather than Red Army occupation pure and simple, the Communist regime proved immune to control by Moscow. Growing tension between Belgrade and Moscow, fuelled by the independent behaviour of Tito, led Stalin to break links with the regime in Yugoslavia in March 1948.[71] The break led to an increased drive for Communist political control in Yugoslavia, what the historian Stevan K. Pavlowitch has termed 'Stalinism without Stalin'.[72] Paradoxically, this drive was justified by anti-Stalinism and the need for unity in the face of a sea of hostile states.[73] For Albania, whose independence had been threatened by Yugoslavia, Tito's split with Stalin was an opportunity, one that was grasped wholeheartedly by Hoxha, who aligned Albania closely with the Soviet Union.[74]

The construction of overt dictatorship in much of the region, and the intensification of that dictatorship in Yugoslavia and Albania, meant, above all, an escalation of repression against opponents, both real and imagined. Building on the foundations of the parallel security states laid in the popular-front era, the dictatorships dramatically expanded their internal security services during the late 1940s and early 1950s. In Hungary, the political department of the police was reorganized several times, eventually becoming the State Security Agency (*Államvédelmi Hatóság* or ÁVH) in 1948. The numbers it employed rose from 9,000 in 1949 to 28,000 a year later.[75] In neighbouring Romania, the internal security services were renamed the *Securitate* in August 1948; employing a relatively small number of officers and a vast army of informers, they had gathered evidence on an astounding 417,916 people by 1951.[76] In Poland, the UB had become a vast organization by 1951, while in Bulgaria, it was estimated that some 70,000 were employed in police-related activities, as opposed to a mere 25,000 at the end of the 1940s.[77] In Yugoslavia, Ranković's security services also grew and new forms of detention camp were opened for 'political' detainees, the most notorious of which was on the island of Goli Otok, off the Croatian coast.[78] The expansion of detention camps accompanied the creation of overt dictatorship across the region; a law passed in Czechoslovakia in 1948, which established 'educational working centres', legalized the practice, in force since February, of sending political prisoners from Prague's Pankrac prison to work camps in the towns of Kladno, Karlovy Vary and Pradubice.[79]

The escalation of repression, like the expansion of the security state, was built on the foundations of the campaigns of anti-fascist retribution pursued in the popular-front era, in that it combined retribution (though on this occasion the scope of retribution was dramatically widened to include those who had opposed the Communists), the elimination of political opponents and propagandistic motives. At the same time, though, it represented a dramatic break from earlier practices, especially in terms of its scale. It also rested on notions that society was divided into supporters and 'enemies' of socialist construction, a practice derived directly from the practice of Soviet Stalinism. The range of enemies identified by the state and security apparatus was enormous. The first targets of the escalation of repression were the representatives of non-Communist political forces and their supporters. In Bulgaria, the show trial and execution of Petkov in summer 1947 initiated a process by which non-Communist political forces were eliminated, while many of their members and representatives were arrested and tried.[80] In Czechoslovakia, the post-Prague *Coup* suppression of non-Communist political forces extended beyond the ranks of non-Communist parties to include representatives of the press. In the aftermath of February 1948, 'the Union of Journalists ... expelled a large number of its members on political grounds', while in the country's universities, action committees 'deprived the rector and a large number of professors their offices and all their functions. Some students have been expelled'.[81] The scope of the repression of former members and representatives of non-Communist parties was extended to those who had belonged to the region's socialist and social democratic parties prior to their liquidation; in Hungary, arrests and show trials of former Social Democrats, including the country's president, Árpád Szakasits, occurred in 1950.[82]

The show trial, in which a senior public figure was tried, often for a conspiracy against the state, fabricated by the security apparatus and signed under torture, became a symbol of the wave of repression which spread across the region during the early 1950s. The most striking of these show trials were those where senior Communists themselves were tried and executed on trumped-up charges of treason against both the system they had helped to create and their country. The early show trials directed at senior Communists involved rooting out assumed enemies within the party who, according to the trumped-up charges they faced, had conspired with Tito to betray their comrades to the capitalist West. This was the easiest to effect in Albania, where Hoxha was keen to cooperate with Soviet attempts to identify and root out 'Yugoslav deviationism', resulting in the trial of the former interior minister, Koçi Xoxe, in May 1949.[83] The trial in Hungary of another former interior minister, László Rajk, on similar charges in September 1949, and his execution the following month began a wave of arrests and trials that convulsed the Hungarian party throughout the early 1950s.[84] In Bulgaria, the trial and execution of Traicho Kostov, the former Communist deputy prime minister, for membership of the 'Titoist conspiracy' followed.[85] While the 1949 wave of show trials was intended to send a message to party members, activists and the population that Tito was little more than the 'chained dog' of Western imperialism, Yugoslavia's split with Moscow had initiated a wave of purges inside the south Slav state. Tito had liquidated all non-Communist opposition by the time of the split, and when a new wave of repression was initiated in 1948, this was against pro-Moscow elements inside the party, in a purge which was a mirror image of those under way elsewhere. According to Ranković, between 1948 and 1952, around 13,500 had been punished for their pro-Moscow stance.[86] The waves of trials on the other side of the divide in Soviet-dominated Eastern Europe rumbled on throughout the early 1950s. In one of the most notable show trials in the region, the secretary-general of the KSČ, Rudolf Slánský, was tried and executed for 'treason' in 1952.[87]

The message that the country's leaders intended to send out, by way of the show trials of senior party figures, was that internal enemies and traitors were to be found everywhere. This bolstered the escalation of repression, as its objects shifted from political opposition to society. Organized religion was increasingly an object of escalated repression during the late 1940s and early 1950s. In part, this was due to the natural suspicion with which the Communists regarded the churches, given the anticlericalism of the region's rulers. It was also due to the fact that churches had, in much of the region, sustained anti-Communist political activity during the popular-front period and continued to do so as the dictatorship was built. In Slovakia and Hungary, for example, political Catholicism in rural areas had shaped a political culture which propelled centre-right parties to victory in elections during the mid-1940s. In Hungary, the reaction in the country to the arrest of its Catholic primate and prominent conservative critic of the regime, Cardinal József Mindszenty, in December 1948, underlined popular

Catholicism's continued hold among sections of the population, particularly women and those living in rural areas. Even in industrial areas, like the town of Újpest, women textile workers who commuted from rural areas greeted Mindszenty's arrest with dismay.[88] In Slovakia, the period after the Communist assumption in power of Prague was accompanied by a wave of arrests of priests who used their position to make anti-Communist statements. By summer 1949 there were reports of violence in a number of villages, as residents attempted to defend their priests from arrest by the security services.[89] In rural Poland, rumours that the state would arrest priests provoked considerable opposition. The way in which political opposition and popular Catholicism fused in the Polish context was illustrated by reactions to the supposed sighting of the weeping of the statue of the Virgin in Lublin Cathedral in 1949. This 'miracle' was interpreted by many believers as a sign of the illegitimacy of Communist rule.[90]

It was not only in predominantly Catholic Central Europe that the state responded to church activity with repression. In western Yugoslavia, where Catholicism was tied to Croatian nationalism, and thus to the issue of collaboration with the NDH and to Slovene anti-Communism, Catholic priests had become targets of state repression as early as 1946.[91] Albania saw increasing measures to limit the influence of Islam and to curb Catholicism.[92] In Romania, during the early 1950s, the focus of the state's attacks on organized religion were Catholic priests and the Uniate Church, which it tried to suppress, deploying considerable brutality.[93]

In the handling of organized religion, the limits as well as the extent of dictatorship were apparent. In view of the importance of both organized and popular religion among the region's rural majority, the regimes sought not simply to suppress, but also to incorporate certain elements of organized religion into the official power structure. In Yugoslavia, while the Serbian Orthodox Church, like the Catholic Church, had been the victim of politically inspired repression during the late 1940s, from 1950 there was a gradual reconciliation, based upon the Church promising to support regime efforts to achieve 'brotherhood and unity', in exchange for the state extending social insurance to priests and regularizing the legal status of churches.[94] In Romania, a bargain had been struck between the regime and the Orthodox Church in 1949, but it was a highly unequal one. It agreed to the nationalization of its assets, making it financially dependent on the state. Though this bargain ensured that Orthodox priests did not face the level of persecution met by Catholics and Uniates, it effectively accepted incorporation into the power structure.[95] In Hungary, where the anti-Communism of both Catholic and Protestant clergy, as well as the jailing of Mindszenty, made a durable institutional settlement between Church and state all but impossible, the regime sought to incorporate the clergy into the power structure through the official, party-sponsored peace movement, limiting their freedom of action and giving them a defined political role.[96] In Poland, a concordat between Church and state had been signed in April 1950, but relations remained tense throughout the early 1950s, given the anti-Communism of much of the clergy and believers. This failure of the state to stem opposition resulted in a further turn to repression, culminating in the arrest of the Polish primate, Cardinal Stefan Wyszyński, in 1953.[97]

The escalation of repression was not merely about the drive for political control, nor was it strictly motivated by the desire of the region's rulers for retribution against groups that had sustained opposition; it was necessitated, in large part, by the radicalism of the regime's policies in the economic and social spheres, as it moved explicitly to pull back from the conciliatory tone of the popular-front period and pressed ahead with the construction of socialism. This was accompanied by a rhetorical attack on social classes perceived to be hostile to socialism, as an intensification of the class struggle was demanded by the region's leaders. This shift was already visible in 1947, on the eve of the onset of overt dictatorship, through campaigns like Poland's Battle over Trade, in which the PPR's, and later the PZPR's, economic supremo, Hilary Minc, launched campaigns against 'speculators' that added up to a generalized attack on private enterprise in the retail sector.[98] In Czechoslovakia, campaigns directed against the 'hoarding of goods' and 'speculation' by retailers, manufacturers and wholesalers in the textile and clothing sector immediately preceded the political crisis of February 1948.[99] The drive against the private sector sometimes resulted in economic show trials. Hungary's oilfields had provided a source of political conflict between their American owners and the Ministry of Industry throughout the 1940s. With the advent of overt dictatorship in 1948, they were simply confiscated by the state and their senior management put on trial for 'sabotage' of the national economy.[100] These provided political cover for the liquidation of private owner- ship in industry, finance and trade through policies of radical nationalization; by 1952, between 97 and 100 per cent of industrial output came from the socialist sector of the economy across the region, and between 76 and 98 per cent of all retail turnover was generated in socialized enterprises.[101]

The 'class war' rhetoric and practice of the dictators was not only directed against businessmen, but also against the rural popu- lation, as the state moved to socialize the agricultural sector and grab as much of the agricultural surplus as possible to feed urban populations. The attack on the individual landholder that resulted was justified through references to the incompatibility between individual patterns of land ownership and socialism. In the words of Romania's dictator, Gheorgiu-Dej, 'We have in the villages an ocean of small individual farms (over 3 million), which after the celebrated saying of Lenin, generate capitalism'.[102] In order to prevent the 'generation of capitalism' in the countryside, the state targeted the 'proto-capitalist' class in the countryside by identifying the wealthier farmers and labelling them 'kulaks'. Though the term was used throughout the region, its precise meaning varied from country to country and, in terms of its implementation, often from village to village. The term had entered official discourse in Yugoslavia in 1946, two years before it became widely used in the rest of the region, and it is difficult to disagree with Yugoslavia's chief ideologist, Edvard Kardelj, that 'the kulak is a political concept'.[103] The countryside was subjected to increased taxation and the intensification of state requisitioning of agricultural produce, introduced in most of the region during the war years. Those identified as kulaks were subjected to more punitive taxation and greater quotas of requisi- tioned produce than fellow farmers, as the state aimed to drive them out of farming entirely. These policies produced penury in many villages across the region, as smallholders struggled to preserve their family landholding in the face of pressure from the state. In western Hungary, in late 1952, 'the farmer got less for his produce, than his seed had cost him', causing 'general hunger … the rural population had to wait in long queues for bread and flour, whilst the family who could get hold of half a kilo of flour was delighted'.[104] This climate provoked both resentment and passive resistance to state attempts to collect taxes and enforce the requisitioning of produce. In one Polish village, in 1952, the residents adopted:

> what might be called a solid anti-political front. The government inspectors who occasionally visit the place are given identical information at each house. Obviously all the people in the hamlet know who has hidden potatoes or illegally slaughtered a hog, but they keep quiet. The inspectors are unable to break through the wall of silence.[105]

Attempts to force peasants into agricultural producer cooperatives – new large-scale agricultural enterprises which were, in theory, owned by the workers, but where production was to take place on an industrial scale under state direction – went together with the increase in deliveries. This was attempted everywhere in the region, including Yugoslavia, which was worried about guaranteeing food to its cities. Smallholders across the region were largely hostile to state steps to end their independence. The Polish countryside was marked by a wave of protest that accompanied collectivization campaigns, which included arson, sabotage and demonstrations.[106] Poorer smallholders tended to join cooperatives, but where they did so, disorganization and under-investment led to miserable living conditions. Remuneration in one Bulgarian cooperative, paid in kind, was so low in late 1950 that the members, 'tired of all the vain promises, and armed with spades and forks ... attacked the co-operative, taking back their cattle and implements.'[107] Opposition rarely turned into open revolt, but where it did it could be spectacular. The largest anti-collectivization uprising occurred in the Bihać region of north-western Bosnia in May 1950, which affected five villages and resulted in 714 arrests.[108] The strength of feeling across Eastern Europe did not result in compromise, at least until Yugoslavia's permanent abandonment of collectivization in 1953, and Hungary's temporary suspension of the process following the death of Stalin in the same year. The countryside was where the dictatorships could be seen at their most brutal, and anti-regime feeling was at its strongest.

Anti-regime feeling was also marked among large segments of

the pre-socialist middle class, especially among those dispossessed by radical nationalization. In the western Hungarian town of Nagykanizsa, in 1949, dispossessed former businessmen waited for a war with the United States that they hoped would bring 'the liberation of the country'.[109] Members of these social groups were subject to routine discrimination in employment and faced the pressure of deportation, particularly when they lived in politically sensitive regions. The 40,320 deported by the Romanian state from the Banat region on the western border in 1951 included 'kulaks and inn keepers' as well as 'former landowners and industrialists'.[110] Yet those targeted by such measures were more than just former capitalists; they included professionals, civil servants and a range of middle-class groups. This could be seen in 1951, when several thousand 'class enemies' were removed from Budapest, in part to ease pressure on housing in the capital as the industrial workforce expanded.[111] Members of the former middle classes were discriminated against in terms of access to education; the future Czech president, Václav Havel, was among those denied educational opportunity in early socialist Czechoslovakia, due to his 'bourgeois' origins.[112] As the state changed the social roles of many in intellectual occupations, in academia and in areas like the arts and journalism, political control increased and non-Communists were purged.

Yet strangely enough, despite the policy of purges and restrictions on the numbers of those of 'bourgeois' origins who could gain access to higher education, middle-class social groups preserved their social positions to a remarkable extent. In Hungary, it was estimated in 1956 that of those employed in professional positions, as many as 60–70 per cent had occupied similar social positions in the pre-socialist period.[113] In some countries, the reason for this lay in the fact that attempts to promote workers and peasants to higher education courses that served as the entry point to such professions never achieved success. This was the case in the Czech lands, where working-class students continued to be grossly under-represented in higher education throughout the 1950s.[114] The demands of the economy for technical expertise in a climate of industrialization created such a demand for educated labour that opportunities were opened for children of former middle-class groups to enter new professional jobs. This seems to have been the case in Hungary[115] and also in Poland, where discriminatory practices were relaxed in 1950, where the family members of an applicant were 'important to production and politically valuable'.[116] Thus, though they were an object of repression, the limits as well as the extent of dictatorship were clearly visible in the way in which the state dealt with members of the middle class.

Both the limits of dictatorship and protest against its policies could be seen at their starkest in the industrial sphere. Just as industrial workers provided a base of albeit conditional support for the regimes in the popular-front era, Stalinist dictatorships mobilized workers through the deployment of class-war rhetoric and a celebration of manual industrial labour at the ideological level. At the same time, the state began to prepare the ground for comprehensive economic planning, pursued with the objective of expanding the industrial sector. Yugoslavia began its first five-year plan before the break with Moscow in 1947, but elsewhere in the region, five- and six-year plans commenced in 1949 and 1950.[117] In order to prepare workplaces for planning, the state reshaped labour relations in factories, mines and on construction sites, replacing existing wage systems with standardized ones that were designed strictly to reward production, as set out in the plan.[118] In order to mobilize workers to increase productivity, labour competition campaigns and the decoration of 'outstanding' workers, known as Stakhanovites, began during the late 1940s.[119] Such campaigns brought the state into direct confrontation with working-class culture; the reaction of one Łódź union official to textile workers mobilized in the labour competition was typical: 'We are fighting for [the right] to work on only one loom, and you work on two looms and take bread away from the others'.[120] The marked unpopularity of these campaigns was underlined when they were combined with increases in production targets for workers that resulted in cuts in wages; in Hungary, such increases in August 1950 resulted in a wave of industrial unrest.[121]

The industrialization drive that central planning entailed brought enormous increases in the size of the industrial labour force across the region; between 1948 and 1953, the numbers employed in mining and manufacturing rose from almost 1.4 million to over 1.6 million in Czechoslovakia, from 0.4 million to 0.9 million in Hungary, from 0.4 million to over 0.7 million in Romania, and from under 0.5 million to 0.6 million in Yugoslavia.[122] The industrialization drive also brought economic chaos. It was based on Soviet demands to expand sectors such as machine manufacture in order to feed an arms build-up, in order that Moscow would be able to fight a third world war, something leaders in the region believed to be imminent, given deteriorating relations between the superpowers and the conflict in Korea, which broke out in 1950.[123] Industry expanded more quickly than did the production of energy and raw materials to support it. The result was that production was frequently plagued by shortages of tools and raw materials, which undermined the attempts of enterprises to fulfil the plan. These combined with severe shortages of labour: by 1952, the Polish trade unions warned that industry was short of around 200,000 workers.[124] As managers attempted to cope with meeting plan targets in a climate of endemic shortage and widespread working-class discontent, a range of informal compromises between workers and lower management resulted, which subverted wage policies that sought to tie workers' performance to the goals of the plan.[125] Given the chaos that reigned, as industrial production was hit by frequent stoppages, earnings became increasingly insecure. Absenteeism and labour mobility in industry rocketed; by 1953, around 12 per cent of Czechoslovakia's industrial workforce changed jobs annually.[126] The state unsuccessfully responded to its increasing lack of control over the working class with repression; but attempts in Hungary, in 1952, to criminalize both job quitting and absenteeism failed to stem the tide of 'work indiscipline'.[127]

Both working-class discontent, and that of the urban population more generally, was fuelled by the impact on living standards of forced industrialization and the economic chaos that accompanied it. In Hungary, working-class real wages fell by an estimated 16.6 per cent between 1949 and 1953.[128] In Czechoslovakia, real wages in 1951 stood at only 86.6 per cent of their 1937 level.[129] Poverty combined with endemic food and goods shortages, which had been a near permanent feature of everyday life in the region since the late 1940s. As early as 1949, discontent caused by food shortages had rumbled in Slovak urban centres like Bratislava, Nitra and Zilina.[130] By 1952, Western observers commented regularly on shortages of food and consumer goods across the bloc: 'food shortages were attributed by refugees to many causes; drought in Poland, changeover from agriculture to industry in Czechoslovakia, food exports from Bulgaria to other nations ... peasant unwillingness to fulfil compulsory delivery quotas'.[131] Such shortages fed a burgeoning black market, which prospered across the region, despite its criminalization and the vigilance of the security services. In Romania in mid-1952, 'certain people' brought 'anything needed to the houses of those they know and trust, on condition that the black market price, which is about three times the free market price, be paid'.[132]

While working-class protest had bubbled beneath the surface throughout the early 1950s, where it had been concerned with workplace issues it was met with repression. This contributed to a situation where large numbers of industrial workers languished in the region's jails and work camps; for example, workers made up 31.6 per cent of those held in Czechoslovak prisons for 'political' crimes in 1950.[133] Continued economic chaos, declining living standards and attempts by the state to reduce further the purchasing power of the population to keep forced industrialization on track caused a breach between the state and the working class. This became painfully apparent in 1952 and 1953, as governments responded to growing shortages, suppressed inflation and generalized economic chaos by implementing currency reforms that effectively confiscated the savings of populations. Reforms, copying one introduced in Poland in October 1950, were introduced in Romania in January 1952, in Bulgaria in May 1952 and in Czechoslovakia in May 1953. The Czechoslovak currency reform provoked not only a wave of strikes across the country, but also one of the most spectacular acts of working-class protest in the region during the early socialist years. In Plzeň, strikes at the town's Škoda works in June 1953 erupted in generalized rioting that led to the occupation of the town hall by demonstrators; the uprising was only put down by military force brought in from Prague.[134]

Three months before the Plzeň revolt, however, an era had come to an end with the death of Stalin. Though this was not clear at the time, Stalin's death would usher in a period of fraught, conflict-ridden consolidation of the regimes that ruled the region. That consolidation would be so problematic for the regimes' rulers because of the deep-seated weaknesses of socialist states. Industrialization and collectivization had brought economic turmoil, while the policies the regimes had pursued had alienated almost every section of society. While the states had lost control of the economy, they were dogged by widespread peasant and working-class protest at many of their policies. Despite their repressive nature, socialist dictatorships were as far away from establishing a stable basis for their rule as the popular-front regimes had been in 1945.

3 Consolidating socialism

Revolts like that at Plzeň underlined the weakness of the foundations on which socialist rule in the region rested at the time of the
death of Stalin. The shift away from Stalinism was a conflict-ridden
and turbulent process, most starkly demonstrated by events in
Poland and Hungary in 1956. Yet by the mid-1960s, socialist rule had
been largely consolidated in most of the states of the region; outside
Albania, which forms an exception to this rule, states had succeeded
in building a social settlement of sorts, which brought relative peace
on the industrial and agricultural fronts. It promised, and to some
extent delivered, a 'socialist consumerism'. It aimed to confront the
problems of the operation of a socialist economy through economic
reform, and the political legitimacy of the state through measures of
de-Stalinization. It accepted a greater role for emergent middle-class
social groups within the socialist polity. The settlement was not a
static, but a dynamic one, and in some countries, it rested on more
fragile foundations than in others. This would be demonstrated by
the political turbulence, most marked in Czechoslovakia and
Poland, that shook the region during the late 1960s.

The death of Stalin, the more conciliatory policies of his
successors in Moscow, and the need for political consolidation in the
face of domestic turmoil in the states of the region brought about the
advent of what have been termed 'new course' policies across
the region. These heralded more conciliatory policies towards the
collectivization of agriculture, with a permanent suspension of the
policy in Yugoslavia – due to domestic, rather than international
pressures – and a temporary suspension elsewhere. In
Czechoslovakia, where Gottwald died following an illness contracted
while attending Stalin's funeral, his successor, former trade union

leader Antonín Zápotocký, told collective farmers in late 1953, that if they wanted to leave, 'we will not hold you back'.[1] Imre Nagy, Hungary's new prime minister, appointed at the behest of the Soviet leadership, was alarmed that Mátyás Rákosi's regime was leading the country to economic collapse and political crisis, and announced a similar relaxation of policy towards agriculture in the summer.

In addition to the suspension of the collectivization drive, which represented a ceasefire in the virtual state of civil war between regime and peasantry in the countryside, investment levels were cut and economies were reoriented to production for consumer need, though this policy was pursued somewhat unevenly across the region. Policies towards industrial workers were relaxed, both in view of the revolt in Plzeň and the more widespread protests in the German Democratic Republic in June 1953, sparked by attempts to raise production norms. While official statistics showed increases in the real incomes of workers across the region, the impact of these policies on working-class working conditions and living standards were distinctly mixed. In some countries, most notably in Hungary, the advent of new-course policies heralded de-Stalinization and a gradual rehabilitation of political prisoners convicted over the previous four years. These policies were limited geographically. In Romania, the limited release of political prisoners that began in 1954 was linked to a shift in focus of the nature of repression and coincided with a new wave of political trials, spearheaded by the trial of senior Communist Lucreţiu Pătrăşcanu, held since 1948 but not brought to trial until six years later.[2] In Czechoslovakia, political trials also continued throughout 1954, the most notorious being those of the so-called 'Slovak bourgeois nationalists', in which the future secretary of the KSČ, Gustav Husák, was jailed.[3]

The limited de-Stalinization initiated by new-course policies had generated serious political crisis by 1956. In Hungary, the appointment, under Soviet pressure, of Nagy as prime minister initiated a power struggle between reformists and allies of Rákosi that split the Hungarian party. Intellectuals, incensed at the 'crimes' committed by the regime during the early 1950s, weighed in on the side of the reformers. As living standards stagnated and the economy continued to be mired in a crisis generated by the effects of over-ambitious industrialization, working-class frustration with the regime grew, while attempts to reverse Nagy's relaxation of the collectivization drive in 1955 met with widespread resistance in rural communities. Nikita Khrushchev's 'secret speech' to the Twentieth Congress of the Soviet Communist Party, which revealed the crimes of Stalin and criticized his 'cult of personality', had an explosive effect in Hungary, giving confidence to the party reformists and leading to a collapse of confidence in the party itself. Soviet moves to seek reconciliation with Yugoslavia intensified this trend, underlining the Stalinist practices of the senior party leadership. In one Budapest factory, workers argued that 'cult of personality was just as marked here [in Hungary] as in the Soviet Union, especially among the top leadership', and that 'in Hungary, like the other people's democratic countries were representatives of Stalin's policies, and the comrades responsible have not been made accountable for their actions'.[4] The party attempted to deal with the mounting crisis by removing Rákosi from the position of party secretary, yet his replacement, Ernő Gerő, inspired little confidence in view of his culpability for Stalinist policies during the early 1950s.

It was not only Hungary which was in open revolt by 1956. Poland was also in ferment; intellectual criticism of the regime had begun in 1955, with savage criticism of the human costs of socialist industrialization, published in the journal *Nowa Kultura*, sparking a ferocious reaction from the party leadership. Economic crisis, low living standards and despotic management in workplaces had produced growing working-class frustration. According to one Łódź worker in 1956, 'I have slaved all my life. I've been told that before the war it was the capitalists who profited from my work. Who profits now? I have a wife, my old mother, and three children to support ... It is a treat when I give the children butter on their bread on Sundays. It was never so bad as that before the war'.[5] This coincided with the suppressed memory of the post-war civil war between the Communists and the sections of the Home Army who had resisted their advance, to produce a deep-seated lack of legitimacy for the regime – a legitimacy that was further shattered by Khrushchev's revelations. With the death of Bolesław Bierut, the country's senior Communist during the early 1950s, within days of the speech, the party was forced to begin a process of reform. Edward Ochab was elected secretary of the PZPR, and Władysław Gomułka, the former secretary of the PPR, expelled from the party and later imprisoned for his advocacy of a Polish national road to Communism, was rehabilitated. The combination of generalized de-Stalinization, factional struggle within the top echelons of the party following the death of Bierut, and widespread popular unrest produced a fragile situation in the country.

Working-class discontent, in particular, became politicized. One party member's opinion was indicative of this shift: 'the luxurious life of our dignitaries is at the expense of ordinary living standards. The rich live off pregnant women, they holiday on the wages of ordinary people.'[6] Politicized working-class discontent exploded in June 1956 at a locomotive plant in Poznań, where the workforce resolved to dispatch a delegation of representatives to Warsaw in support of their largely material demands, in which a substantial wage increase figured prominently. After the delegation was rebuffed by the government, the Poznań workers determined to send the delegation back to Warsaw. When it failed to return, workers took matters into their own hands, staging an uprising not dissimilar to that seen in Plzeň three years earlier. The uprising was suppressed, leading to as many as 300 casualties.[7] While party leaders denounced the Poznań events as being the work of 'enemies of socialism', the deep-seated working-class discontent they revealed gave impetus to those groups arguing for reform. By mid-October, Gomułka was first secretary of the PZPR, and after intervention from those parts of the party leadership opposed to reform, he was given Moscow's blessing. Working-class ferment in the fevered atmosphere of 1956 had secured a degree of change in the leadership of the country, though the degree to which that change would shape the lives of ordinary Poles was far from clear.

Events in Poland were eagerly watched in Hungary, where the crisis of socialist rule was advanced by late summer 1956. Budapest's industrial workers drew the conclusion that 'the riots broke out in Poznań … not because of the enemy and foreign spies, but because twelve years after the end of the war living standards remained low'.[8] Gerő was unable to impose his authority on the crisis-ridden party, as intellectuals and students rallied around Imre Nagy, seeing him as a potential Hungarian Gomułka. The regime's rehabilitation of the victims of the political trials of the early 1950s, and its attempts to improve relations with neighbouring Yugoslavia, further contributed to the crisis, while large sections of the working class were deeply frustrated with the regime, given low living standards. Social explosion resulted, triggered by a demonstration organized by Budapest students on 23 October, which was supported by intellectuals and, to the surprise of the organizers, by large numbers of working-class youth. As sections of the demonstration laid siege to Hungarian Radio, the situation turned ugly when armed defenders of the radio station fired on the crowd. This, in turn, triggered a generalized uprising and the almost total collapse of the socialist state, as sections of the regular police and army defected to the increasingly broad popular movement, demanding an end to socialist rule. Initial attempts to use Soviet troops to restore order foundered on the strength of popular unrest, while Imre Nagy, appointed prime minister to deal with the situation, was forced into taking ever more radical positions.

By the beginning of November, power had been effectively transferred to 'national committees', which echoed similar organs that took power in the wake of the Red Army advance in 1944–5, and workers' councils in the factories. A multitude of political parties had been hastily founded, while the Hungarian Workers' Party was disbanded and replaced by the Hungarian Socialist Workers' Party (*Magyar Szocialista Munkáspárt* or MSZMP), led by János Kádár, a senior Communist imprisoned as a result of a political trial in the early 1950s. In addition, Nagy transformed his government into a multi-party popular-front administration, announced multi-party elections and Hungarian neutrality. These measures were steps that the Soviet Union was not willing to countenance. Furthermore, the speed of events and the violence that accompanied them shocked many Communists, who feared that the revolution would turn into a bloody 'counter-revolution'. Kádár was among them and he disappeared in early November, returning at the head of a 'Revolutionary Workers' and Peasants' Government' when Soviet troops attacked Budapest to crush the revolution on 4 November. The bloody suppression of the revolution by Soviet troops and Hungarian paramilitary units loyal to Kádár lasted into 1957. Judicial reprisals that followed the consolidation of the Kádár regime resulted in some 22,000 convictions, for offences connected to political activity during the revolution, of which an estimated 229 people received death sentences.[9]

Hungary's experience underlined the fact that repression was a necessary but insufficient condition of stabilizing socialist rule.

Kádár's regime faced a serious crisis of legitimacy, as strikes rumbled on through the early part of 1957. At the heart of the crisis lay the paradox that while Kádár claimed to rule on behalf of the working class, his restoration of socialism rested on the violent suppression of a revolution driven in large part by industrial workers. As workers' councils were dissolved and their leaders subjected to judicial reprisal – branded 'agents of counter-revolution' by the regime – Kádár and his allies moved to restore their shattered links to the working class. The MSZMP asserted its identity as a 'workers' party' and moved rhetorically and practically to cast itself as the authentic representative of the skilled, urban working class.[10] This was underpinned by large wage increases, an expansion in social benefits and the reversal of Stalinist policies towards work organization and remuneration in the factories during the late 1950s.[11]

While the Hungarian regime's attempts to rebuild its links to the working class were the most marked, in view of the depth of the crisis it experienced during 1956, right across the region, states attempted to repair the damage done to their links with industrial labour during the era of socialist industrialization in the early 1950s. In Poland, where the forces of protest had not experienced the dramatic defeat that they had in Hungary, and where it could be claimed they had secured a partial victory, the working class became more assertive as a result of 1956. During 1957, strikes broke out across the country, hitting heavy engineering factories, the railways, power generation and public transportation. Much strike action was localized and was defused through the politics of compromise rather than outright confrontation.[12] While the relatively independent works' councils in the factories were sidelined by the regime, industrial peace was bought by increases in living standards: the real incomes of those living from wages rose by 4.9 per cent per annum between 1956 and 1960.[13] The events of 1956 and the subsequent stabilization of Gomułka's rule in the factories established the basis for a relationship between the regime and the working class in Poland that would dog it through the remainder of its existence. Polish workers, emboldened by the effects of protest, proved willing to strike for improvements in living and working conditions, while the state was forced to respond by buying industrial peace.

In those states where the regime had not been shaken to its foundations, the turn towards more conciliatory policies in the factories was less visible, but marked, nevertheless. In Czechoslovakia, in view of the events of June 1953 in Plzeň, moves to pacify the working class were in evidence immediately when the government introduced and then, within days, revoked a package of laws designed to criminalize job quitting and absenteeism in the workplace.[14] The growing unwillingness of authorities to take steps that would have a detrimental effect on working-class living standards became more evident through the 1950s. In the Ostrava region, this unwillingness resulted in a situation, in 1955, where decrees designed to improve 'scientifically determined' work targets resulted in generalized wage increases, largely because of the refusal of authorities at all levels to countenance wage reductions.[15]

Attempts to protect the incomes of the male, skilled élite of the region's industrial working class resulted in the tacit acceptance by the regime of the informal patterns of workplace bargaining, which had sprung up between workers and management in the face of the operation of the socialist economy. This pattern of tacit acceptance blunted the impact of state attempts to increase labour productivity and eroded both payment-by-results wages and labour competition. The impact of these processes can be measured by the growing percentage of workers paid according to the lowest production targets established for so-called 'hand work'. In Czechoslovakia in 1961, 47 per cent of all industrial workers were paid in this way, with 55 per cent of workers in the mining industry and 65 per cent in machine manufacture all working under these preferential, and according to the authorities, 'exceptional' norms.[16] In Hungary, by the mid-1960s, the ability of certain élite groups within the work-force to bargain successfully with management had created a situation, according to sociologist István Kemény, where the skilled élite were able to act as informal leaders of working-class action to secure preferential wages.[17]

These tacit settlements between the regime and industrial workers had several important socio-political consequences. First, in contrast to regime claims to represent the whole of the working class, they privileged a skilled élite and disadvantaged other more peripheral groups. In Hungary, this was dramatically revealed in a 1969 survey of Budapest's gigantic Csepel Metalworks complex: it showed a workforce sharply bifurcated into a skilled élite, with considerable countervailing power, and a peripheral group, who were relatively marginal within the informal power relations of the factory.[18] The differential power of different groups within the working class was visible not only in individual factories, but also between workers in different sectors. Traditionally male, heavy industrial sectors did better, in terms of the earnings of workers, than feminized sectors in light industry. In Czechoslovakia, average earnings in mining in 1967 were almost one and a half times those of the average industrial worker; workers engaged in consumer goods production earned only 83 per cent of the average.[19] Similar patterns of differentiation within the working class could also be found in Poland from the mid-1950s onwards.[20] Second, this resulted in a decline in the differentials between manual and traditionally white-collar occupations, as the regime's rhetorical workerism came to be reflected in wage policies. This was particularly marked in Czechoslovakia, where the pay of engineers declined from 165.4 per cent of that of a manual worker in 1948, to only 126.6 per cent in 1963. Administrators' pay fell from 124.5 per cent of that of a manual worker to 83.7 per cent over the same period.[21] Third, tacit compromise with the skilled élite on the shop floor placed real limits on the attempts of managers and the authorities to rationalize production, particularly where such moves ran into resistance from those privileged by the regime's unspoken settlement with the working class. During Hungary's 1968 economic reform, managers in a heavy industrial factory in the western city of Győr attempted to capitalize on the new climate by rationalizing production and increasing production targets. Their efforts were beaten back by well-organized go-slows, instituted by 'key' workers in the plant.[22]

While workerism, on both rhetorical and material levels, played a central role in the consolidation of socialist rule by the mid-1960s, rural communities across the region were reshaped through more subtle policies than the violent collectivization drives pursued during the 1950s. In two of the states of the region, Yugoslavia and Poland, the regime entirely abandoned agricultural collectivization as a goal. In Yugoslavia, this abandonment coincided with the pauses in collectivization campaigns elsewhere in the region that were initiated as part of the new course. Faced with endemic food shortages in the cities, popular unrest in the villages and the collapse of agricultural production during 1952, Tito's regime moved to base its agrarian policy on individual land ownership during the spring of

1953.[23] While lip-service was paid to the creation of agricultural cooperatives in Yugoslavia during the late 1950s, in reality, private farms came to dominate. The shift of individual producers from subsistence to market production, visible during the 1960s, was stymied by low rates of overall investment in the sector.[24] In Poland, the events of 1956 led to a similar outcome, with delivery quotas and taxation of individual smallholders reduced, as the state tacitly accepted individual landholding. As in Yugoslavia, a smallholder-dominated rural economy suffered from a lack of investment in Poland, while the village population was burdened by poor social and physical infrastructure. By the mid-1960s, standards of living were estimated to be a full 30 per cent lower in the villages than in the major urban areas.[25]

Elsewhere in the region, collectivization was largely completed during the late 1950s and early 1960s. In Albania, while the private sector had accounted for 91.3 per cent of agricultural production in 1949, this had fallen to 18.3 per cent by 1960.[26] In Romania, when the regime announced the completion of collectivization in April 1962, 93.4 per cent of the total arable land area was in the socialist sector.[27] The peak of the collectivization drives in Bulgaria was somewhat earlier, with 80 per cent of the land collectivized by 1956.[28] Czechoslovakia and Hungary conformed more closely to the overall regional pattern; in Czechoslovakia, 80 per cent of the agricultural population were either cooperative members or employees of state farms,[29] while in Hungary, private-sector farms accounted for only 3.3 per cent of agricultural land by 1962.[30]

The new cooperatives, however, differed from Stalinist practices, as the collectivization drives of the late 1950s fitted the pattern of what Nigel Swain has termed 'neo-Stalinist collectivization'.[31] New collectives were based on a settlement which sought to reconcile the demands of large-scale socialist production with elements of the traditional cultures of labour in agrarian communities. Agricultural cooperatives were riven by struggle in much of the region during the 1960s, as the authorities, management and members fought over the question of the balance between socialist labour within the collective and private household production. In new cooperatives in Romania, restrictions on the ownership of livestock and the use of private plots provoked conflict that was solved only through negotiation between agrarian households and the authorities.[32] Such conflict ensured that private plots, on which household production continued to occur, assumed a more sizeable role in production than that intended by the state. In 1970, in Albania, private plots accounted for only 3.5 per cent of agricultural land, but constituted 23 per cent of the total value of agricultural production.[33] In Bulgaria, in 1960, while private plots represented between 8 and 9 per cent of the cultivated area, they accounted for around a quarter of all production.[34] In Hungary, the integration of private plots into the structure of the cooperatives was less a matter of informal accommodation than a deliberate policy of compromise with the agrarian population, to some extent unique in the region.[35] The paradoxical survival of remnants of the private sector in agriculture, after the conclusion of successful collectivization, formed the basis of a shadow economy of semi-legal private activities and favours that coexisted with the state sector.[36]

The rural economy of favours was generalized as a result of the mass migration of labour from agriculture to industry, which was one of the major social consequences of the changes of the 1960s. It was even marked in countries such as Poland, where collectivization was abandoned after 1956, as substantial migration to the cities led to an ageing class of farmers throughout the 1960s.[37] In the western Hungarian county of Győr-Moson-Sopron, local labour exchanges were flooded with village dwellers seeking employment in industry after the successful conclusion of collectivization in the county.[38] Across the region, a class of 'worker peasants' – those who combined work in agriculture with labour in industry – became a significant social group, particularly, but not exclusively, in south-eastern Europe. In Romania's Pitești car plant, by the beginning of the 1970s, 57.5 per cent of the workers commuted from rural areas.[39]

While the paradoxical integration of the remnants of the private sector into the socialist economy in rural areas and the greater blurring of the boundaries between agricultural and industrial labour laid the foundations of the large shadow economy in the 1960s, the attempts of regimes to create a socialist consumerism gave it enormous impetus. Increased consumer goods production had formed one of the foundations of new-course policies, pursued across the region from 1953 onwards. Slow but gradual improvement in the supply of industrial consumer goods was discerned in Czechoslovakia from 1954.[40] Poland's thaw from 1956 onwards was accompanied by the relaxation of restrictions on the provision of certain private services. It also accelerated a trend, visible since 1954, towards the creation of a new consumer culture, which existed in the pages of Polish magazines and the designs of new shops – at least in the country's major cities.[41] In Hungary, the promotion of a consumer culture was underpinned by the regime's policy of increasing living standards after the 1956 revolution. Magazines promoted cosmetics and clothing, in particular, from the late 1950s onwards, while new self-service stores were opened in Budapest.[42] Evidence from industrial communities in the Hungarian capital during the early 1960s suggested that socialist consumerism had begun, if somewhat unevenly, to transform the established patterns of working-class culture.[43] By the end of the 1960s, socialist consumerism had transformed the daily life of most ordinary Hungarians. Two sociologists, in a study of a western Hungarian industrial enterprise recounted that:

> there were those who were fully absorbed in the acquisition of consumer goods ... Others were making an investment in starting a family and were bearing the enormous expense of building or buying some accommodation ... At the same time there were also workers who were already busily satisfying their demands for additional consumer durables: they had their TV sets, washing machines, motor-cycles, and were now spending money improving their apartments, buying refrigerators or even cars.[44]

The hegemony of this consumerist ethic led to the spread of the informal economy in the country, as workers found their wages from socialist enterprises insufficient to achieve their goals in the private sphere. In consequence, in 1969, party officials reported that 'a substantial section of the working class uses its free time in order to take on additional work'.[45]

If the extent of Hungary's socialist consumerism was exceptional within the Soviet bloc, then Yugoslavia's was the most unusual among the socialist states of the region. During the first half of the 1960s, a real socialist consumerism developed in the country, as personal disposable income rose at a rate of 9 per cent per annum in real terms, while between 1960 and 1970, the number of radio sets per 1,000 inhabitants more than doubled, and car ownership rose from 2.9 per 1,000 in 1960 to 35 per 1,000 in 1970.[46] As historian Patrick Hyder Patterson has demonstrated, this increase in living standards, and in the ownership of consumer goods, was accompanied by the creation of a consumer culture generated by a cohort of marketing and advertising professionals, freed from ideological constraints by economic reform.[47] In part, Yugoslav consumer culture received its impetus from the relaxation of restrictions on Yugoslavs working abroad, implemented in 1962, which ensured a steady flow of hard currency into the country's households, along with direct experience of the consumer cultures of Western Europe's post-war economic miracle. By 1969, the number of Yugoslavs working abroad was estimated to have reached 800,000, papering over serious problems of unemployment in many parts of the country.[48]

Yugoslavia's socialist consumerism was tied to its unique post-1948 geopolitical position as a socialist, non-Soviet bloc state, and to the distinctive socialist economic model it had developed, in part as a response to that geopolitical position. Following Tito's split with Stalin in 1948, Yugoslavia had been in a difficult political position, which fed economic instability. In part, this situation ameliorated as Yugoslavia alleviated its problems by exploiting its unique geopolitical position, securing economic and military aid from the United States, anxious to weaken Soviet power at the height of the first cold war.[49] The need to place the Yugoslav economy on a firmer footing combined with the ideological imperative of developing an alternative socialist economic model to the Soviet one, in order to bolster the legitimacy of the regime in offering an anti-Stalinist, distinctive road to socialism. During the first half of the 1950s, the Yugoslav regime shaped a new socialist economic model based upon the principle of 'self-management'. This involved the widespread decentralization of political decision-making, from the federal government in Belgrade to the country's constituent republics; and in the economic sphere, making individual enterprises financially accountable for their production. All employees would be mobilized through their direct control over the assets of firms. The principle of self-management was enshrined in successive Yugoslav constitutions from 1953 onwards, as economic planning was relaxed and market elements assumed a greater, if not a decisive role, in the new economic system. By the end of the 1950s, Tito's regime had shaped a distinctive, decentralized socialist economy in the country.[50]

Self-management underpinned a growth in living standards in the late 1950s and early 1960s, which effectively transformed the country, leading not merely to an increase in the standard of living, but also to the arrival of modernity in settlements across the country. The spread of running water to villages, the increase in industrial and white-collar employment and, of course, the arrival of modern mass consumerism, marked the 1960s.[51] Yet Yugoslavia's decentralized economic system resulted in several serious problems, not least of which was mass unemployment, all but unknown elsewhere in the region. Officially registered unemployment rose from just above 5 per cent in 1952 to somewhere slightly below 10 per cent in 1968.[52] The pattern of economic growth had intensified inequalities between the republics, with Croatia and Slovenia's economies growing at significantly more than the average for Yugoslavia as a whole between 1952 and 1960, while Macedonia and Montenegro had grown by markedly less.[53] Furthermore, many socialist enterprises were commonly recognized to be dogged by problems of productivity and efficiency, leading to further flawed reform in the mid-1960s, which, in turn, led to increased inflationary pressure and little improvement in the overall performance of enterprises.[54] Decentralization also concentrated power, wealth and status in the hands of enterprise managers and white-collar staff, and that generated working-class resentment. In 1972, in a public opinion survey in Croatia, while 43.8 per cent of those responding identified the meaning of self-management as 'management of the means of production by the working class', 20.4 per cent identified managers as the chief beneficiaries, with 8.5 per cent pointing to white-collar workers and 11.7 per cent to the political élites.[55] By the end of the 1960s, after the failure of reform during the middle of the decade, the economy was stagnant, and it seemed merely a matter of time before economic difficulties generated political turbulence.[56]

While the development of Yugoslavia's unique socialist economic model had been a product of a political break with Moscow and, in turn, had generated a unique socialist consumerism, states within the socialist bloc were forced to look to economic reform during the 1960s. The relative social peace of the 1960s in the westernmost states of the region, which rested on workerism, compromise with a newly collectivized agrarian population and efforts to promote socialist consumerism, proved increasingly difficult to finance as the decade progressed. Romania and Bulgaria, on the region's south-eastern periphery, proved to be partial exceptions to this rule, as the 1960s were characterized by dynamic economic growth.[57] Elsewhere there was clear evidence of economic stagnation by the early 1960s. In Czechoslovakia, industrial expansion which exceeded the supply of raw materials, unrealistic plan targets and the poor quality of industrial production for export choked the economy as early as the end of the 1950s. Measures to correct these problems, which consisted of cuts in investment funds, in turn generated economic crisis and a significant recession by 1963.[58] In Hungary, political stabilization had been bought through increases in living standards that were not supported by the stagnant economy, resulting in rising state indebtedness from 1959 onwards.[59] As in Czechoslovakia, industry suffered from low productivity, and attempts to finance rising incomes through increasing exports were dogged by the poor quality of production.[60]

In both countries, economic stagnation and the desire to maintain growth in living standards stimulated debate on economic reform, underpinned by similar discussion in the Soviet Union, initiated by the economist Yevsei Liberman, who suggested decentralization of the economy and the replacement of plan targets with financial incentives.[61] In Czechoslovakia, the party came to accept the need for economic reform in 1965, taking its first tentative steps in this direction the following year. Full-scale economic reform in the country would be subsumed under the general cultural and political liberalization of the country in spring 1968. The eventual fate of reform would be connected to the fate of the Prague Spring more generally.[62] In Hungary, economic reform was both more comprehensive and more permanent. Hungary could with some justice claim, after Yugoslavia, to have developed an economic model distinct from the practice of comprehensive economic planning. Decided upon in 1966 and implemented in 1968, Hungary's New Economic Mechanism dismantled the apparatus of centralized economic planning, replacing it with indirect state control over more autonomous state enterprises, which were instructed to maximize their profits. Indirect control was established through state setting of prices and the taxation of enterprises, which were shielded from the impact of the world market by administratively determined prices and the maintenance of the state monopoly over foreign trade.[63]

The New Economic Mechanism combined with socialist consumerism to create an environment characterized by consumer choice that was unprecedented among the countries of the region, save Yugoslavia. Yet its introduction sparked considerable working-class discontent, as in a number of respects it posed real challenges to the Kádár regime's workerism, which had been a central plank of its stabilization following the 1956 revolution. Workers resented the increasing power of enterprise managers over the workplace, and their ability to benefit disproportionately from profit-share premiums that were designed to reward enterprise performance. As in Yugoslavia, this fed resentment; in 1969, workers 'spoke of the leading role of the intelligentsia, and some that management are a "new class"'.[64] In addition, with the introduction of market mechanisms into the consumer sector, many workers felt they were losing out in an atmosphere of greater social differentiation; in the aftermath of the introduction of the reform, workers spoke, incorrectly, 'about a reduction or a stagnation in real incomes'.[65] Beginning in 1969, such discontent was used, first by sections of the party apparatus and then by the managers of large enterprises, to blunt the impact of economic reform. This process was to gain impetus during the 1970s in the international climate that followed the suppression of the Prague Spring.[66]

While substantial reform in both the Hungarian and Yugoslav cases threatened to provoke working-class discontent at growing social differentiation, the lack of real reform in Poland set the wheels in motion for working-class frustration and later rebellion. Throughout the 1960s, the Polish regime attempted to boost the economy through increasing investment within the established structures of central planning. By the middle of the decade, the problems of stagnation and low productivity that plagued its neighbours became increasingly apparent. In 1966, the central committee of the PZPR warned that 'there are still serious problems in the investment process ... We are still building too dearly and too lengthily'.[67] Gomułka, however, resisted pressure for economic reform and insisted on continuing policies of selective investment within existing structures. This led to only modest increases in the real incomes of industrial workers – 3.2 per cent annually between 1961 and 1965, falling to around 2 per cent between 1966 and 1970.[68] Low investment in agriculture and the generalized atmosphere of economic stagnation led to the emergence of serious meat shortages by 1967.[69] This poor economic record caused Gomułka's workerism to unravel. The Polish regime's failure to construct a durable settlement with the working class was dramatically exposed in December 1970, when increases in the price of food and consumer goods provoked strikes and riots in the Baltic ports of Gdańsk, Gdynia and Szczecin, which led directly to the fall of Gomułka and his replacement with Edward Gierek. The violence and anger evident in these demonstrations was demonstrated by the 45 deaths and 1,165 persons injured as a result.[70]

Despite the uneven progress of economic reform across the region, generalized economic modernization between the mid-1950s and 1970 led to an increase in the numbers and social role of white-collar occupational groups – those classified by the regimes as 'the cultural and technical intelligentsia'. This dimension of social change and the growth of educational opportunity formed part of, and at same time posed considerable challenges to, the social settlements reached during the 1960s. In Poland, by 1960, those engaged in white-collar and professional work accounted for 22.9 per cent of those gainfully employed; a figure far greater than the 5.6 per cent share of the total labour force they had represented in 1931.[71] In Hungary, there were nearly three times as many people employed in jobs that required higher educational qualifications in 1970 than had been the case in 1941; there were half as many again as had been employed in similar positions in 1960.[72] In the more peripheral south-east European states, white-collar employment mushroomed, though it reached an absolute level that was proportionately lower than in countries like Poland and Hungary; white-collar workers in Bulgaria, for example, made up only 16.2 per cent of the labour force by 1965.[73]

The development of socialist industrial economies, the growth of social policy bureaucracies during the 1960s and greater professionalization in each of these sectors increased the social weight of these groups. In Poland, for example, from 1960 onwards, the central committee of the PZPR demanded that industrial managers obtain appropriate qualifications as a condition of remaining in employment.[74] In social policy fields, a greater emphasis on professional autonomy and expertise transformed both state policies and the positions of professional groups. In Hungary, during the 1960s, academic psychology came to play a greater role in the development of state child welfare policies.[75] In Yugoslavia, with its decentralized economic structure and its burgeoning consumerism, advertising and marketing professionals shaped a distinctive consumer culture during the 1960s.[76]

In addition to the growth in white-collar workers, their growing professional autonomy and influence on policy in certain areas, the expansion of higher education played a central role. With the relaxation of the class-based quota systems, typical of the 1950s, which restricted middle-class access to growing universities, increasingly, the children of middle-class parents had marked advantages in gaining the qualifications that led to white-collar jobs. In Yugoslavia, for example, students made up 1.3 per cent of the total population in 1970 – four times the proportion that had studied 20 years previously. Yet this had not broken the hegemony of élite social groups. In 1950, children of white-collar fathers made up 51 per cent of all students, and those of professionals, 8 per cent. By 1970, those coming from white-collar families made up 39 per cent of the total intake, while those from professional backgrounds represented a further 21 per cent.[77] Yugoslavia was far from a unique case. In Poland, in the academic year 1967–8, only 25.8 per cent of all first-year students were of working-class origin, while 54.3 per cent were from white-collar social backgrounds.[78] This effectively allowed large sections of the pre-socialist middle class to reproduce their social position by becoming members of the socialist regimes' cultural and technical intelligentsia. This is well illustrated by the Hungarian case where one sociological survey, in 1964, found that of those who were members of families headed by a middle-class or upper-class father in 1938, 56.5 per cent had gained a managerial or professional position by the mid 1960s, and a further 24.3 per cent were employed in other white-collar positions.[79]

This growing cultural and technical intelligentsia, linked closely to the pre-socialist middle class, existed in an uncomfortable relationship with political regimes that stressed workerism. They tended to stress the value of professional expertise above class origin, and asserted the value of acquired knowledge over ideology. The tensions this clash caused were particularly visible in the universities. In Czechoslovakia, they crystallized around issues such as the compulsory teaching of Marxist-Leninism, though they were also fed by more mundane concerns about overcrowded classrooms and uncomfortable accommodation.[80] Outside the universities, large sections of this group invested considerably in cultural and political de-Stalinization. The relaxation of repression, the gradual redefinition of the role of élite intellectuals and the retreat from socialist realism, under way since the mid-1950s, had created greater room for freer cultural expression, although firmly within politically proscribed limits. The growth of white-collar employment and higher education had created a mass constituency for artistic production, as this group came to define themselves as an intelligentsia, basing their identity on intellectual expertise. The growth of a 'cultural welfare state' through subsidized book publication and the spread of cultural centres and theatres underpinned this.[81]

The difficult relationship between the regime and this social group proved the most significant source of strain on the settlement of the 1960s, as individual regimes explored different routes and encountered various problems with their own cultural and technical intelligentsias, as part of a continuing process of retreat from the political postures of early socialism. The striking exception to this rule was Albania, where Enver Hoxha's break with Moscow in 1961 led to the reorientation of the country's foreign policy towards China, and intensified policies of isolation and class struggle at home. By the late 1960s, Hoxha had begun to pursue his own version of Mao's 'cultural revolution', effectively banning religion, intensifying industrial development, revolutionizing the education system and forging ahead with policies designed to promote gender equality.[82]

Other states sought to integrate their cultural and technical intelligentsia through distancing themselves from the ideological practices of early socialism. One of the most notable of these attempts was in Romania, where, from the late 1950s onwards, the regime recast the basis of its legitimacy, deploying an ideology of national communism to bolster its rule. One of the challenges to doing this was to confront anti-Russian sentiment on the part of the Romanian population, which was undertaken by Gheorgiu-Dej when he negotiated the withdrawal of Soviet troops from Romania in 1958.[83] Attempts to set Romania's regime on a national-communist course were continued after Gheorgiu-Dej's death in 1965 by his successor, Nicolae Ceauşescu.[84] Ceauşescu's effective deployment of Romanian nationalist ideas, and his incorporation of many of those ideas in the ideology he used to legitimate his regime, forged the basis of a political settlement between intellectuals and the state. Intellectuals invested considerably in national ideas within the framework of the Romanian state.[85]

Romania and Albania were both unusual cases, and the 1970s would underscore their divergence from the East European mainstream. In all the other countries, cultural liberalization was pursued to varying degrees, as part of a pact with the cultural and technical intelligentsia. Liberalization threatened the stability of the regimes the least in Bulgaria and Hungary. In Bulgaria, the early 1960s saw Todor Zhivkov's regime relax censorship, allowing both the publication of Bulgarian translations of significant numbers of Western works and the creation of a vibrant domestic literary culture.[86] In Hungary, Kádár's conciliatory policies towards social groups traditionally hostile to socialism, announced at the MSZMP's 1962 congress, had led to the creation of a liberal cultural policy during the middle of the decade. Many joined the philosopher Agnes Heller in hoping that the Hungarian regime's drive for economic reform 'would lead to political reform'.[87] In the universities and research institutes, revisionist Marxist groups argued for greater democratization of the political system in order to ward off the danger that socialism would degenerate into technocracy, while a wave of Maoist political activism swept Budapest's student body in the late 1960s.[88] Yet despite protests in research institutes at Kádár's support for Moscow during the suppression of the Prague Spring, intellectual dissent never seriously threatened the political system.

While it was working-class rebellion in the Baltic ports that would eventually bring him down, Gomułka's regime was shaken by dissent from the intelligentsia during the late 1960s. This was because, while elsewhere the 1960s were marked by cultural liberalization, in Poland, from 1963 onwards, the regime sought to roll back the gains achieved in 1956. The result was a war of attrition between intellectuals and the party, which culminated in student protest, triggered by the regime's attempts to censor a play in Warsaw in February 1968.[89] By early March, this had turned into a generalized and violent confrontation between Warsaw's students and the police, which quickly spread to provincial towns during the month and explicitly challenged the political hegemony of the PZPR.[90] The regime responded by deploying class-based rhetoric and seeking to play on the anti-Semitic sentiments of the Polish population in order to mobilize the support of working-class Poles against the students and intellectuals. Gierek, who was to head the regime two years later, attacked the demonstrators as 'the usual enemies of the Polish People's Republic, the descendants of the knives of the old regime, revisionists, Zionists, and supporters of imperialism'.[91] The defeat of protests was secured by the use of over-whelming force on the part of the security forces, and the mobilization of popular anti-intelligentsia sentiment under the slogan, 'the students back to the lecture hall benches! The writers back to their desks!'[92] It would be the rebellion of the working class, and not the dissent of students and intellectuals, that would prove fatal for the Gomułka regime.

Yugoslavia had developed its own brand of socialism by the mid-1960s, but further reform, required to correct the problems of the self-management system, threatened the balance of power within Tito's regime. Yugoslavia's parallel security state, attached to its military, with close links to the leadership of the party in Serbia and fronted by the head of the state security services, Aleksandar Ranković, represented a powerful break in reform and bolstered the *de facto* hegemony of Serbia within the federation. Ranković's dogged opposition to reform and his illegal surveillance of senior party leadership figures led to his dismissal in 1966. The curbing of the power of the country's parallel security state brought consider-able cultural liberalization in its wake. This liberalization opened up the space for the articulation of demands for greater national independence and cultural autonomy for the country's constituent republics.[93] As in Hungary, cultural liberalization produced a wave of revisionist Marxist thinking among intellectuals across the republics who sought the reform and democratization of Yugoslav socialism. This spilled over into the student body, but led to only limited student protest. In June 1968, student marchers clashed with police on the streets of Belgrade.[94] The political consequences of reform and liberalization would only be felt fully during the first part of the 1970s.

The most dramatic of the upheavals generated by the attempts of the regime to seek a settlement with the cultural and technical intelligentsia was in Czechoslovakia. The country had been ruled since the mid-1950s by Antonín Novotný; up until 1957, the regime had been headed jointly by him and Antonín Zápotocký. The period of Novotný's rule, from 1957, was marked by caution on the economic front, a continued commitment to workerism in the factories, a relaxation of repression compared with the Gottwald era, but clear resistance to too great a measure of either cultural liberalization or de-Stalinization. Increasingly, however, Novotný's basic conservatism fitted ill with the considerable pressure from the Soviet Union for real de-Stalinization and the mounting unrest in Czechoslovak society, particularly among the cultural intelligentsia and students. It also clashed with the clear need to reform the country's economic structures, given the stagnation of the Czechoslovak economy, visible in the early 1960s. By 1967, the clash between a regime unwilling to countenance reform and overwhelming pressure for change had created a political crisis in the country. This crisis was not only marked by public criticism of the regime by prominent writers, but also, in October, by increasingly militant protest by students in Prague, which in turn led to violence, and then to further protest.[95]

The increasing militancy of students and the intelligentsia, combined with Novotný's stubborn resistance to change, produced a split in the party between conservatives and reformists, who rallied round the secretary of the Slovak party, Alexander Dubček. Against a background of growing student protest, Novotný's departure and replacement with Dubček in January 1968 was brokered by the Soviet leader, Leonid Brezhnev.[96] As the new party secretary, Dubček advocated the wholesale reform of his country's socialist system, in order to open it to the aspirations of the young, the students and the cultural and technical intelligentsia. Enshrined in the action programme of the KSČ in April 1968, and in Dubček's policy pronouncements, was a vision of a fully democratized socialism in the country, in which the KSČ would act as the leading force in

Czechoslovak society, one in which free cultural expression would be allowed and one which would be characterized by considerable pluralism.[97] The radically reformist course pursued by the Dubček leadership opened the lid on a torrent of forces that demanded liberalization and open discussion of the country's recent past and its future direction. The effective lifting of press and literary censorship led to a radical widening of the views that could be expressed openly in print; free public discussion spread in Prague and other major cities; while previously taboo subjects, such as the effects of the repression of the Gottwald era on Czechoslovak society and the political trials of the 1950s, were openly discussed for the first time. By summer, increasingly radical demands for wholesale democratization that openly threatened the foundations of the socialist system were beginning to be heard in Prague, though the government, and Dubček's regime as a whole, remained unwilling to countenance anything more than a thoroughly reformed socialism.[98] Yet sections of the KSČ, around former supporters of Novotný, like Vasil Bil'ak and Alois Indra, remained in senior positions and refused even to accept the legitimacy of Dubček's reform socialist project.[99] More significantly, it provoked outrage from more hardline East European leaders, led by Gomułka, who had resisted student pressure himself earlier in the year, and who accused Dubček of presiding over 'counter-revolution'.[100] However, it was the opposition of Leonid Brezhnev and the Soviet leadership that proved fatal to the Prague Spring; by July, he was demanding that Dubček rein in many of the social forces that had been unleashed. Dubček refused to countenance repression and, in response, Moscow moved on the night of 20–21 August, sending 165,000 troops from the Soviet Union and other East European countries to suppress the Prague Spring.[101] The use of troops to crush Czechoslovakia's attempt to create its own distinctive socialist model was a political turning point of enormous proportions. The Soviet Union, by resorting to military intervention, spelled out the external limits under which Soviet bloc states could create political settlements with the populations they ruled. It heralded a partial reverse in attempts by regimes to integrate the cultural and technical intelligentsia right across the bloc, as we shall see in chapter 7. It also effectively destroyed hopes that a truly reformist socialism could be created within the geopolitical confines of the post-war international settlement in Europe, thus setting the stage for oppositional politics right across the region during the 1970s and 1980s, and the eventual collapse of socialist regimes in 1989.

4 A society based on productive labour

Behind the mutations of the region's socialist regimes between the 1940s and 1960s, as well as the political turbulence that accompanied them, lay a profound social transformation. Within the boundaries of the individual nation states of the region, capitalism was abolished as industry, agriculture, trade and commerce were nationalized. Businesses were incorporated into the structures of nationally bound socialist economies, while the states of the region proclaimed their intention of creating a society in which all performed productive labour within the socialized sector of the economy. During the early years of the dictatorships, when the regimes were at their most utopian, and at their most despotic, the states and their ruling parties envisaged the incorporation of their societies through socialist labour almost as a moral crusade. Yet none of the regimes was able to create new cultures of socialist labour on a *tabula rasa*. To differing degrees, all had to reckon with inherited cultures of work in agriculture, industry and white-collar professions. The reproduction of these inherited work cultures in the circumstances of socialist transformation limited the regimes' room for manoeuvre. As the needs of political consolidation superseded early socialist dreams of outright transformation, accommodation to established work cultures characterized the ways in which states sought to continue the project of creating a society based on productive labour.

The shift from popular-front regimes to overt socialist dictatorships during the late 1940s was accompanied by a rash of constitution-making that sought to legally enshrine the transformative project of the states, defining them explicitly as 'workers' states'. Hungary's 1949 constitution stated that 'the basis of the social order of the Hungarian People's Republic is work'. The basis of citizenship was to perform labour and thus to contribute to the generation of the social product. As the state was to direct 'the construction of socialism', labour was to be performed in the socialist sector.[1] Bulgaria's 1947 constitution set the state the goal of ensuring that the socialist sector would form the basis of something it termed 'unified people's ownership'.[2] 'Work' was not only the basic determinant of the social order, but the nature of that work was also to change fundamentally. With the abolition of capitalist property relations, the state sought to abolish alienated labour, which was the product of those property relations. With nationalization and the consequent abolition of private property, the relationship of workers to their work was to change significantly. As Czechoslovakia's former trade union leader and Stalinist prime minister, Antonín Zápotocký, argued in late 1951: 'In the past we were not interested in production and its prosperity. Capitalist production exploited the workers … We are the masters today … and we must approach the problems of the economy differently'.[3]

As was discussed in chapter 2, most output in industry and activity in retail trade were concentrated in the socialist sector of the economies of the region by 1952. Chapter 3 has shown that, outside Poland and Yugoslavia, campaigns of agricultural collectivization were concluded by the early 1960s. These transformations entailed radical changes in the way in which the region's inhabitants worked. They radically transformed expectations and attitudes towards questions of status and property within society. These shifts were often bitterly opposed by many of the social groups that were affected by them, and, as we have seen, the opposition and occasional open protest they generated had profound political consequences for the socialist regimes themselves. The focus here, however, is on the nature and direction of the changes in the everyday lives of Eastern Europe's worker-citizens and the consequences for their identities. This chapter examines the changing experiences of industrial, agricultural and intellectual labour in turn, in order to assess the extent of change in the region's workplaces and ascertain how far socialist regimes were able to create societies that were constituted of socialist worker-citizens.

Industrial labour was absolutely central to the creation of socialist society, right across the region. To some extent this was because the industrial working class had constituted the most secure base of support for the left during the popular-front years. The most fundamental reason for the prioritization of industrial labour by socialist states was the centrality of a vision of socialism as a modernized, industrial society in which the working class would enjoy a central role. This vision was promoted in the propaganda posters of the first post-war decades, which underlined the centrality of the factory to the emerging socialist society, and in the use of images of industrial reconstruction and of construction, literally and as metaphors for a new society emerging from the ruins of war.[4] The male skilled worker and the heavy industrial plants in which he worked played a central role in the official imagery of transformation; regimes presented a gendered vision of the future that rested on the ingenious, class-conscious, skilled male worker.[5] The early socialist regimes' visions of industrial reconstruction did not rest merely on the hegemony of the industrial working class in society, but on what one senior Bulgarian functionary in 1951 termed 'a new attitude' among the workers 'towards their State, towards labour and towards socialist property'.[6] The image of the class-conscious worker, who acknowledged the need for sacrifice and selfless labour in the interests of socialist construction, was a central figure in regime propaganda during the industrialization drives of the early 1950s, figuring prominently in cultural artefacts like the works of Polish socialist realist painter, Aleksander Kobzej.[7]

Yet the social reality of the region's working class conformed uneasily to such propagandistic visions when overt socialist dictatorships were institutionalized at the end of the 1940s. First, the industrial working class comprised only a minority of the population in all the states of the region. In 1948, those employed in mining and industry accounted for only 11 per cent of the total population and 38.5 per cent of the labour force outside agriculture in Czechoslovakia – the most industrially developed state of the region. For Poland and Hungary, industrial employment accounted for 6.2 per cent and 4.7 per cent of the population respectively, and 33.2 per cent of the Polish non-agricultural labour force and 22.3 per cent of the Hungarian.[8] On the region's south-eastern periphery, industrial communities were islands of urban, proletarian life in economies dominated by small-scale agriculture. In Romania, working-class traditions were concentrated in several workplaces in distinct areas, like Bucharest's Griviţa railway repair yards, the Resita steel mills and the coal mines of the Jiu Valley.[9] Yugoslavia's working class was concentrated in similar islands of industry, like railway construction in Croatia, the Slovenian coal mines and steel mills, and the armaments plants in Sarajevo and Kragujevac.[10]

Even in the more industrially developed western states in the region, the new regimes confronted working-class cultures inherited from the inter-war years. Czechoslovakia's industrial working class, concentrated in industrialized Bohemia and Moravia, had generated a specific working-class culture in the period of the First Republic. Stratified by sectoral differences, a majority of the workforce was concentrated in enterprises with fewer than 250 employees in 1930, while a large proportion of the workforce lived not in urban areas, but in villages; rural dwellers made up around half the workers in Brno's armaments plants in 1939. Furthermore, in the country's most industrialized areas, in north-western Bohemia, a majority of the workforce retained ties to the land, maintaining a 'worker-peasant' existence. Working-class political action was moderate, if not unpolitical, highly decentralized and centred on the enterprise – a situation exacerbated by the divided trade union movement.[11] In Hungary, from the late nineteenth century, industrialization led to the development of distinct occupational, sectoral and local working-class identities, which were shaped by the circumstances of industrialization in given localities. In Budapest and major cities, strongly hierarchical shop-floor cultures were established, which privileged an élite of male and largely urban skilled workers. The skilled élite was the most likely to be unionized and to participate in the labour movement. Skilled workers sat at the apex of a hierarchy where women, the young, those commuting from rural areas – not to mention the semi-skilled and unskilled – were placed in a subordinate position within shop-floor culture. Outside the major cities, working-class cultures differed; yet hierarchical social gradation was common even here, if only between those who lived in company housing that surrounded industrial establishments and rural, unskilled or seasonal workers.[12] Despite the enormous social disruption that resulted from war and its consequences in Poland, in industrial centres like Łódź, a strong working-class culture survived into the post-war years and provided a moral economy in the city's factories, which governed patterns of working-class protest.[13]

State attempts to lay the foundations of its socialist transformation in the factories would quickly force the regime to confront directly these established working-class cultures. The regime banned independent trade unions, substituting them with its own 'transmission belt' organizations. Management remained centralized and enterprises were integrated in a vertical, hierarchical structure of decision-making to facilitate economic planning. Worker participation in industrial production was restricted to the labour competition and the various work movements that sprang up on the shop floor. At the same time, wage relations were transformed as hourly based forms of payment were eliminated and remuneration was tied tightly to production. These measures were designed to individualize wage relations and subordinate performance at work to the goals set out in early economic plans.[14]

The drive for increased production, state control over the shop floor and the individualization of work relations were bitterly resisted by workers. Labour competition campaigns, in which workforces were mobilized to radically increase their production, represented one marked focus for such resistance. From the late 1940s onwards, this involved the selection and promotion of certain individuals as outstanding workers, or Stakhanovites, who were to act as the focus for campaigns designed to increase production.[15] Frequently, such resistance was explained by the fact that campaigns to increase production, as in Hungarian industry during 1949 and 1950, preceded measures to increase work targets, thus leading to cuts in wages.[16] Often, however, it was the blatant infringement of the moral economy of working-class communities that the introduction of Stakhanovism represented, which provoked both resentment and resistance. In Bucharest's Elena Pavel textile factory, where the fulfilment of production targets was low because 'looms are made of scrap iron and break down twenty times a day', one worker, Ghergina Servan, was promoted by factory management as a Stakhanovite. To do this they put her 'to work on looms which had been overhauled by foreman Stefanescu ... [she] was given the best cotton thread ... whilst her looms functioned perfectly, her neighbor's looms were constantly breaking down'.[17] Given the deep-seated unpopularity of Stakhanovites, many sought to reintegrate themselves into the culture of the plant where they worked, thus subverting it as a movement to transform working-class attitudes towards their work. In Czechoslovakia, the clash between the belief of most workers in the equality of all, and the Stakhanovites, was frequently resolved through the acceptance of the collective ethos embedded in established shop-floor cultures by the Stakhanovites themselves.[18]

Established working-class cultures were also profoundly challenged by the policies that the regimes pursued to recruit labour to meet the demands for socialist industrialization. During the late 1940s, in western parts of Poland and the Czech lands, new labour policies had been pursued as the state attempted to replace deported German labour. The need to replace German forced and voluntary labour was a major concern in Czechoslovakia's Ostrava mines,[19] while the wholesale removal of Germans from the Wrocław region of western Poland forced the recruitment of an entirely new and 'genuinely Polish' workforce.[20] The shift towards policies of socialist industrialization, during the late 1940s and early 1950s, necessitated further expansion of the workforce and led to the pursuit of policies which explicitly challenged established working-class culture. Across the region, crash training courses were to be introduced to train new skilled workers, challenging cultures of seniority in the region's factories, mines and on its construction sites. Most radically, however, working-class masculinity was to be challenged through a policy of introducing women into areas of industrial work where they had been unrepresented previously, as part of a policy that explicitly sought to redefine ideas of gender within the societies concerned.[21]

From the late 1940s onwards, economic plans in Czechoslovakia had stated as an objective 'that the number of gainfully employed women will be increased'.[22] Albania's economic plan stated, in 1952, that by the end of the plan period, 25 per cent of the country's workers should be women.[23] Hungary's plans went further, stipulating that enterprises were 'not to place women into occupations that have been generally filled by women … women should be directed to every occupation … except those which their physical strength prevents them filling'.[24] Such egalitarian intentions were frustrated both by the sexism of enterprise management and the hegemony of working-class masculinity on the region's factory floors. In 1952, the Polish press noted with concern that some heavy industrial enterprises did not hire women, because 'either they have no confidence in the women's ability or because they want to avoid responsibilities connected with maternity protection'.[25] Many male workers were deeply hostile to the demands of newly recruited women for equality within workplaces, despite the support the state gave to such demands. When women workers in one provincial Czech industrial plant in 1952 complained that their work was harder, yet was paid far less well than that of male workers, they were upbraided by one of the plant's male Stakhanovites, who told them, 'isn't it enough that you are earning 700 *koruny* a week? What more do you want?'[26] Yet such male resistance to equality in the workplace played a central role in the frustration of early campaigns for equality in the workplace. While female employment increased in sectors that traditionally employed women, like textiles or postal services, their employment in traditionally male, skilled, heavy industrial jobs remained the exception rather than the rule.[27] Paid consistently less than men, women would increasingly perform the role of a reserve of cheap labour that regimes could draw on, following the failure of the drives of the early 1950s for equality through socialist labour.[28]

While the regimes failed to transform established working-class cultures, either through the promotion of new work methods or through the promotion of gender or generational equality, there was more generalized resistance. This often took the form, as it did in Czechoslovakia, of a marked antagonism to the politicization of the workplace.[29] The deep-seated poverty of industrial workers, as living standards across the region declined as a consequence of socialist industrialization, constituted another serious source of discontent. In Hungary, this led workers to complain of 'a blood-sucking government'.[30] In one factory in Romania's Huneadoara county, poverty led to problems of widespread theft, so that workers could participate in the black economy.[31] As we saw in chapter 2, this poverty and resentment provoked various forms of reaction on the part of industrial workers, ranging from open protest to more individualistic strategies of job quitting, which seriously undermined the industrialization drives under way across the region, provoking draconian if ineffective action by the state.

Chapter 2 examined the chaos in socialist production that resulted from the explosion of shortages that accompanied the industrialization drives. With lower-level management desperate to fulfil plan targets, space was created for the generation of a range of informal compromises at factory level that were in place already during the first half of the 1950s. Such compromises often took the form of management caving in to working-class pressure for lower work norms, or targets, thus raising wages. In Bulgaria, enterprises were instructed to base their norms on 'Stakhanovite performance'; instead, the trade unions noted that norms were easier to reach when based on the performance of the average worker.[32] By 1953, informal bargaining between the skilled élite of the working class and foremen was endemic in Hungarian industry, shaping a series of decentralized, informal compromises in which production was effectively informally negotiated.[33] In Czechoslovakia, this pattern of informal compromise went still further, with local functionaries of the monopoly trade unions asserting their independence from the state as early as 1953, and using this independence to create an informal 'alliance' between local unions and factory workforces against some of the campaigns of mobilization that were initiated in Prague.[34]

Informal compromise at enterprise level formed the social backdrop to the institutionalization of regime workerism – the creation of a settlement between the state and industrial workers across the region, discussed in the previous chapter – that was fundamental to the consolidation of socialist regimes after they had been shaken by the crises of the mid-1950s. In that such compromises invariably involved accommodation to working-class culture in the factories, in the mines and on construction sites, workerism involved retreat, both from attempts to transform work practices and utopian attempts to destroy the inequalities and hierarchies that had characterized working-class culture. Regime workerism, during the late 1950s and 1960s, was driven and, in turn, drove such informal compromises that also preserved working-class culture in the enterprise. In Czechoslovakia, where workerism was at its most entrenched, industry was characterized by a considerable degree of equality of earnings between skilled workers and white-collar staff. Earning differentials between workers in different sectors conformed to the moral economy of a male, heavy-industry-dominated working-class culture. Women earned far less than men by the mid-1960s, while workers in light industry were worse paid than those in mining or steel production.[35]

Elsewhere, workerism strongly affected the internal stratification of the working class as its ranks were expanded radically during the 1960s. In Poland, the total number of manual workers rose from just over 4.3 million in 1960 to 6.4 million a decade later.[36] As the workforce expanded, an 'income aristocracy', consisting of workers in energy production, mining and heavy industry, enjoyed the highest earnings and greatest countervailing power on the shop floor.[37] Other groups, like the growing number of worker-peasants, who combined work in industry with labour on an agricultural smallholding and who made up 12.2 per cent of the workforce in 1973, or women, who made up 40 per cent of all workers, found themselves in a less favourable position.[38] In Hungary, between 1960 and 1970, the total numbers employed in industry rose from 1,347,945 to 1,835,556; and those in construction increased from 289,056 to 370,044 over the same period.[39] An influx of workers into factories from agriculture reshaped the working class; by 1970, over 130,000 from a total of 220,000 manual workers in rural and suburban Pest county commuted into Budapest every day. Such workers found themselves – along with women and younger workers – in a peripheral position within the industrial workforce, where élite positions were monopolized by male, urban, skilled workers.[40]

It was, however, on the south-eastern periphery where the continued industrialization of the 1960s resulted in a real transformation of the working class, in part because of the restricted size of the industrial workforce during the pre-socialist period. In Romania, according to official statistics, the working class accounted for 23.7 per cent of the country's population in 1956. This figure had risen to 39.9 per cent a decade later.[41] Neighbouring Bulgaria witnessed a similar increase, from 29.2 per cent in 1955 to 42 per cent ten years later.[42] Across the south of the region, workers migrated from agriculture into industry on a large scale, without leaving rural communities, creating a situation in which worker-peasants became a significant social group in their own right. In Yugoslavia, around 4.5 million people had left agricultural employment between 1945 and 1970, with the result that by the end of the period, 45 per cent of rural households had one member or more working for wages. In both the most industrialized republic – Slovenia – and in one of the least developed republics – Macedonia, this figure was higher still.[43] In Romania's Braşov county, by 1973, as much as 50 per cent of the workforce in most factories consisted of commuting worker-peasants with connections to the land.[44] Many more had connections to the land through relatives. In Bulgaria in 1967, only 26.1 per cent of workers came from a family headed by an industrial worker – on the other hand, 39.7 per cent came from the families of individual peasants, and a further 21.8 per cent from those who were members of agricultural cooperatives.[45]

While the spread of the worker-peasant identity created a large body of industrial workers with access to the shadow economy, and thus a safety valve, it created tension between them and urban workers and, at the same time, affected the informal social contracts that evolved within south-east European enterprises. With the exception of miners' strikes in the Slovenian coalfields in 1958 and a strike wave in the late 1960s, in Yugoslavia, a social contract emerged where the short, wild-cat strike became a tool in highly decentralized workplace bargaining.[46] In Bulgaria, by the late 1960s, enterprise management made frequent concessions by reducing work norms in order to prevent the largely worker-peasant workforce migrating to other jobs.[47] In Romania, similar informal settlements, based on low production norms and job security, developed to accommodate worker-peasant workforces, who commuted long distances and returned home to a 'second shift' in agriculture.[48]

The blurring of the boundaries between industrial and agricultural labour, which was particularly marked in south-eastern Europe by the end of the 1960s, was accompanied by a wholesale transformation in the nature of work in rural areas that resulted from the collectivization of agriculture. Whereas industrial workers had constituted a minority of the labour force across the region, those engaged in agriculture constituted a majority almost everywhere during the inter-war years. While only 33 per cent of relatively industrialized Czechoslovakia's population were dependent on agriculture in 1930–1, in the south-eastern European states (Albania, Bulgaria, Romania and Yugoslavia), the proportion ranged from 72 per cent to 80 per cent. In Hungary and Poland, majorities depended on the agrarian economy for their existence.[49] Histories of agricultural development had left a legacy of highly differentiated patterns of land ownership, property and work relations across the region. A legacy of long-term development and waves of land reform had left agriculture in Czechoslovakia, Hungary and Poland characterized by large units, while Romania, Bulgaria and Yugoslavia were largely characterized by small-scale peasant farming.[50]

The immediate end of the Second World War brought about a major transformation in agrarian property relations across the region, as the creation of popular-front regimes was accompanied by radical land reform. In Czechoslovakia, the first wave of post-war land reform was closely connected to the expulsion of ethnic Germans and 'anti-fascist' retribution, as around a third of agricultural land in the Czech lands, and 10 per cent in Slovakia, was transferred to 122,000 new owners.[51] In Poland, post-war land reform dovetailed with the expulsion of Germans from the western regions of the country and the need to resettle those driven from territories that had been incorporated into the Soviet Union. Poor peasants from within the pre-1939 borders of the state made up 50 per cent of land reform's 5 million beneficiaries, while those from the eastern territories lost to the Soviets contributed another 40 per cent.[52]

Elsewhere, while ethnic, anti-fascist retribution formed an undercurrent within land reform policies (in Yugoslavia, for example, 40 per cent of all land available for distribution as part of the 1945 land reform was confiscated from ethnic Germans[53]), it aimed more explicitly at the restructuring of class relations in rural communities. In Hungary, official land reform was preceded by land seizures in the overpopulated and radical east of the country, which were eventually legitimized and spread to cover the whole country by government action in 1945. Land reform destroyed the stranglehold of great estates over the agrarian sector, creating instead a rural economy dominated by individual smallholding. Hungarian land reform had 642,342 beneficiaries, of whom 370,963 had been manorial servants or wage labourers prior to 1944.[54] Romania's post-war land reform was partly directed against ethnic Germans and collaborators, but more centrally aimed to eliminate all large farms and estates, marking properties of more than 50 hectares for restructuring, with land over this amount made available for redistribution to the rural poor.[55] In Yugoslavia's reform, the upper limit was set at 45 hectares, with the further provision that those farms which employed agricultural labourers were marked for expropriation.[56]

While the post-war waves of land reform did not entirely eliminate the highly differentiated patterns of land ownership that had existed in the inter-war period, they produced an agricultural sector dominated by small-scale private agriculture. The role of subsistence farming increased: by the late 1940s, subsistence farms accounted for a quarter of the agrarian land area in Czechoslovakia and Poland and half of the same in Hungary.[57] During the period of popular-front rule, most Communist parties vocally supported private subsistence farming; indeed in Hungary, in 1946, the MKP sought to mobilize poor smallholders against the political right with a campaign entitled 'We Will Not Give the Land Back'.[58] Yet this support did not survive the transition from popular-front rule to socialist dictatorship, suggesting that in most countries in the region it was a short-term political strategy designed to cement the relationship between the emerging regime and the rural poor.[59] The beginning of the construction of socialism heralded the pursuit of two interconnected policies: the first was based on the need to feed the industrializing cities and was, in effect, a policy of class-based taxation, but it was always connected to the second, which involved the elimination of private ownership and the socialization of the agricultural sector.

The first of these policies involved sharp increases in the taxation of land and the compulsory delivery obligations – that is to say, the amount of produce farmers were legally obliged to deliver to the state at fixed prices that had been in existence since the war years. These increases sharply discriminated against wealthy farmers, often termed kulaks after the Soviet example, in order to drive them out of agriculture entirely. In Yugoslavia, the kulaks, defined as 'enemies in the village who wish to aggravate the union of peasants and workers that was created during the war', were first identified in 1946, two years before the rest of the region.[60] In Romania, party campaigns targeted the *chiaburi*, the local term for kulak, as an 'odious and shrewd' element of life in the villages.[61] Wealthy farmers bore the brunt of discriminatory taxation and compulsory deliveries; however, as the regime sought to drive more smallholders into socialized agriculture and feed the growing industrial areas, all farmers became subject to this process.[62]

The second policy involved an attempt to generalize the socialized sector in agriculture. Socialized agricultural enterprises took one of two forms: the first were state farms – centrally managed agricultural enterprises – which were only ever a minority phenomenon; the second were agricultural cooperatives – the hegemonic socialized agricultural enterprise. Within the agricultural cooperative, the individual member was the nominal owner of the land which was held and farmed in common. While several different types of cooperative were established, and they varied from country to country, the state aimed to integrate as many farmers as possible into the 'higher' type of cooperative – that is to say, where a member's tie to their land was weakest. In these forms of cooperative, while farmers retained a small private plot for subsistence production, agricultural work was organized industrially on commonly farmed land. Remuneration was calculated on the basis of the overall earnings of the cooperative, which were distributed between the members on the basis of the number of 'work-units', a scientific calculation of work done, completed by each member.

Collectivization was both unsuccessful and deeply unpopular during the early 1950s. By 1952, only 9 per cent of those active in agriculture in Czechoslovakia were employed on state farms and 34 per cent were members of collectives; in Hungary, the respective figures were 12 per cent and 25 per cent; and in Poland, 12 per cent and 5 per cent.[63] Such figures were typical for the region as a whole. At the heart of the problem lay low levels of investment, given that the state prioritized industrialization, and the fact that only the poorest smallholders joined the new cooperatives in the late 1940s. In the Romanian village of Taga, 16 smallholders attempted to found a cooperative with 20 hectares of land from a total of 661 available locally.[64] In Hungary, in June 1949, of those who had joined cooperatives, around 70 per cent had been agricultural labourers, while another 29 per cent had possessed properties of less then 4 hectares prior to joining.[65] In one Bulgarian village, those who joined the new cooperative were 'men with only one goat to their name'.[66] The lack of capital, land and equipment made for chaotic production on early cooperative farms; the president of one early Hungarian cooperative remembered that 'among the members there was neither a horse nor a cow'. Gradually, with the help of the authorities, this problem was solved as the cooperative managed to acquire for itself four horses and oxen. The first year was extraordinarily difficult, given that 'in the first year the land was not properly ready for growing sugar beat, and the labor force was weak. The co-operative couldn't pay them, and so they all went to get casual work'.[67] Chaotic production often resulted in penury for the membership. In one cooperative in Poland's Wrocław province, founded in 1950, 'potatoes and beetroots looked like overgrown bushes. The peasants have had enough of such farming. They are saying – the more we work, the less we get'.[68]

During the 1950s, weak agricultural cooperatives were forced to exist in a deeply hostile environment. The state's taxation measures, backed by severe repression and despotic confiscations of land in order to bolster the cooperative, resulted in a state of near civil war in the countryside between rural residents and the representatives of the regime, as we saw in chapter 2. During the first half of the 1950s, party leaders blamed the parlous state of the countryside on 'mistakes' and 'excesses'. In 1951, the Romanian Communist Party's central committee blamed a 'lack of adequate propaganda ... and brutal methods employed in forcing individuals to join collectives' for the problems.[69] By 1953, however, the decay of the authority of the regime in rural communities had become so great, and the disruption to food supplies for industrial centres so considerable, that most states witnessed a pause in their collectivization drives, as we saw in chapter 3. In two states, Yugoslavia and, eventually, Poland, these pauses turned into a permanent suspension of the collectivization drives. Private farming on a small scale would remain dominant in both the Polish and Yugoslav countryside until the collapse of socialist dictatorship at the end of the 1980s.

Elsewhere, the collectivization drives were renewed in the mid- and late 1950s, this time, far more successfully than in the early part of the decade. Bulgaria was somewhat exceptional in that its agriculture was substantially collectivized earlier than in the rest of the region, as its campaigns had been characterized by less of a pause during the mid-1950s than elsewhere.[70] In Czechoslovakia, renewed collectivization began in 1956 and ended in 1960; by the end of this second campaign, 67 per cent of all agricultural land was held by agricultural cooperatives, and a further 15.6 per cent by state farms, while a residual private sector survived only in the less fertile, mountainous regions of Slovakia.[71] In Romania, the pause in collectivization led to a brief consolidation of small-scale agriculture. In December 1955, 45.2 per cent of rural families owned smallholdings of up to five hectares, while their real incomes had increased substantially – by 86.6 per cent – when compared with their 1951 level. This was ended by a renewed collectivization drive at the end of the 1950s; by 1962, cooperatives covered 77.4 per cent of all agricultural land and state farms owned a further 17.6 per cent.[72] In Hungary, collectivization was resumed in 1958, after the upheavals of the 1956 revolution, spearheaded by a determined campaign in which party activists from the cities invaded the villages to persuade and coerce smallholders into cooperatives.[73] By 1960, 60.3 per cent of all agricultural land was in the hands of the cooperatives, with state farms owning a further 16.7 per cent.[74]

Many of these newly established cooperatives were established in the teeth of peasant opposition; despite the fact that collectivization policies had been modified to ensure their success, the lack of consent on which they were based was revealed in their poor performance. Collectivization campaigns, and the passive resistance they engendered, were blamed for the poor performance of Czechoslovak agriculture in 1961 and 1962.[75] In Bulgaria, many of the new cooperatives suffered from similar problems, of a lack of machinery and disorganization, to those that had been set up in the early 1950s. As one member remembered, 'we worked all day in unbearable heat, doing everything by hand just like before, except now the blocks of land were endless ... The work was hard and the pay very low'.[76] In Hungary, many of the heads of households surrendered their land to cooperatives and then left agriculture entirely, leaving other family members to work in them. In 1961, almost 75 per cent of cooperative members were over 40; in some cooperatives, as many as 60 per cent of the membership did no work in the collectives.[77]

Faced with the continuance of deep-seated problems, the state was forced to win support for the cooperatives among a membership which had largely refused to consent to their foundation. To some extent, this was achieved, as rationalization and investment in agriculture led to increased mechanization, in turn boosting productivity and increasing members' incomes.[78] This was a long-term process; in the shorter term, the promise of social security for cooperative members also played a role. The extension of pension provisions, for example, to include members of agricultural cooperatives, had been granted in 1951 in Czechoslovakia and in 1958 in Hungary, and played a part in persuading members of the benefits of cooperation in those countries.[79] Increasingly, however, the ability of the cooperatives to protect the incomes of their members against the insecurities of labour in agriculture was central. Because of agricultural labour's seasonal nature, the growing ability of cooperatives to provide work throughout the year played an important role. This possibility was generated by the increasing specialization and diversification of cooperative activities as they came to encompass small-scale industrial production. In Romania, for example, cooperatives had been allowed to engage in small-scale industrial and service activities to provide employment for their members since 1956, though their further expansion was prevented from the mid-1960s onwards.[80]

Far more central, however, to the consolidation of agricultural cooperatives was the generalization of informal practices in the organization of production and remuneration, which effectively allowed established agrarian work cultures to reproduce themselves within the framework of the collectives. This was especially marked in patterns of overall labour organization within the cooperatives. In early cooperatives in Romania's Olt Land, rural households sustained by networks of kin formed the basis of work teams, being held responsible for parcels of land.[81] While mechanization eroded the basis of this 'traditional' division of labour on the land during the 1960s and 1970s, the family household unit remained 'the basic unit of production in almost all … non-mechanized activities'.[82] The spread of sharecropping in Hungarian cooperatives during the second half of the late 1950s provided a basis for the integration of 'traditional' agrarian work culture into the framework of the collective farm.[83] This would become more general during the 1960s, even after the substantial extension of mechanization.[84]

Measures such as the extension of sharecropping contracts on Hungarian cooperatives formed part of a more general shift away from the work-unit system of remuneration. This was necessary given the income insecurity that this system of distributing the revenue of the cooperative engendered, in the face of attempts to consolidate cooperatives. In Czechoslovakia, the abandonment of the work-unit system, and its replacement with conventional, industrial-style wages for work completed, took place in the mid-1960s.[85] In Romania, while work-units dominated, from the mid-1960s onwards they began to be complemented with other systems of remuneration that shaped wage relations in the cooperatives.[86]

The area in which informal compromises between cooperatives and their membership were most marked, and where continuities with pre-socialist agrarian work cultures was most visible, was in the role of private plots within cooperatives, as we saw in chapter 3. In Bulgaria, where the private plots existed as subsistence farms within the collective, they provided a means through which aspects of individual, pre-socialist peasant culture were transferred into the cooperative.[87] Given their productivity, their scope was extended in the 1970s, and the limits on the individual ownership of livestock abolished.[88] In Hungary, the period between the late 1950s and the mid-1970s witnessed the integration of labour on the private plot, within the work of the cooperative, to an extent that was greater than elsewhere in the region.[89] In Czechoslovakia, while the average size of private plots, on paper at least, had fallen from 0.42 hectares per member in 1965 to 0.26 hectares in 1975, in the latter year their importance was underlined by the fact that the private sector in agriculture, which included private plots, produced 48 per cent of all eggs and 15 per cent of all meat.[90]

In both industrial and agrarian spheres, socialist states attempted to redefine the meaning and nature of work, yet were forced to accommodate themselves to pre-existing cultures of labour. Intellectual labour represented a different challenge to the regimes, given its highly differentiated nature. During early socialism, the regimes were dependent on the diverse forms of intellectual labour, in part because of the dependence of their social transformation on expertise, but also because their attempt to shape a socialist culture was crucially dependent on intellectual labour. Intellectual workers, however, were able to assert their autonomy and use their control of the categories of culture and expertise to redefine their roles as the dictatorships were consolidated.

Socialist industrialization, the collectivization and mechaniza-tion of agriculture and the expansion of state services all placed a premium on expertise. With the expansion of industry, state rhetoric proclaimed:

> The new intelligentsia in the countries of the
> people's democracy is being formed ... from the
> ranks of the leading workers, from the new
> section of the working class which, jointly with

> the graduates of the higher educational establish-
> ments, constitutes the core of the working-class
> intelligentsia, the core of the leading staff of the
> new intelligentsia … The best part of the old
> intelligentsia in the people's democratic
> countries is also taking an active part in socialist
> construction.[91]

The need to create a 'new intelligentsia' was not only demanded by the absolute numbers of highly qualified employees that socialist transformation required, but also by the marked distrust of existing white-collar staff by the state. Often this distrust was an extension of Stalinist class-war rhetoric; this was especially the case in the factories, where engineering and technical staff had been identified with pre-socialist management and thus were deemed legitimate targets of suspicion. In Budapest's United Lighting and Electrics factory, in 1952, the plant's engineers and foremen were blamed for subverting state labour policy, something that party propagandists argued was rooted in their political pasts as 'former social democrats'.[92] In certain professions, like medicine, it was related to the impact of nationalization on working conditions and resentment at what were felt to be attempts to destroy their professional autonomy. In Bulgaria, 'physicians and dentists were among the few professionals allowed the right of private practice. Then came the nationalization of medicine in 1949, followed by a regulation that all medical workers up to 60 years of age were obliged to hold a state job. If any physician or dentist under this age limit refused to comply, his license to practice was withdrawn'. One former medical researcher from Czechoslovakia complained that 'the revolution and regimentation' of his profession was making 'it increasingly difficult for physicians to exercise their profession according to pre-Communist standards'.[93]

The solution to these problems was conceived as a major expansion of training and technical education in order to create a new intelligentsia from the ranks of the working class. Crash training and retraining programmes in enterprises were established to allow workers to train to become foremen or engineers; the training of skilled workers was professionalized with the introduction of new technical schools; schools for engineers were established; and universities were to be opened to the working class, through the creation of so-called 'workers' faculties' and the introduction of forms of affirmative action in university entrance policies. In Romania in 1951, in the energy sector, 71,000 employees were reported to be taking retraining courses, while the country's 17 workers' faculties had 2,516 students enrolled.[94] Alongside these measures, mainstream university curricula were reorganized to transfer the productivist culture of the dictatorships into the lecture hall. In Czechoslovakia, university curricula were reorganized unevenly from 1948 onwards, with the goal that student learning should be brought 'close to production and practical life'.[95]

As we saw in chapter 2, policies of affirmative action in terms of higher education entrance were only of limited effectiveness as, despite extensive class-based discrimination, the children of middle-class parents were relatively successful in gaining university degrees and thus intellectual jobs. Regime higher educational policies, however, did change the nature of the universities radically. Besides the introduction of class-based quotas for university entrance, opportunities to study liberal arts subjects were restricted, while technical and vocational degrees were significantly expanded. One prospective university applicant in Czechoslovakia remembered that:

> … only three students from our school will be permitted to register at the Department of Philosophy, and this quota includes those who are intending to study languages. The Principal advised me to learn descriptive geometry and try to register, at least, in the School of Technology …[96]

Faculties were purged of academics whom the regimes regarded with suspicion; in Poland, the regime justified its purges with reference to the view that 'our students are not receiving a cohesive Marxist-Leninist worldview'.[97] University curricula were also thoroughly Stalinized; one refugee summed up his experience of this in the Law Faculty at Kraków in 1951: 'Every course, even postal law, starts with instructions on the base and superstructure of Marxist philosophy. This basic preamble includes Stalin's contributions to Marxism, quotations from the classics of Marxism, and a constant repetition of the superiority of Soviet science'.[98]

The reorganization of academia formed one plank of a programme to transform the labour of intellectuals in the cultural sphere. The role of cultural intellectuals was to be transformed and they were to become key players in the battle of emergent regimes to bring 'socialist culture' to the population. In post-war Yugoslavia, Tito's regime, in a shift typical of the region, spent large sums on the various cultural trade unions in order to boost the material benefits available to cultural intellectuals. In return, it sought the active cooperation of the country's intellectuals in shaping a 'new' culture, aimed at mass enlightenment, which would transcend what had been seen previously as 'bourgeois' forms.[99] This drive to transform intellectuals into disciples of cultural enlightenment was marked in the role they played in democratizing mass media, in particular, radio. In post-war Hungary, they played a central role in creating 'new' radio programming that aimed to ensure that the voices of industrial workers and the rural poor were heard for the first time in the mass media.[100]

The transformation of the social role of left-wing cultural intellectuals into carriers of cultural enlightenment during the late 1940s, and their material dependence on the state-provided resources of the cultural trade unions, left them vulnerable when overt socialist dictatorships were created. The Stalinization of cultural life within the Soviet bloc led to the subjection of cultural intellectuals to new pressures. The plan that transformed industry during the early 1950s was applied to the sphere of high culture, as writers were subjected to plan targets and explicit demands for certain kinds of work.[101] The institutionalization of 'socialist realism' as a dominant, regime-imposed style across painting, sculpture, architecture, literature and music severely restricted the freedom of expression of intellectuals, and was used as a stick to beat individuals. It also aimed at the wholesale remaking of both high and everyday culture within socialist societies.[102] Yet even within the deeply conformist climate promoted by repression and institutionalized socialist realism, beneath a surface of outward conformity, artists were able to subvert certain aspects of the official line through the deployment of personal networks and the judicious exploitation of patronage and personal protection.[103]

Within the context of early socialism's transformation of intellectual labour, there was a re-emergence of continuities, with pre-socialist notions of intellectual identity, which were to become powerfully visible during the first stages of the consolidation of the socialist regimes that followed Stalin's death. Members of the technical intelligentsia began, in the climate of chaos that characterized the early planned economy, to assert their expertise in marked opposition to the ideological practice of the regime. One engineer in Budapest's United Lighting and Electrics factory blamed the sidelining of technical expertise in the organization of production in the plant for the decline in the quality of its products in 1957. For him, 'the pre-war United Lighting and Electrics was one of the few plants in Hungary which could compete with the Americans ... as a consequence of the socialist re-organisation of production the quality of ... [its] products fell'. His argument rested on the fact that the recovery of the competitiveness of the factory relied on a reassertion of the role of the technical expertise of engineers in production.[104] With the politics of consolidation, other intellectuals began to reassert a claim, deploying a discourse of expertise to influence policy. This was particularly true of economists, who asserted the value of policy prescription, based upon empirical research, to correct the malfunctioning planned economy; bodies like the Institute for Economic Research of Hungary's Academy of Sciences advanced these arguments powerfully from 1954 onwards.[105]

Within the cultural realm, the effects of the reproduction of continuity in intellectual identity within socialist contexts were more dramatic and more problematic for socialist regimes. The combination of the notion of intellectual as independent thinker and the socialist notion of intellectual as bringer of cultural enlightenment combined to produce a situation where cultural intellectuals, especially writers, became the conscience of their nations during the initial period following Stalin's death. In Poland, writers, younger members of the cultural intelligentsia and even students became the most radical public advocates of wholesale political reform in 1955 and 1956. Taking advantage of factional struggle in the PZPR and a relaxation in censorship, periodicals like *Nowa Kultura* were prepared to publish such demands.[106] In Hungary, in the run-up to 1956, writers played a similar role in exposing what they saw as the crimes of dictatorship and opening the space for broader intellectual mobilization around demands for radical reform of the system.[107]

Open dissent of this kind was severely suppressed after the 1956 revolution in Hungary, yet in the years that followed, as the repressive post-revolutionary climate was relaxed, the reconfiguration of intellectual identity that had emerged during the mid-1950s was given scope for restricted expression, as part of a settlement between the regime and intellectuals.[108] In Poland, relations between the state and the writers, as with the cultural intelligentsia as a whole, were characterized by an uneasy truce throughout the 1960s.[109] The preservation and the extension of the intellectual identities that emerged in the 1950s would form the basis of the spread of the identity of the cultural and technical intelligentsia as a group in socialist society over the course of the following decade. As we saw in chapter 3, the consolidation and spread of this particular identity had major consequences for the institutionalization of social settlements that allowed the regimes to consolidate their rule throughout the 1960s. They also played a profound role in shaping the nature of the challenges to socialist regimes that emerged during the decade.

5 Remaking the private sphere

The attempts of socialist states to build societies based upon the performance of productive labour succeeded at the cost of a retreat. This retreat involved the abandonment of visions of outright social transformation in the workplace and accommodation to established work cultures that had reproduced themselves during the early phase of socialist transformation. Yet the retreats made by the state in the workplace were neither the most radical nor the most significant for the legitimacy of the regime. Socialist states attempted to remake the contours of everyday life, promising new forms of socialist living for their worker-citizens across the region, based upon the creation of new communities to underpin their project of shaping a society based upon productive labour. This offensive involved the shaping of new model communities; influenced the design of housing; underpinned the social and consumer policy goals of the new states; and aimed to reshape the boundaries between public and private spheres. While it was less explicitly concerned with the reshaping of class identities than was the project of transforming Eastern European workplaces, it nevertheless posed substantial challenges to established identities based upon gender and generation.

In transforming everyday culture during the early 1950s, however, the state was faced with severe constraints of resources, as investment was diverted into the cold-war industrialization drives. Life in the region during the early socialist period was consequently characterized by penury. This clashed with the aspirations of members of households in the climate of the post-war years; increasingly, individuals and family units aspired to material security and a depoliticized existence, while many, particularly the young, demanded greater personal autonomy. Socialist consolidation involved an accommodation that occurred on several fronts with households in the region. Its attempts to transform the gendered boundaries between public and private were substantially modified; and there was a gradual relaxation of policies that demanded cultural conformism, thus involving an accommodation with those who sought greater personal autonomy. Most significantly, the regimes adapted to social aspirations for greater, privatized material security, though these patterns of adaptation were never even across the region.

The attempts to remake households and communities were intimately tied to regime attempts to shape a society that was based on the performance of socialist labour. Production was central to the early socialist public sphere as it was conceived by the regime. This can be seen in the way in which socialist citizens' participation as citizens was closely related to labour. By the early 1950s, for example, most party members were members of their workplace cells rather than members of the party organization where they lived. Of the recorded members and candidates for membership of the party in Hungary's Fejér county in 1952, the overwhelming majority were members of workplace-based organizations.[1] Assumptions of the centrality of socialist labour to the public sphere were extended to the design of model socialist communities during the 1950s. The industrialization drive of the early part of the decade witnessed a rush to shape such communities, of which the most spectacular were attempts to build entirely socialist cities, like Nowa Huta in Poland, Sztálinváros in Hungary or Dimitrovgrad in Bulgaria. These model communities were to serve as examples to their national societies of what new socialist communities would look like. Nowa Huta, built adjacent to the city of Kraków, was to play a particular role in signposting a socialist future. As one party propagandist proclaimed, 'Kraków is awakening to a productive life. The stagnant city of half-feudal customs, and lord and pauper traditions has surrendered its place to a socialist city'.[2] For the residents of the Hungarian village of Nagykarácsony, 20 kilometres from Sztálinváros, the new city was to act, both literally and metaphorically, as a beacon for a new way of life:

> At night the fires of Pentele's [Sztálinváros's] chimneys light the sky; their sparks like sparkling

red stars breaking apart the darkness. Above the former prairie and the banks, the woods and the gardens they rise, lighting the tractors stood in the fields.[3]

These new cities, as projections of the regime's vision of the future, were explicitly organized around socialist industrial labour. Nowa Huta was organized around the Lenin Steel Works, a flagship of the Polish state's drive to industrialize the country. Sztálinváros was likewise organized around the Stalin Steel Works, the undoubted flagship of the country's first five-year plan. The new Hungarian city's urban form was organized explicitly around the twin poles of political power and socialist labour; at one end of the city stood the factory, divided from housing by a kilometre of woodland and linked to public buildings by a main street, which led from the factory gate at one end of the city to a square flanked by the party headquarters and city hall at the other.[4] Model urban spaces were also to contain model urban homes. Warsaw, reconstructed from the devastated state in which the Second World War had left it, was to be reshaped as a new socialist city. This involved the planning of 120,000 new urban homes, to be contained in six-storey apartment blocks built in socialist realist style. Such homes had a specific social role; they were 'not only a place of rest for the working man. They are also a place where one can work on self-improvement, a place where one may work out many of the ideas about efficiency that present themselves in professional work'.[5] Housing in the new towns, however, was designed in such a way that it would not become a focus for private economic activities; in Sztálinváros, local council officials were charged with ensuring that no pigs were kept in newly constructed flats, while urban design offered residents no individual garden space in which vegetables could be grown or chickens kept.[6] Households living in socialist model housing were to be consumers of food produced in socialist enterprises only, and played no role in self-provisioning themselves.

The assumptions of household behaviour that were implicit in the designs of model housing across the region formed one element in a broader policy of shaping the household and its social role that was based on a reconstruction and reform of the family unit. The need for family reconstruction rested on the pressure to restore a sense of stability following the enormous disruption to households that had occurred as a consequence of the population loss and upheaval of the Second World War. This had not only brought severe material dislocation, but had disrupted the hierarchies of gender and generation within and between family units, creating acute social problems and unleashing new aspirations in the post-war context. As we saw in chapter 1, the human cost of the war, particularly in states like Poland and Yugoslavia, was staggering, significantly altering the age structure of the population. War in most societies of the region brought about an ageing of the total population, as the proportion over 65 increased significantly. At the same time, the proportion of the population under 14 fell, thus creating a premium on relatively scarce youth.[7] Absolute losses of population created a push for pro-natalist policies, while subverting generational hierarchies through underlining the importance of youth. The effects of the loss of male combatants, the conscription of labour to work in Germany, the deportation of prisoners of war by the Germans, and then the deportation of civilians by Soviet troops, forced the role of the management of many households on women. While women suffered as victims of the violence that war brought in its wake, for example, the mass rapes that accompanied the arrival of the Red Army in Budapest,[8] war also involved the adoption of new roles by women that challenged established hierarchies of gender. In Yugoslavia, for example, female participation in partisan activity was substantial: around 100,000 served on the side of Tito's Communists, of whom 25,000 died.[9]

Post-war and early socialist policies, in so far as they impacted on gender and generation, moved simultaneously in two contradictory directions. On the one hand, they aimed at restoring a semblance of pre-war normality, particularly as far as restoring gendered hierarchies and reconstructing the heterosexual family as the basic social unit were concerned. On the other hand, the politics of socialist transformation sought, not particularly successfully, to channel the energies released by the wartime subversion of gender and generational hierarchies. The restoration of traditional gender roles in politics was particularly visible during the mid- and late 1940s. It was particularly evident in Yugoslavia, where the Anti-Fascist Women's Front had played a central role in challenging established gendered hierarchies by mobilizing women for partisan struggle during the early part of the decade. With the consolidation of Tito's rule, it was reined in and transformed into something called the Conference for the Social Activity of Women, strongly subordinate to the regime.[10] While the retreat was less radical, Hungary's transition to overt socialist dictatorship was marked by the elimination of independent women's organizations and the creation of a monopoly transmission-belt organization.[11]

Legal regulation enshrined the two-parent, heterosexual family as the basic unit of society, though this legislation attempted to set family relationships on a more egalitarian footing than had been the case before the war. Czechoslovakia's socialist family code, which protected 'motherhood, marriage and the family', came into force in 1950; though it removed the legal distinctions between legitimate and illegitimate children and argued for marriage as a relationship of equal partners, it enshrined the family as a basic social unit.[12] Hungary's family law, passed two years later, was similar in nature; it also sought to enforce the norm of a two-parent heterosexual family, providing a legal underpinning for a battery of social policy measures that aimed to enforce this, effectively outlawing single parenthood.[13] The rash of laws that institutionalized the two-parent heterosexual family as the basic household unit across the region, between 1947 and 1953, not only represented an attempt to impose 'normality' on the household after the disruptions of war, but also formed the backdrop to the aggressive promotion of parenthood by regimes concerned to use pro-natalist policies to replace population losses and create a future labour force. In Romania, where the birth rate declined in the immediate post-war years, the socialist state revised the penal code in 1948 to make attempts to end pregnancy a criminal offence, as part of a largely unsuccessful pro-natalist policy.[14] Hungary's early socialist pro-natalist drive was associated with the policies of the Stalinist minister of health, Anna Ratkó. Rights to abortion were first curtailed and then revoked outright; access to birth control was restricted; motherhood was promoted; and childlessness was actively penalized, through a childlessness tax.[15] In Poland, post-war pressure to relax the restrictive provisions of the 1932 ban on abortion was resisted in the interests of reversing population loss, laying the foundations for aggressive pro-natalist policies in the 1950s.[16]

Yet while early socialist social policy involved the reconstruction of the heterosexual family unit and the aggressive promotion of motherhood through pro-natalist policies, in other respects it aimed at a radical and egalitarian reconstruction of gender relations and identities. While established working-class identities were constructed around masculine norms across the region, and notions of divides between public and private spheres in all societies were sharply gendered,[17] socialist regimes challenged these ideologies by promoting women in the workplace as men's equals. To a considerable extent, this reflected the commitment of socialist states to gender equality in a society organized around productive labour, which could only be achieved through the promotion of socialist labour as a 'calling' for the region's women.[18] Notions of a gendered divide, where women managed the household while men earned a living wage to support their families in production, were to be replaced by a model of cooperation, based on equality between men and women in production and in the home. This was neatly illustrated by one piece of Czechoslovak propaganda about the worker Ludmila Gabolova, who took employment in a southern Moravian industrial enterprise during the early 1950s. 'She is working', reported the propagandist, 'to the great satisfaction of the foreman, as the first woman blacksmith. She is working together with her husband. She heats and presses the cut casts while he operates the hammer, or vice versa'.[19]

While attempts to mobilize women for socialist labour on the basis of equality with men were characteristic of the whole region, with the notable exception of Yugoslavia,[20] as we saw in chapter 4, they encountered stiff resistance when male monopolies over certain skilled positions were challenged. The campaigns also challenged established ways in which gender structured notions of the legitimate division between public and private spheres across the region. The public realm of work was largely constructed as a masculine realm, while the private was normally identified with the feminine. In working-class communities in Hungary, at the end of the 1940s, for example, male workers believed in their role as breadwinners, and thus their entitlement to a family wage. This income, it was believed, should be sufficient to support a woman in the pursuit of the management of the household; women, where they worked, worked to provide a supplementary income, according to this moral economy, and therefore male earnings and jobs should be protected before those of women.[21] In rural communities, similar gendered notions structured divisions between public and private and legitimate access to work; in the isolated villages of the mountainous regions of south-west Poland, notions that women were best located as 'carers and nurturers' in the private sphere, while men participated in the 'public' activity of farm management, were hegemonic.[22] Similar notions were deeply inscribed on gender identities in both rural and urban communities across Yugoslavia, despite deep-seated regional differentiation that in turn shaped those identities.[23]

In a situation in which, as a consequence of wartime dislocation, women had taken on new roles, new aspirations for greater female personal autonomy emerged. This was used by the regimes to mobilize the minority of women who sought to use the state's campaigns to assert their independence and equal worth alongside men in production. The propaganda of the Polish regime was keen to capitalize on this, claiming in 1951: 'We now have thousands of women employed as motorists, conductors, machinists, tool makers, tractor drivers, carpenters, armament workers. Have they not all of them crossed that barrier which until now has barred them from "men's professions"?'[24] In 1949, one Prague worker complained to officials in the British Embassy of a marked feminization of the city's workforce: 'waitresses are replacing waiters, women act as traffic police, and also work in all kinds of factories'.[25] Amid the sexism of many male workers, the low wages and the poor working conditions, the enthusiasm that to some extent sustained these campaigns in the early 1950s rapidly disappeared. Attempts by the regime to restructure gender relations and the place of the household within society, based on productive labour, foundered, as an ideal of social privatization spread among the societies of the region.

The spread of social privatization and the defence of household autonomy, which was in part a consequence of this, stemmed from the failures of the socialist economies of the region to satisfy the material needs of households. As far as the architects of the socialist order were concerned, the needs of households were to be satisfied through a mixture of collectively provided services and industrially produced goods. Household self-provisioning of foodstuffs was to be abolished and then superseded by a new, socialist consumer sector. Nationalization was to lay the basis for this new sector. In

Bulgaria, the state sector accounted for 12.9 per cent of retail turnover in 1947, rising to 51.3 per cent by 1951. In Czechoslovakia, state and cooperative enterprises mushroomed as a result of the nationalization drive; small-scale private pharmacies in Prague were liquidated during 1949 and 1950, becoming part of 'Medica', a large, quasi-monopoly state chain.[26] As retail trade was brought under the control of the state, access to its benefits were to be distributed according to performance in work. As early as 1949, the Czechoslovak trade unions approved the creation of 'special shops selling goods in short supply and giving priority to shock-workers'.[27]

The reality of the state sector in retail fell far short of its promise during the first half of the 1950s, as the retail networks suffered from serious under-investment. One Polish escapee described the situation:

> In spite of a considerable expansion in socialized trade, the number of retail stores is still insufficient. Last year the press devoted much space to the defective distribution of retail outlets and their scarcity in various sometimes thickly populated districts. However, the essential weak point is ... the incompetence of the whole trade set-up ... the shortage of trained sales personnel, and the red tape covering commercial trans-actions.[28]

With the crisis in agriculture brought about by conflict in the countryside over collectivization, urban areas across the region suffered from severe food shortages that plagued state shops. In November 1951, Czechoslovak prime minister, Antonín Zápotocký, admitted that 'the regular supply of food and consumer goods are our greatest worry and also the source of complaints and dissatis-faction'.[29] One Albanian farmer, who escaped to the West in the same year, reported that 'sugar, kerosene, salt, coffee, edible oil, clothing, shoes and dairy products are hardly ever to be found, and when they are available prices are prohibitive'.[30] By 1952, 'during the summer months it ... [was] ... almost impossible to buy meat, vegetables and fruit' in Bulgarian cities.[31] Outside the Soviet bloc, in Belgrade, the American anthropologist, Barbara Kerewsky-Halpern, remembered that in the early 1950s, 'men went unshaven for razor blades were scarce and so was hot water'.[32] During the severe shortages of household fuel that gripped Budapest in 1952, in the city's apartment blocks, 'the frequent coal shortages forced the building superintendent to limit providing hot water to at best once a week.[33]

The severe discomforts caused by the shortages of basic goods were exacerbated by the serious problems of material poverty, as wages declined across the region in the face of forced industrialization, as we saw in chapter 2. Furthermore, in urban areas, the diversion of investment in housing construction led to poorly maintained and frequently overcrowded housing in industrial areas. In Belgrade, Barbara Kerewsky-Halpern recalled living in 'a communal flat, sharing a kitchen and WC with three other families'.[34] While the state attempted to alleviate housing shortages in Budapest through confiscating large flats and dividing them into smaller ones to accommodate more families,[35] overcrowding remained the norm for most urban residents. In Warsaw, 'families were raised in small, one- or two-room apartments in which the living room often doubled up as a bedroom for more than one generation and the "blind" kitchen was a windowless gallery'.[36] Coping with the demands of shortage, poor living standards and overcrowded housing often fell on women, who also combined the demands of shopping, home-making, child-rearing and labour. This produced distinctive problems. In Hungary, in early 1953, female workers on the morning shift in the Újpest Yarn Factory complained to the factory trade union organization because they had to rise at four in the morning on weekdays to be sure of being able to buy meat. If they tried to buy it after their shift it was simply unavailable.[37]

In the face of poverty, family units pooled resources in order to cope. In working-class Łódź, 'if a family consists of five persons, each of them takes turns collecting pieces of clothing. The bachelors, as can be seen, lead the most miserable life, being unable to dress themselves decently'.[38] Increasingly, households sought self-sufficiency and independence from the state distribution network through pilfering. During Hungary's winter shortages of household fuel, according to a miner's wife from the town of Komló, the family went to the nearby woods to cut wood illegally, which was only possible to do 'on Mondays and Fridays, when no-one was there to look after the wood', because if they were caught, they faced a heavy fine.[39] Low wages and severe goods shortages in urban areas led to the emergence of a shadow economy, as urban workers with access to goods sought to supplement their meagre incomes. Bucharest's railway employees illegally bought foodstuffs from the peasants, while working on trains travelling in rural areas, to sell to urban residents at home on the black market.[40]

Rural households, given the impact of taxation and the collectivization drive on their incomes, as well as their greater access to foodstuffs, were both eager and more able than their urban counterparts to participate in a black market. In a situation in which work from wages was characterized by deep-seated insecurity, and the provision of goods characterized by severe shortages, their desire to hold on to their land as a guarantee of independence was reinforced, even in the face of repression. The logic of the attachment to land as a source of independence in the face of persistent shortage was well articulated in Hungary's Zala county by one local man, who told the local party committee that his wife had told him: 'it [the land] is there to help us live, because of it we have not starved, but if it is taken away from us, we will [starve]'.[41] Across the country, in the mining town of Tatabánya, workers eagerly joined limited state campaigns to help build private individual family housing for urban workers, in part because this would provide space for the household to become self-sufficient in the face of the shortage economy.[42]

Behind the trends towards social privatization, rooted in the operation of the economy, lay a desire for improvement in the material conditions of households after the political upheavals and considerable privations of the Second World War. When set against these aspirations for greater stability and comfort, the first years of the construction of socialism were seen as a continuance of the upheavals of the war. This lay behind the tendency of many in the region to compare unfavourably the material situation of their own household in the mid-1950s to the living standards they enjoyed before the onset of war. In one Polish village, 'starved clerks come to the village when harvesting goes on and walk around doing their chores and look for food and we ask them when it was better: in the Sanacja time [under Piłsudski], or now, in the People's Democracy'.[43] In Czechoslovakia, such sentiment was spread by the fact that in the early 1950s, overall living standards and patterns of consumption were closer to those of the war years than those of the inter-war period, fuelling nostalgia for the first Czechoslovak republic in the country.[44] Given that regime attempts to legitimate itself rested, in part, on claims of rebuilding the country after a damaging war and also increasing living standards, such popular sentiments were highly dangerous. They were combined, however, with the growing willingness of Western radio stations, operating a campaign of psychological warfare in the climate of the first cold war, to broadcast contrasts between the miserable standards of living in the socialist countries with an image of Western states characterized by consumer plenty.[45] In states like Hungary, which had borders with the capitalist West, such propaganda was widely listened to and played a role in shaping popular attitudes. By 1954, one miner in the Tatabánya mines was heard to claim that, 'A worker can't give his family the comfort that a western worker enjoys, as they have to work much less than we do. In the United States they only have to work four hours and they earn enough to have their own property in their old age, their own car and house'.[46] During strikes in Ostrava that followed Czechoslovakia's currency reform in June 1953, miners were heard to state: '... we do not trust you! We shall fall to America! America tells us the truth!'[47]

The consequences of the operation of the planned economy for everyday life had frustrated aspirations for the modification of gendered identities and roles, as well as underlining the poverty of the household realm. The contrast between the hunger for the improvement of the material conditions of households and the bleak realities of everyday life had severely corroded the limited legitimacy of early socialist regimes. The marked alienation of young people, whose aspirations had also been reshaped by the crisis of the Second World War, sparked serious social protest during the mid-1950s. The new regimes had sought to play on young people's aspirations for greater autonomy from their elders and a more prominent social role, in order to promote the transformation of social life. During the late 1940s, Croatian youth was instructed by its Communist leaders to 'carry to its end the democratization of the schools and throw out of school those professors who want to provoke us'.[48] In Czechoslovakia, after February 1948, young people had been placed by the party in the vanguard of its attempts to transform workplaces: 'Young miners in the Ostrava coal basin have started a Stakhanovite movement. Young heroes of Labour in the

Liberice Iron Works have been rewarded with chocolate and poultry.'[49] In Hungary's Bánhida power plant, young workers had played a central role in early labour competition, antagonizing their elders, who were anxious to protect traditional working practices.[50]

Yet, in other areas, the expression of the aspirations of post-war youth found outlets in certain cultural forms that sat uneasily with regime attempts to turn them into a vanguard of the construction of socialism. Among Yugoslav youth, American cultural forms, like jazz, enjoyed tremendous popularity. This led to leisure patterns described by cultural policy functionaries as being of the 'warped Western variety'.[51] In the poor villages of south-eastern Hungary, in 1947, the social investigator, István Márkus, noticed rural youth's fascination with the United States, one fuelled by an obsession with 'cars, technology and motoring', stimulated by visits to the cinema in the nearest large town.[52] As popular-front regimes gave way to overt socialist dictatorship, the state and youth were drawn into conflict. In a minority of cases these conflicts took explicitly political forms. As the socialist state was consolidated in Czechoslovakia during 1948, for example, those arrested and tried for the distribution of 'subversive pamphlets' were described as mostly 'very young'.[53] Popular culture was, however, a more frequently contested battle-ground than politics *per se*. Jazz and dance music, residually popular among the youth of the region, were frequent targets. In Romania, the regime attacked 'cosmopolitan influences … still apparent in, for example, the slow waltzes of Miss Xanou … which are cheaply sentimental and reflect the influence of the … languorous melodies from the bad memories of the past, that pitiful time of nightclub music'.[54] At the University of Košice in Slovakia, the authorities focused on the dress and habits of the student body, targeting those who wore 'American striped socks' or who frequented 'coffee houses'.[55]

Youth was not only deeply frustrated at the relentless pressure for cultural conformity on which the early socialist dictatorships insisted, but was also profoundly alienated, given the poor conditions on the region's construction sites and in factories or overcrowded lecture halls. In Nowa Huta, for example, by the mid-1950s, the failure of the authorities to control groups of young workers who were perceived as unruly and undisciplined was a matter of constant concern for local authorities.[56] Nowa Huta's

Hungarian sister city, Sztálinváros, was equally plagued by violence between gangs of alienated youth, which reflected the existence of a powerful and resistant youth subculture in the country's first socialist city.[57] The alienation such patterns of hooliganism and violence revealed pointed to the regime's deep-seated loss of legitimacy among youth, who found their aspirations for greater independence and status frustrated by the practice of early socialism. This loss of legitimacy formed the background to the widespread participation of youth in some of the crises, like the 1956 revolution in Hungary, which shook socialist rule across Eastern Europe.

By the mid-1950s, the social foundations of socialist rule across the region were virtually non-existent. The desire of households for greater material security had been frustrated utterly; the desire for greater independence for women had been subsumed under the idealization of traditional notions of the household that had resulted from the social privatization of the early years of the decade; while youth's aspirations for greater freedom had been curtailed by material misery and the restrictive cultural policies of the dictatorships. Consequently, the emphasis on greater cultural liberalization and the attempts of regimes to promote greater material well-being, which formed part of their early attempts at consolidating their rule, were met by a society hungry for change. The material hunger was evident in the popularity of campaigns to support those building private houses in Hungary's mining areas in the early 1950s, simply because of the promise of economic independence that such homes brought.[58] It was also evident in exceptional events like Slovenia's 1950 March of the Brooms, when the Yugoslav authorities permitted the opening of the border between them and Italy for residents of the divided town of Gorica/Gorizia. The border was overrun by thousands of Yugoslavs, largely women, eager to acquire consumer goods easily available in Italy that could not be procured in socialist Yugoslavia.[59]

This popular hunger for greater material improvement provided the backdrop from below to one of the most spectacular, but also one of the quietest retreats made by socialist regimes in the face of the need to consolidate their rule. They quietly abandoned their attempts to create a new, distinctively socialist material culture, replacing it, in the artefacts that became the objects of socialist consumerism, with an engagement with patterns of Western consumer culture. The consumer culture that had been promoted during the early 1950s reflected a culture based upon universal entitlement to housing and goods, which emphasized the fundamental sameness of the region's worker-citizens. Hungarian shop windows in this period, wrote one design critic in 1951, 'amount to objective displays signaling the steady rise in our living standard', rather than being the 'capitalistic eye-catchers' of the past.[60] Yet these visions of a socialist material culture were being subverted from within the apparatus, which sought to shape a consumer culture characterized by greater consumer sovereignty, even when the realities of shopping were characterized by poverty and chronic shortage. From October 1951, enthusiastic civil servants inside the Ministry of Internal Commerce in Budapest began to survey the preferences of consumers in the Hungarian capital's grocery shops. Emboldened, they began to ask for comments on specific products, in order to ascertain how far consumer choice could be harnessed to boost quality.[61] In 1950s Yugoslavia, an emergent cohort of advertising professionals argued more aggressively for the development of a modified version of a Western consumer culture in their state. As one professional wrote of Western consumption and advertising in 1957, '… thanks precisely to that sort of advertising their products are in great demand here in Yugoslavia and, unfortunately for our manufacturers, they persistently tend to force out domestic products of the same sort and of even better quality'.[62]

During the late 1950s, at least at the level of discourse, if not always at the level of practice, a more self-consciously differentiated consumer culture, taking its cues from Western norms, became more prominent. Despite the slow improvement in material conditions in Poland after 1956, a range of new periodicals promoted, at the level of image, at least, a new consumer culture. They were so popular that in 1959 they were attacked by the PZPR for celebrating 'western culture'.[63] In Hungary, immediately after 1956 and with the speedy consolidation of Kádár's rule, trade periodicals were filled with images of a new consumer culture. The journal of the Ministry of Internal Commerce celebrated new 'American-style' self-service shops, which opened in Budapest and large provincial towns, new styles of furniture for flats, new fashions and unusual consumer goods, such as the electric guitar, promoted in 1959.[64] In Yugoslavia, the public visibility of advertising grew in an expanding print media as a culture of consumption was formed.[65] In the Soviet bloc, at least, much of this shift was concealed by campaigns during the early 1960s to publicize Khrushchev's promise that 'full Communism' could be built by 1980. 'Full Communism', in much of the propaganda of the period, was interpreted as being a state of generalized abundance of consumer goods.[66]

This significant retreat involved the regimes renouncing the goal of shaping a socialist material culture and instead accepting that the world of goods would be shaped by a local version of a consumer culture that accepted Western forms. It was, however, not the only retreat that would be made during this period. Central to this was the accommodation of the regime to the demand that it focus its living standards policies around the material needs of households, rather than those of worker-citizens as individuals. As part of this, the creation of secure domestic spaces for East European households became a central social policy goal in the decade and a half that followed the crises of the mid-1950s. The building of large numbers of housing units in the region's cities became a central plank of this policy, while the promise of improving housing conditions became central to the legitimacy of the regime. It was this logic that lay behind promises, such as that made by Gomułka's regime in 1960, to build 75,000 new flats in Warsaw alone over the course of the following five years.[67] The monumental architecture that had characterized socialist realist housing development was replaced by new, industrial methods of flat construction, based upon units to be contained in 'panel-houses' that could be industrially manufactured and quickly assembled. These blocks of flats transformed the urban landscapes of the region. In Budapest, the first apartments of this kind were built in the early 1960s. The beginning of full-scale panel construction was heralded by the opening of Hungary's first factory for manufacturing the components in 1967. During the first half of the 1970s, the Hungarian capital's peripheral working-class districts found their low-rise family housing replaced wholesale by new high-rises.[68]

Despite major housing construction projects, from the mid-1950s onwards, there remained a severe urban housing shortage right across the region, exacerbated by the continual increases in industrial employment that successive waves of socialist industrialization brought in their train. These shortages resulted in waiting lists for urban apartments; in one Bulgarian urban centre, a wait 'of only three years' was reported.[69] This formed the backdrop to the spread of commuting on the part of worker-peasants throughout the 1960s, as was discussed in chapter 4. In some states, like Yugoslavia, the poor quality of new, urban housing led many migrants to the towns during the 1960s to retain their homes in the villages as weekend residences.[70] Hungary developed its own social contract with rural and suburban dwellers by institutionalizing a system of state support, consisting of a mixture of grants and cheap state-subsidized loans for those seeking to build or extend private houses, as early as 1955.[71] Even in states like Bulgaria, where housing improvement in the villages mobilized substantial private resources, it formed one base of an informal economy of favours in rural communities, given the persistent shortcomings of the socialist economy.[72]

The new consumerism of the late 1950s and early 1960s was centred on the home, and was both informed by and, in turn, reinforced new notions of domesticity. Furnishing the home was seen as a key component of the consumer culture, promoted by design and advertising professionals across the Soviet bloc from the mid-1950s onwards.[73] In Poland, attempts by design professionals, during the late 1950s, to promote furnishings that would transform small, new apartments into 'fashionable' homes, demonstrated the clear links between the new discourses of consumerism and improvement in the housing stock.[74] Newer housing tended to promote more consumerist and individualistic forms of behaviour – something that was underlined by the findings of sociological surveys of daily life in Budapest's working-class suburbs, as living standards rose and the ownership of consumer goods spread during the early 1960s. In older housing, constructed in the nineteenth century, the ownership of consumer goods like washing machines and televisions was lower than on newly constructed housing estates. Mentalities on the new estates were different; while in older housing, residents offered to share the use of a fridge with their neighbours, on newer estates, residents hardly knew who lived next door.[75]

Given the way in which the new consumerism of the late 1950s and early 1960s was centred on the domestic sphere, it was also deeply gendered in terms of its appeal and its nature. In Yugoslavia, in 1968, the most commonly found household consumer items were either those, like television and radio, which existed to provide privatized leisure within the bounds of the home, or those which were designed to assist with housework: 37.7 per cent of Yugoslavs owned a gas or electric stove, 25.2 per cent a refrigerator, and 15.1 per cent a vacuum cleaner.[76] In the context of a gendered division of household labour, in which women undertook a disproportionate share of the responsibility of housework, this feminized aspects of consumer culture.[77] This gendered division of housework across the region was remarkably constant during the mid-1960s. In 1965, in Bulgaria, women spent an average of 28.6 hours per week on child-care, compared with 12.8 hours spent by men; the equivalent figures for Czechoslovakia were 40.7 and 15.1 hours; for Hungary, 41 and 7.9 hours; and for Poland, 38.9 and 12.4 hours.[78] Furthermore, as the female members of households shunned inadequate, collectively provided services across the region, they invested in household consumer goods. In Czechoslovakia, in 1970, for example, 80 per cent of households owned a washing machine (though not an automatic one, as they were not yet available in the country), 52 per cent had a vacuum cleaner and 60 per cent possessed a refrigerator.[79]

While central aspects of the new consumer culture reinforced domesticity and the gendered ideals that were implicit within it, in other respects it challenged them, by articulating, in a limited way, female aspirations for greater social recognition and independence. This was done through the promotion of feminine fashion, particularly marked from 1956 onwards. Polish periodicals concerned with fashion deviated from Stalinist practice, promoting new styles of female dress.[80] In their Hungarian counterparts, as we saw in chapter 3, fashion and cosmetics were strongly promoted by the late 1950s.[81] In Bulgaria, the promotion of fashion from the early 1960s onwards was not merely related to cultural liberalization, but was also directed against the supposedly traditional customs of the country's Turkish minority.[82] In Hungary, the combination of a new fashion culture and the influx of young, unmarried women from rural areas into light industrial employment in the late 1950s and early 1960s, created a limited space for a consumerist sphere of female independence that modified, albeit in small ways, established concepts of gender.[83]

The spread of a new consumer culture went some way to

meeting the aspirations of young people for greater freedom. The promotion, at least at the rhetorical level, of consumer artefacts like the Hungarian electric guitar, discussed earlier in this chapter, underlined the links between the consumer cultures promoted during the period and the gradual penetration of Western popular culture into the region. This intensified during the 1960s, as the popular enthusiasm for Western rock music, beginning with The Beatles, spread across the region, giving rise to a series of domestic rock groups that imitated their style, led by those like Poland's Czerwone Gitary, Bulgaria's Bundaratsie and Czechoslovakia's Olympic.[84] The spread of popular music had been aided and was further spread by Western broadcasters. Radio Free Europe's Géza Ekecs, broadcasting under the name of László Cseke, became a national figure in Hungary as a result of his *Teenager Party* programme, which broadcast to the country from 1958.[85] As we shall see when we discuss the politics of the official youth movement in the next chapter, the regimes regarded with alarm the hold Western popular culture, especially music, enjoyed over East European youth. Reformists, however, often met these criticisms head-on; in the western Hungarian county of Vas, the local party newspaper wrote in 1963: 'Youth in our country are not angry, young people are not hoodlums or hooligans, they are not impatient ... Young people are not impatient and angry in general, but they are critical and merciless toward conservative tendencies'.[86]

The liberalization visible in certain aspects of consumer culture was only one small element of liberalization in so far as it was directed at women. Far more significant was the outright abandonment of the crude pro-natalism of the early socialist years, which had raised the birth rate in some countries at the cost of an explosion in illegal abortions and significant strains on the household. In Hungary, the legalization of abortion in 1957 was greeted with enthusiasm by Budapest textile workers, who saw it as granting them immeasurably greater personal freedom from what they had seen as the unreasonable demands of a state that expected them to bear children in conditions of material penury.[87] In Poland, abortion was legalized in 1956, albeit in the face of vociferous opposition from the Catholic Church.[88] In Czechoslovakia, while abortion was legalized in 1957, access to it was curtailed by new legislation in 1962, which introduced charges for those seeking an abortion, motivated by the concerns of policy-makers about the birth rate.[89] The most radical volte-face was in Romania, where abortion was legalized initially in 1957, and then criminalized in 1966, as the regime returned to pro-natalist policies reminiscent of the early 1950s, which formed part of Ceauşescu's attempt to shape a distinctive national communism that rested, in part, on a policy of raising the birth rate.[90]

Ceauşescu's pro-natalism, which gathered pace throughout the 1970s and rested on the criminalization of abortion, extreme restrictions on access to contraception and relatively low levels of financial assistance to families with children, was at one extreme in the region. Other states sought to promote maternalism with the carrot of social policy measures far more than they used the stick of restriction. Czechoslovakia's restrictive abortion legislation of 1962 was accompanied by the limited extension of paid maternity leave and the introduction of unpaid maternity leave. Yet by the late 1960s, it had become clear that even these measures had proved insufficient to halt the persistent post-war decline of the birth rate. The post-Prague Spring government responded by introducing explicit financial recognition of motherhood in 1970, through introducing a monthly salary for those mothers in work who had a second child, paid to the mother up to that child's first birthday.[91] In Hungary, official maternalism rested almost entirely on social policy measures, introduced on the eve of comprehensive economic reform. In 1967, the state introduced GYES, a provision which compensated mothers with two and half years of financial support for temporarily leaving work to have a child, a provision that was extended two years after its introduction to give three years of financial support.[92]

While the spread of social provision for mothers, outside Romania, did represent a more benign form of maternalism than the crude pro-natalism of the early 1950s, by making motherhood central to social policy, regimes accommodated traditional notions of gender, which represented a retreat from the, albeit flawed, egalitarianism of the early socialist years. In the workplace, protective legislation was passed that was justified in terms of protecting women who were either pregnant or of childbearing age. Bulgarian legislation passed in 1953 banned 'overtime, night work, heavy and arduous' work for all pregnant women and mothers with children under the age of eight. In addition, women were to be banned from working in 'hazardous occupations', of which there was a list.[93] In the workplace, such measures were often used not to transfer women workers from dirty or dangerous workplaces, but often to exclude them from the best paid jobs.[94] As maternalist policies became marked during the 1960s, protective legislation was often extended. In Hungary, in 1965, large numbers of jobs in construction and mining were declared off-limits, given that they were deemed to harm 'the lives and well-being of women'.[95]

While the growing emphasis placed by regimes on maternalism represented an accommodation of traditional notions of gender in both the household and the workplace, this did not mean that the socialist states retreated from the goal of incorporating women into society based on productive labour, though it implied that they would not be incorporated as men's equals. At the level of rhetoric, socialist regimes continued to emphasize socialist labour as a 'calling' for women well into the 1970s.[96] At the same time, absolute levels of women's employment continued to rise, yet they tended to be concentrated in traditionally feminized sectors. This was true even in Albania, which was the most radical of the region's regimes in terms of its rhetorical commitment to female equality within socialist labour. In 1961, women accounted for 73.7 per cent of workers in textiles, 69.7 per cent in the health services, 60 per cent in food processing and 50 per cent in retail.[97] This pattern of gendering of female employment was typical across the region. In neighbouring Yugoslavia in 1970, for example, women made up 66.3 per cent of the workforce in textiles, 68 per cent in the health services, but only 41.4 per cent in retail and trade.[98]

The accommodation of the regimes to the material aspirations of East European households had other consequences than those that were visible in terms of the subtle reshaping of gendered identities. While, as we saw in chapter 3, the growing improvement in the material conditions that underpinned the spread of socialist consumerism bolstered the legitimacy of the regime, the spread of a new consumer culture throughout the 1960s imposed unspoken limits on the regime's authority and legitimacy. The achievement of material security for the household was dependent on participation in the semi-legal shadow economy outside either the household or the state sector. The informal economy of favours that had existed during the generalized state of penury, which characterized early socialist society, survived into better material times. It was particularly marked in the realm of housing provision. Housing construction in rural Bulgaria, for example, was plagued by shortages of skilled labour and necessary materials. Given the nature of many of these shortages, building a house as a secure domestic space was something that took years and was dependent on the deployment of elaborate networks of personal contacts to procure the necessary materials.[99] In urban Poland, during the 1960s and 1970s, the promise of material abundance presented in consumerist discourse was belied by the reality of severe shortages of basic goods – often foodstuffs – in the climate of a malfunctioning and largely unreformed economy. Workers often coped, acquiring scarce foodstuffs by mobilizing connections with relatives in rural areas, or friends in industrial enterprises with access to goods and services in short supply.[100] In relatively unreformed economies, by the early 1970s, the clash between the expectations generated by improved material security and, albeit limited, socialist consumerism produced marked criticism of the performance of planned economies, which brought into question the attempts of regimes to legitimate their actions through pointing to industrial development. As ordinary Romanians complained during the decade: 'Why ... do we only make things that machines can use and not that people can use'.[101]

In the reformed socialist economies, like the Hungarian and Yugoslav, participating in extensive socialist consumerism was connected to participation in the informal economy. In Hungary, the creation of an informal economy had its roots in the country's successful, final collectivization drive, which had ensured the integration of small-scale agricultural production and the work of cooperatives. The dramatic improvement in housing conditions during the 1960s and early 1970s gave it further impetus. Private family housing and the construction of flats through flat construction cooperatives substantially involved both the legal private sector and the shadow economy; in practice, both played a major role in the maintenance and repair of shoddy, state-built housing.[102] By 1979, around a third of all maintenance of flats and housing was performed by those working in the informal economy. This was, however, the tip of the iceberg; the repair of clothing, motor vehicles, electrical goods, telephones and personal services were all areas where the influence of the shadow economy was marked.[103] Participation in this informal economy was essential to many who wished to be able to afford to participate fully in the country's socialist consumerism. Participation in this semi-legal private sector was an important factor in the erosion of class- and work-based identities in Hungary during the 1970s, which provided a social dynamic that would eventually contribute to the crumbling legitimacy of the regime in the 1980s.[104]

While the relationship between household consumption and informal economies destabilized regime legitimacy, in different ways, in relatively reformed and unreformed socialist economies alike, socialist consumerism was also corrosive of the foundations of legitimacy; above all, it invited the region's worker-citizens to compare their lot with the capitalist West. The opportunities for doing this were at their greatest in Yugoslavia, given its open borders. Indeed, the transfer of money into Yugoslav households from the growing numbers of family members working in the West was important for sustaining socialist consumerism. In the remote Bosnian village of Planinica in the mid-1960s, social relations had been reshaped, with members of several households leaving the country to take on temporary, unskilled work in Austria. Combined with the expansion of domestic industrial employment, this had allowed urban consumer culture to penetrate this remote location; the consumption of wealthier families came to be marked by 'the purchase of skirts for teenage girls ... the acquisition of European-style furniture such as beds, tables and chairs ... or the introduction of Italian-made synthetic raincoats'.[105] The relative freedom of travel open to Yugoslav citizens allowed them to develop a culture during the 1960s and 1970s of day trips to Western cities like Trieste or Graz, which lay just over the border.[106] 'Shopping across the border' formed part of middle-class identity in socialist Yugoslavia, as well as informing domestic consumer culture; but most centrally, it served to demonstrate for many the assumed 'superiority' of Western consumer culture over the domestic variant.[107] Yugoslavia was, however, somewhat exceptional given the high degree of openness of its borders. Behind the closed borders of the Soviet bloc, few citizens had direct experience of Western consumer culture. But during the 1960s and 1970s, partly as a result of the efforts of Western broadcasters, information from relatives living in the West, and the increasing penetration of Western popular culture into the countries of the bloc, Eastern Europeans were becoming increasingly aware of the superior standard of living and material comfort of Western Europeans. In Hungary, this awareness was underlined by one worker in the mid-1970s, who identified life in the West as living with 'two cars of my own'.[108]

These unfavourable comparisons ate away at the legitimacy of the regimes, only truly becoming serious when states could no longer offer material improvement to their populations. Their most spectacular failures came with reining in the aspirations of youth. While the new consumerism of the late 1950s attempted to provide new fashions to satisfy their aspirations in the field of consumption, the 1960s were marked by the gradual incursion of Western popular culture into the region. As we saw in chapter 3, the persistence of youth alienation and rebelliousness formed the backdrop to the spectacular student activism that marked the late 1960s across the region. This clash of aspirations seriously shook elements of state attempts to shape their own socialist public sphere – the subject of the next chapter.

6 The socialist public sphere and its limits

Eastern Europe's post-war political settlement rested on key retreats by its ruling socialist regimes. First, their attempts to transform the meaning of work had been abandoned, and instead, their projects of building a society organized around productive labour had been achieved only through the states' accommodation of established cultures of labour. In the workplaces and communities of the region, its rule by the end of the 1960s rested on an uneasy, and ultimately destabilizing, class compromise between working class, cooperative peasantry and intelligentsia. Second, within communities and the private sphere, the state retreated from its attempts to reshape radically the role of the household, and relations of gender and generation within them, by creating a more collectivist, work-based and egalitarian society. The pressures of the early socialist years and the subsequent shifts towards consolidation had forced the state to recognize the demands of households for autonomy and welfare; by the mid-1960s, support for a regime was tied to its success in promoting an individualized consumerism that rested on modified, and certainly not remade, hierarchies of gender in both the household and society.

Yet this post-war settlement was institutionalized through a political system that was widely regarded as illegitimate. Effective single-party socialist rule had been imposed on polities whose civil societies were highly differentiated at the end of the 1940s as the dictatorships were built. The climate of the early cold war encouraged the rulers of the region during the period of early socialist rule to base their rule on a mixture of paranoia, extreme coercion and mobilization. This strategy of governing exacerbated the legitimacy deficit of the regimes, helping to generate the serious crises of socialism in Eastern Europe during the mid-1950s. This meant that the strategies of governance pursued by the region's rulers shifted considerably. Attempts were made by rulers to seek inclusive sources of legitimacy for their rule, which in some states included marked attempts to develop a national communism, and in others involved more conciliatory policies towards social currents that had been regarded as anti-socialist during the early socialist years. The social scope of the apparatus of repression was reduced – and became less intrusive – though the threat of state violence was selectively deployed against potential political dissent. The outcome of the crises of the mid-1950s, furthermore, convinced large sections of the population of the permanence of socialist rule and thus, greater acceptance of, but not support for, the political system. This, in turn, promoted a process by which the remnants of pre-socialist civil society and state, party and other social organizations became enmeshed, shaping a distinctive socialist public sphere by the mid-1960s, characterized by both small-scale accommodation and conflict. Yet the varied motives of citizens for participating in this socialist public sphere, and the fact that many who worked within this framework on a day-to-day basis actively opposed the socialist regimes, prepared the ground for some of the crises of the late 1960s.

The shift in the bases of legitimation of the region's socialist regimes set the stage for the shaping of the socialist public sphere of the 1960s. As we saw in chapter 2, as pre-socialist civil societies were abolished during the late 1940s, the new states moved to shape a public sphere that was based on clearly demarcated boundaries between supporters of the regimes' programme of social transformation and perceived enemies. Members of the latter group were identified rhetorically either as 'supporters of the old regime', 'clerical reactionaries', 'fascists', 'enemies', 'counter-revolutionaries' or even 'right-wing social democrats'. The distinction between 'us' and 'them' was used to justify and perpetuate a large apparatus of repression, resting on powerful state security agencies, networks of informers and a large prison camp system. On the other hand, those identified as supporters of the new system became the objects of mobilization, designed to support revolutionary change. Collectivization in the villages, labour competition in the factories, and numerous campaigns in communities were designed to reinforce a notion of legitimation through revolution. Revolutionary change within societies of the region was linked at the level of regime rhetoric to the concerns of the first cold war – in part, at least, as a consequence of the construction of overt dictatorship across the region. Mobilization for the revolutionary transformation of local institutions was linked by propagandists to a global struggle, in which an insurgent imperialist capitalism attempted to prevent 'peace-loving' peoples from constructing socialism in their own states. Measures like Hungary's Korea labour competition campaign in August 1950 linked, at an ideological level, drives for improved productivity in Hungary's factories, the fulfilment of the country's first five-year plan and the conflict over the Korean peninsula, on the other side of the world.[1]

Yet in the climate of penury that accompanied much of the revolutionary mobilization of early socialism, such a strategy of mobilization produced a serious crisis of legitimacy, which expressed itself forcefully during the crises that hit socialist regimes during the mid-1950s. As the regimes shifted their emphasis from revolutionary mobilization to political consolidation, the strategies they pursued to legitimate their rule changed perceptibly. Outside Yugoslavia, which was different due to its split with Stalin in 1948, early socialism had been marked by conformity to the pre-eminence of the Soviet Union. This acceptance of Soviet pre-eminence had been marked both at the level of direct political rhetoric and in economics and culture. As far as Bolesław Bierut, secretary of the PZPR, was concerned, speaking in 1952, 'the Polish workers owe everything they hold most dear to the Communist Party of the Soviet Union: their liberty, independence, the rapid development of industry and national culture and the growth of internal strength'.[2] At the time Bierut was declaring his loyalty to the Soviet Stalinist model, Tito's Yugoslavia was distancing itself from Soviet practice. Tito's attempts, during the early 1950s, to develop alternative economic models, in part underlined his regime's anti-Stalinism and his own state's 'national' distinctiveness. Early self-management would, for Tito, 'be the beginning of democracy', something that would constitute 'a radical departure from Stalinism'.[3] The upheavals of the mid-1950s, however, produced a situation in which the regimes sought to modify the Soviet-centred doctrine of the early 1950s and assert relative autonomy from the Soviet Union. At the height of the turmoil of October 1956 in Poland, Gomułka insisted that a reformed Soviet bloc should be based on the notion that 'each country should have full independence, and the right of each nation to a sovereign government in an independent country should be fully and mutually respected'.[4]

The shift from acceptance of Soviet hegemony to what has been, in some cases, misleadingly termed 'national communism', represented a shift in the bases of legitimation, and went further in some states than others. Behind the rhetoric, however, it represented a far more subtle shift than it appeared at first sight. The regimes continued to pay rhetorical lip-service to notions of socialist internationalism, even as they asserted their independence from the Soviet Union; in 1957, representatives of the Romanian Communist Party, which would go furthest in using national ideology to legitimate its rule, proclaimed that 'the workers' movement is international in its very substance. The fundamental characteristic is expressed by proletarian internationalism, by the ideology and policy of international solidarity of all workers.'[5] As assertions of the internationalism of communism post-dated the shift away from the crude pro-Sovietism of the early socialist years, the deployment of national ideas by the region's ruling parties had pre-dated it. During the popular-front period, Communist parties, as we saw in chapter 2, consciously mobilized national ideas and symbols to give themselves and their policies of national reconstruction legitimacy.

Even during the period of the construction of overt socialist dictatorship, national ideas and forms did not disappear from the ideological armoury of the ruling parties. The regimes themselves were based resolutely upon notions that socialism could be built institutionally within the borders of national states, echoing Stalin's belief in 'socialism in one country'. Societies based on productive labour were bounded by national borders. In the town of Komárom/Komárnő, split by the Danube and the border between Czechoslovakia and Hungary, Slovak textile workers living on the northern bank sought to retain their jobs in the Hungarian plants on the southern bank as the planned economy was built in 1949. In order to escape the nationally bound logic of the separate planned economies operating on either side of the river, employment contracts had to be exchanged and approved by national planning offices in Prague and Budapest, in order that workers be allowed to continue to cross the bridge over the Danube each morning to go to work.[6] Commitment to the institutions of nation states was bolstered by notions of 'socialist patriotism', that each citizen had a duty to make sacrifices in the interests of their 'socialist fatherland'. Socialist patriotism was contrasted with the enemies of both 'chauvinism' and 'bourgeois nationalism'. These enemies were ideological constructs, designed to stigmatize manifestations of nationalism that undercut the stability of the early socialist nation states across the region. This was most evident in the 1954 Czechoslovak show trial of leading Slovak Communists in Bratislava, including Gustav Husák, for 'having conspired with the intention of separating Slovakia from the Czech working people and putting a wedge between Czechoslovakia and the Soviet Union'.[7]

During the later 1950s, the modifications of an official national ideology, based on notions of socialist patriotism, were nevertheless real and represented a shift to promote distinct nationally bounded settlements in the states of the region, as the regimes moved towards consolidation. This shift was underlined by the reconciliation between Belgrade and Moscow, sealed in June 1956, by a meeting between and joint declaration by Khrushchev and Tito, which proclaimed that 'the parties hold the view that the paths of socialist development vary according to the country and the conditions that prevail there. They agree that the diversity of forms of development of socialism is a positive factor'.[8] As the region recovered from the crises that shook the regimes, which culminated in the months that followed Tito and Khrushchev's declaration, notions of national diversity shaped the ways in which regimes sought to legitimate themselves as they consolidated their rule. In all countries, this consisted of de-emphasizing the political hegemony of the Soviet Union and involved some accommodation of pre-socialist national identities, though the patterns of this accommodation varied substantially across the region.

The most substantial shift towards an explicitly national-communist form of legitimation occurred in Romania. As we saw in chapter 3, in 1958, the Gheorgiu-Dej regime successfully secured the withdrawal of Soviet troops from Romania, thus heralding an accommodation with a traditionally anti-Russian, pre-socialist Romanian nationalism. This accommodation was continued and extended by Gheorgiu-Dej's successor, Nicolae Ceauşescu, after 1965. While the extension of this policy during the 1970s will be discussed in chapter 7, it did manifest itself in Bucharest's decision not to support Soviet intervention in Czechoslovakia in 1968 to end the Prague Spring. Within politically exceptional Albania, part of the Soviet bloc until 1961, the development of the cult of personality that surrounded Enver Hoxha sought to identify him as the creator of 'a new Albania', playing on 'the absence of a nationwide myth' to generate a new version of Albanian national identity, with him at its centre.[9] Bulgaria's regime under Todor Zhivkov had developed a more subtle engagement with pre-socialist national identities. While external loyalty to the Soviet Union was assiduously maintained throughout the 1960s and 1970s, Zhivkov's rule was marked by anti-Macedonian undercurrents; growing and ever more overt policies directed against the cultural identity of the Turkish minority; and the promotion of cultural nationalism throughout the 1970s, associated with the political rise of Zhivkov's daughter, Liudmila Zhivkova.[10]

Yet the search for distinctive roads to socialism did not result in the socialist regimes' unproblematic accommodation of pre-socialist national identities everywhere. In the Polish case, Gomułka began his rule by concluding an agreement with the Soviets in 1957, which laid down that 'the temporary stationing of Soviet forces in Poland can in no way affect the sovereignty of the Polish state and cannot lead to interference in the internal affairs of the Polish People's Republic'.[11] Despite such beginnings, the hopes generated by Gomułka's deployment of the rhetoric of national self-determination were quickly frustrated, as the regime came to rest on a fragile compromise between radicals and conservatives within the party leadership that stymied the prospects of meaningful reform and set the stage for the crises of 1968 and 1970, which were discussed in chapter 3. In Hungary, the attempts of the regime to develop its own distinctive socialist model were developed in opposition to patterns of pre-socialist national identity, which Kádár and his allies identified with the political practice of the inter-war Horthy regime and those sections of the population that bitterly opposed socialist rule, as an alien imposition on the country. During the late 1950s, after the suppression of the 1956 revolution, security forces remained deeply paranoid about the influence of revisionist sentiment towards Transylvania, anti-Semitism and popular religion on large sections of the population.[12] During the late 1950s, as the suppression of the revolution continued and agriculture was collectivized, the Kádár regime 'insisted ... on its character as an authentic government of the workers'.[13] With the relaxation of repression during the early 1960s, Kádár offered a compromise to all social groups, based on at least outward conformity, which promoted a more inclusive socialist patriotism than that advanced during the previous decade. Outlining the settlement in 1962, Kádár proclaimed that:

> Everyone who is striving for the cause of socialism and peace must be united on the basis of the socialist policy of national unity. We must bring together Communists and those outside the party, politically active supporters of the regime and those who today are still wavering, the indifferent, those who hold to a materialist world-view and people of a religious disposition alike. The construction of socialist society is a matter for the nation as a whole.[14]

In the region's two multinational states, the gradual development of distinctive roads to socialism entailed a continuing rhetorical emphasis on a more inclusive socialist patriotism than that advanced in the 1950s, even if it was not as inclusive in either state as in Kádár's Hungary. Yet while in Yugoslavia the state sought to accommodate itself to the differing national identities that existed within its borders, in Czechoslovakia, the regime moved in the opposite direction, seeking to replace the identities of Czechs and Slovaks with a unitary Czechoslovak one, at least prior to 1968. The KSČ's 1958 congress set as a policy goal, 'the completion of the cultural revolution and the strengthening of the unity of peoples'.[15] This was followed by the creation of a constitution in 1960, which not only tightened party control of the state, but subordinated Slovak governmental and party organs to those in Prague, in the name of institutionalizing 'democratic centralism'.[16] Since the mid-1940s, as we saw in chapter 2, Yugoslavia's socialist patriotism had been based on the twin principles of the 'brotherhood and unity' of the peoples of the south Slav state. Its notions of a distinctive Yugoslav road to socialism had been given substance by its development of a distinctive political, economic and social model of 'self-management, as we saw in chapter 3. As Andrew Baruch Wachtel has pointed out, while prior to the early 1960s the unity of Yugoslav peoples took pride of place in the Tito regime's cultural and nationality policies, from this date emphasis was increasingly placed on brotherhood.[17] Greater decentralization and democratization of Yugoslavia's political system, enshrined in the 1963 constitution, gave impetus to the process of accommodation of the range of national identities that existed within the state.[18] Both centralist and decentralist solutions to national tensions, however, generated considerable turbulence, which shook the political system as the 1960s progressed.

These shifts in the bases of legitimation of the regimes were combined by the transformation of the apparatus of repression. The parallel security states that had been developed during the popular-front era, by Communist parties across the region, had been an important tool in securing their political hegemony. Furthermore, their dramatic expansion, described in chapter 2, as the states of the region came to be ruled by overt socialist dictatorships, had confirmed their role as a crucial tool of regimes intent on social transformation. The radical expansion of armies, militias, regular police forces and, most crucially, state security agencies and their networks of paid and unpaid informers, had marked the early 1950s in the region. The huge increases in the regular prison populations and those sentenced in the networks of work camps attached to mines and construction sites across the region had also under-pinned early socialist rule. While the re-examination of the political trials of leading Communists had sparked the measures of de-Stalinization that shook the region during the mid-1950s, it was the deep-seated popular anger generated by the widespread nature of repression that gave the process its impetus.

Given the breadth of discontent and the radicalism of the regime during the early 1950s, representatives of the parallel security state played an overt role in daily life. In factories, farms and communities, the size of the security state meant that individuals came into contact with it on a daily basis. Poland's state security agency, the UB, contained an industrial department that 'sends an inspector into every industrial enterprise. This undercover man organizes a network of informers among the employees'.[19] In the western

Hungarian border town of Moson Magyaróvár, one former worker remembered that:

> at the dairy there was an ÁVO [secret police] department which tried to make me an informer. They reasoned that I was declassed [of former middle-class origin], that I had to work in a menial capacity, and as a result was dissatisfied with my environment and therefore would gladly inform on my fellow workers. This sort of thing was very difficult to refuse. They tried to blackmail people to become informers in the factory and other places.[20]

Even small open acts of protest could be met with severe retribution. During the unrest in Ostrava that followed the Czechoslovak currency reform of 1953, mine management attempted to use the local militia to force miners back to work.[21] Yet the state security agencies not only sought to suppress open protest, but also fed the paranoia of the regimes about opposition by collecting information on almost any kind of non-conformist behaviour. In Moravia, during the early 1950s, for example, local representatives of Czechoslovakia's state security agency, the StB, instructed informers to 'find out which citizens listened to foreign broadcasts or planned to escape from the country'.[22]

Where substantial political conflict over de-Stalinization emerged during the mid-1950s, public discussion was not only confined to the issues of show trials, but was also fuelled by the enormous anger over the apparatus of everyday repression. In Poland, this was sparked by the defection to the West in December 1953 of a senior official of the state security agencies, Józef Światło, and the subsequent decision of Western radio stations to broadcast his revelations about state security agency activities to Polish citizens over the course of the following two years. According to the British-born observer of Polish affairs, Flora Lewis, this led police informers to tell 'friends and fellow workers that they had been forced to spy ... "Black" or underground news rolled like a snowball, gathering accretions. People who had been interrogated by police or arrested and later released began to tell of the tortures they had never dared mention'.[23] In Hungary, the release of political prisoners that began with the advent of Imre Nagy's new course in 1953, lifted the lid on deep-seated public anger at the everyday actions of the state security apparatus. By late 1955, in Budapest's Standard Telecommunications factory, according to Sándor Rácz – who was later to play a prominent role in the workers' council movement during the 1956 revolution – 'the world had changed a great deal. One after another the informers had been found out, and they had become the objects of general hatred'.[24]

In Poland, and even more dramatically in Hungary, hatred of the state security agencies played a central role in the upheavals that convulsed both countries during 1956. In Poznań, rioting was triggered by the rumour that workers' representatives dispatched to Warsaw had been detained by the officials of the UB. Both the prison and the UB headquarters in the town figured prominently among the objects of hatred of the rioters.[25] In Hungary, during October 1956, as the revolution spread from Budapest to provincial towns, the demonstrations that began on their main streets frequently targeted the local headquarters of the ÁVH – the Hungarian state security agency. In some towns, like Moson Magyaróvár, those guarding the buildings fired on unarmed crowds, giving force to the revolution at local level, just as the decision of the guards of Hungarian Radio in Budapest to fire on demonstrators on 23 October had sparked the revolution nationwide.[26] The most notorious and controversial incident of the revolution was the battle between demonstrators and ÁVH officers for control of the Budapest Party Committee building at the end of October, in which the violence of the state security services and the anger of the crowd against them were starkly revealed, both by the violence of the battle and the lynching of the building's defenders by the demonstrators after their defeat.[27] After the Soviet intervention and the suppression of most of the armed groups that opposed Kádár, sporadic armed resistance was often provoked by police intervention to arrest those it perceived to be responsible for the revolution. In the mining town of Tatabánya, company housing was defended by armed groups of residents, into mid-December, against police attempts to arrest those active during the revolution.[28]

The crises of the mid-1950s underlined that the presence of the parallel security state in everyday life, far from protecting the regime, actually served to underline its lack of legitimacy, and often provided the spark of protest that destabilized it. Furthermore, the outcome of the political crises of the mid-1950s stabilized the regimes by encouraging a climate in which populations learned to accept the permanency of their socialist political orders, though the social roots of this acceptance varied from country to country. In Hungary, it was built upon the tangible sense of psychological shock at the violent defeat of the revolution and the wave of state repression that followed. The culture of defeat was bolstered by the widespread belief of many anti-socialist Hungarians that the West had broken promises, made in radio broadcasts, to intervene to free them from the Soviet yoke.[29] While Kádár's conciliatory policies, were built on the culture of defeat created during the period of repression of the late 1950s, they were also underlined by the implicit threat of repression, if certain groups failed to accept the social bargain they were offered.[30] The growing acceptance of socialist rule was based on collective amnesia about the events of 1956, the threat of repression and the development of a broad social contract that differed significantly from the class-war politics of the early 1950s. In Poland, the very fact of the transition from Ochab to Gomułka was sufficient for the PZPR to overcome the crisis of 1956 and gain a measure of support from society. Gomułka's relative popularity remained high, as living standards increased during the late 1950s, pressure was relaxed in rural areas with the abandonment of collectivization and a degree, albeit small, of de-Stalinization occurred.[31]

The ripples created by the events of 1956, particularly the Hungarian Revolution, were felt throughout the region. In Czechoslovakia, they were felt through dissent within the ranks of the party and writers, along with limited working-class discontent and demands for the punishment of those responsible for the repression of the early part of the decade.[32] In Romania, the events over the border in Hungary sparked sporadic protest, particularly among students in Cluj and Timişoara in Transylvania and the Banat. Such protest, which given the presence of a Magyar minority in the region had the potential to explode into widespread unrest, was successfully contained by the regime in Bucharest.[33] The containment of protest, the defeat of the 1956 revolution in Hungary itself, and the support of Tito for Soviet intervention all played their part in reinforcing perceptions of the permanence of the socialist regimes outside Hungary.[34] This gradual acceptance, however, came between the late 1950s and the mid-1960s, as the socialist post-war settlement, described in chapter 3, was tacitly accepted among large sections of the populations.

This process of consolidation enabled and was strengthened by a shift in the behaviour of the dictatorships' parallel security states, which fundamentally modified the nature of repression across the region. While huge parallel security states were maintained, and in many cases extended, into the 1960s, they became less intrusive, in terms of their presence in the daily life of the region's citizens, and more selective in their prosecution of political disobedience. Increasingly, states came to rely on the threat, rather than the fact of overt repression to maintain the boundaries of legitimate public discourse or action. In Hungary, during the period of the initial waves of post-revolutionary repression, the ÁVH was formally disbanded, but was subsequently quietly restructured, with those entrusted with state security having to report to the Political Investigations Department of the Ministry of the Interior. This department continued to maintain a large staff of officers and informers throughout the 1960s and 1970s, particularly within the churches. It was, however, to interpret its role of the defence of the state in a more limited way. As far as the party leadership was concerned in 1970:

> … socialist legality is a great achievement of our party and our state. The strict maintenance of this principle is a basic demand we place on the Ministry of the Interior. [The state security agencies] … guarantee the defense of every law-abiding citizen. At the same time however they must take action against any law breaker, whoever they are and whatever their position.[35]

In neighbouring Romania, as Gheorgiu-Dej shifted towards a national-communist strategy, the use of state security agencies to purge the party and government apparatus continued during the late 1950s. During the early 1960s, however, the prisons and work camps operated by the parallel security were dismantled, with the numbers of political prisoners falling from 17,613 in 1960 to 9,333 in

1964.[36] Yet this should not be interpreted in any sense as a measure of liberalization; the *Securitate* remained a large organization, dedicated to dealing with acts of explicit political dissidence. Under Ceauşescu, their role and methods were refined and extended to include, by the early 1970s, the detention of political 'dissidents' in psychiatric institutions.[37] A similar shift occurred in Czechoslovakia from 1956 onwards. By the period that immediately followed the suppression of the Prague Spring, the StB was, according to dissident Milan Simečka:

> a different kind of StB from the secret police of the 1950s … It is no longer boxed about with myths, such as being the protector of the revolution, of socialism and of the people's peace and tranquility. In fact it protects nothing more than static order and the safety of its masters …[38]

Just as the 1960s were marked by a shift in the function and social role of the parallel security state across the region, the formal political institutions of the party state also changed in nature, especially in so far as they related to the rest of society. For much of the period following the institutionalization of overt socialist dictatorship, the ruling parties, trade unions, youth and women's organizations had acted in tandem as agents of campaign-based mobilization, to drive forward the construction of socialism. Repression and mobilization became two sides of the same coin, as the parallel security state combined with formal political and social institutions to generate an apparently seamless apparatus of control. The party employed propagandists – 'people's educators' – in all walks of life. Their function was to support the political campaigns initiated by the party leadership. In Hungary, for example, throughout the 1950s, the Stalinist leadership attempted to finance its industrialization programme, in part, through the so-called 'peace loans'. The population would 'voluntarily' pledge to 'loan' 10 per cent of their annual income to the state. It was ultimately the job of the people's educators to solicit these contributions from ordinary Hungarians. These 'loans' were far from popular. The people's educators were confronted with the complaints of the population, their dissatisfaction with state policies and sometimes their outright opposition. Such information would be used in two ways. First, and most important, it was used to identify 'enemy behaviour' among the population – the identities of such 'oppositional elements' would be passed on to the state security agency. Second, it was used to compile 'reports on the climate of opinion', which provided a distorted view of the state of public opinion across the country.[39]

The public face of mobilization was presented through political ceremony and staged demonstrations, which involved citizens displaying their passive support for leadership on occasions such as May Day, or the anniversary of the October Revolution in the Soviet Union. The degree to which, in the early 1950s, these were staged affairs was underlined by Milovan Djilas, who remembered his role as a senior member of the Yugoslav party leadership in choreographing these events, when he recounted that he specified:

> ... the number of posters to be used in the May Day celebration, of which leaders and how large, how many thousands of citizens should attend ... how many floats, how many, how much, all down the line. That brought an end to both criticism and spontaneity, from the top and from the bottom ...[40]

Even after the apparatus of mobilization had been relaxed, centrally organized, formulaic demonstrations came to define socialist political ritual. However, as the nature of formal political institutions changed, these political ceremonies came to lose much of their political meaning, assuming the role of an ideological façade that concealed some of the realities of socialist rule in the region.

As socialist regimes consolidated their rule, the nature of their ruling parties changed. While socialist rhetoric still remained central to their practice, the class-war rhetoric of the early 1950s was diluted by the forms of political discourse that accompanied the shift in the bases of legitimation of socialist rule. Increasingly, the membership of the ruling parties became more technocratic in nature than it had been in the late 1940s. Indeed, the initial purges in the membership of ruling parties in Hungary and Romania that followed the creation of overt socialist dictatorship during the dying years of the 1940s, led to an increase in the proportion of industrial workers among party members in both countries.[41] Yet in Hungary, almost immediately after the suppression of the 1956 revolution, the systematic deproletarianization of the ranks of the party and its domination by managerial and administrative personnel were underlined by statistics, which showed that only 29.2 per cent of party members were employed as industrial workers in 1957.[42] Though these kinds of statistics reflected the promotion of working-class activists from the shop floor into management and administrative positions during the 1950s, over the course of the following decade the ruling parties opened their doors to members of the cultural and technical intelligentsia. In Romania, by the end of the 1960s, 41 per cent of medical doctors, 52 per cent of engineers and 47 per cent of all schoolteachers were reported to be members of the Romanian Communist Party.[43] Similar trends were visible elsewhere. In 1949, only 26.7 per cent of members of Poland's PZPR were employed in white-collar positions; two decades later, this figure had reached 42.8 per cent.[44] Among Yugoslavia's League of Communists, those in white-collar occupations made up 13.6 per cent of the membership in 1948 and 43.8 per cent 20 years later.[45]

The ruling parties were not the only bodies that changed as the social settlement between regime and population strengthened during the mid-1960s. In those states like Poland, where the ruling party enjoyed a 'leading role', in concert with other front parties, these organizations, nominally distinct from the ruling party, were little more than a façade for single-party rule. Social organizations like the trade unions were a different matter entirely. During the late 1940s, independent trade unions had been effectively nationalized, incorporated into the mechanisms of rule of the party state at national level. In the factories their role was limited to assisting management in increasing productivity, managing certain aspects of enterprise social policy, and enforcing health and safety rules. As the party retreated from its campaigns of mobilization in the workplace, official unions lost much of their direction. In Czechoslovakia, as we saw in chapter 4, the official unions gained a degree of independence from the state in representing their members. This was, however, exceptional; in much of the region they became little more than distributors of cash and holiday places to workers, backing the management in the workplace. In those states where the workforce was completely remade by the influx of worker-peasants in the 1960s, such as Romania, official unions lacked all relevance for the workforce as interest representation organizations. Because of their utter ineffectiveness they became deeply unpopular in the workplace.[46] Within this framework, many of the institutions operated by trade unions became depoliticized and effectively domesticated. Socialist brigades in Hungary, for example, intended, from the late 1950s onwards, as the instruments by which rationalization of the workplace would be furthered, were transformed into institutions which reflected the interests of networks of friends, providing a focus for cultural and leisure activities by the early 1970s.[47]

The domestication of Hungary's socialist brigades were just one example of how the functions of party-related social organizations were appropriated at the local level by Eastern European citizens for essentially non-political uses. This process drove an intermeshing of social activity with state organs, creating a public sphere in which society and state became enmeshed. This was, however, not always a conflict-free process, with official youth organizations posing a particular problem for the regime throughout the 1960s. Given the aspirations of many young people for a greater measure of cultural and social liberalization, as we saw in chapter 5, they found themselves on a collision course with those party leaders who, like the Bulgarian leadership, argued that they 'should mercilessly burn with a hot iron all manifestations of admiration for what is foreign, of a nihilistic attitude toward our country, toward the past achievements of our motherland and people'.[48] The cultural facilities operated by official youth organizations often became the battleground for such struggles between the regimes and youth. In Czechoslovakia, given the constraints on the music that could be played in official facilities, young people set up a network of underground clubs outside the official framework. When the StB moved against unofficial musical clubs in Bratislava in 1967, it found a total of 16 operating regularly in the city.[49] Youth organizations, however, were often characterized by an internal tension, between the need to satisfy the aspirations of their members for depoliticized leisure and those of their country's rulers for outward ideological conformity. In Budapest's Csepel Metalworks, for example, the meetings of the youth organization emphasized the last requirement, while the organization's club provided a space for music and dance, where alcohol could be consumed unofficially, despite a ban on its consumption on the plant site.[50] Sometimes, similar patterns of compromise and accommodation could be found beyond the local level in the practices of official youth organizations at the national level. In Poland, for example, the official youth daily, *Sztandar Młodych*, provided a space where developments in Western popular music were reported and their popularity in the country openly discussed, often to the consternation of party conservatives.[51]

While the activities of official organizations were often appropriated for non-political purposes, and while some, like youth organizations, became battlegrounds between the regime and sections of the population, the enmeshing of state and society had other aspects. The relationship between the state and organized religion was a highly complex one throughout the 1960s, characterized as much by mutual accommodation as opposition. As we saw in chapter 2, during the early 1950s, anticlerical regimes had regarded organized religion as intrinsically oppositional. Religious leaders had frequently found themselves the objects of state repression, which resulted in religious organizations across the region being forced into positions where they could operate only on terms that were favourable to the state.

While the gradual relaxation of the mid-1950s affected organized religion, the relationship between the Church and state was characterized by a mixture of accommodation and mutual distrust. This was particularly the case in Catholic Central Europe, where organized religion continued to exert a hold over certain sections of the population and could act as a focus for certain acts of political protest. This was illustrated by the temporary upsurge of religious observance that followed the suppression of Hungary's 1956 revolution. In contrast to the pre-revolution years, when church congregations in the capital had been made up of elderly women, during Christmas 1957, in one industrial district, 25 to 30 per cent of the congregations were aged between 18 and 20. In another similar district, some 60 per cent of those attending the Christmas morning service were male manual workers. During 1958, it was noticed that a significant minority of manual workers in one district spent ten minutes in their local church before and after work each day.[52] Religion also played a role, even among those no longer observant, in shaping the cultural identities of populations, thus conferring on it a degree of political power and relevance that could be used to undercut the authority of socialist regimes. In celebrations of the millennium of Polish Christianity, in May 1966, Cardinal Wyszyński, Poland's primate, was able to assert that 'nowhere else is the union of Church and nation as strong as in Poland, which is in absolute danger'.[53]

While orthodoxy never presented the direct challenge to socialist rule that the Catholic Church was able to present in Poland, religious identities connected to orthodoxy played a central role in the construction of national and other cultural identities across south-eastern Europe, limiting the ability of the regimes to build anticlerical states.[54] Islam played a similar role, particularly in Bosnia-Hercegovina, where religious and national identities were both confused and intertwined. The fundamentally anti-religious Yugoslav state recognized the way in which religious identity shaped broader cultural identities in Bosnia as early as 1948, when the census recognized the existence of a nationality category of 'Muslims nationally undetermined'. By 1961, the state had recognized that the identity of Muslim could be an ethnic identity, while the census, ten years later, recognized it was possible to be a 'Muslim in the sense of nationality'.[55]

Despite undoubted pressures towards secularization in East European societies during the post-war period, religion played a considerable role in shaping cultural identities across the region. Most crucially, in some contexts (particularly, but not exclusively the Polish one), this gave religion a central political resonance – one that could be used to undercut the legitimacy of socialist rule. State security agencies attempted to maintain tight control over religious organizations. Throughout the 1960s, despite the relatively conciliatory policies that were pursued toward the Catholic Church, the Hungarian state security agencies maintained a network of informers among priests and congregations.[56] This coexisted with the ambiguous collaboration of many priests with the regime through the official peace movement, which had begun in the 1950s, as we saw in chapter 2. A pact with the Vatican was sealed by Kádár in 1964, creating a climate of mutual acceptance, if not trust, between the regime and Hungary's Catholics. Yet it was outside Catholic Central Europe that collaboration between the regime and organized religion was at its most marked. The unequal bargain struck by the regime and the Orthodox Church in Romania, in 1949, persisted and was extended as Gheorgiu-Dej, and then Ceauşescu, shifted to an explicitly national-communist strategy of legitimation. By recognizing the legitimacy of the socialist regime in Romania, the Orthodox hierarchy helped legitimize national communism in return for a measure of religious freedom.[57]

At the same time as churches at both national and local levels collaborated with socialist regimes and their agencies, religious institutions and identities could also shape the basis of opposition. This was at its clearest in Poland, where the Catholic Church under Wyszyński proved both able and willing to assert its independence from and opposition to socialist rule. Religious identities also played a part in motivating smaller-scale acts of protest against the state. In Hungary, relatively liberal policies towards the Church created space for forms of religious organization beyond the supervision of the authorities that could not be found elsewhere in the region. These often took the form of unofficial prayer or study groups of practising Catholics, whose existence was noticed from the mid-1960s.[58] In Czechoslovakia, where the anticlerical state never accepted the rights of the religious to associate freely, the existence of prayer and study groups was effectively criminalized, forming the basis for a religious underground, motivated by suspicion of and opposition to the party state.[59]

While religion as both an institutional and a cultural phenomenon existed in an ambiguous relationship to socialist regimes, and varied enormously across the bloc, popular nationalism, as we have seen, could be used by regimes to bolster their legitimacy, as in Romania and Albania. This was, however, not an option that was open to all socialist regimes. In Poland, for example, Gomułka was forced to articulate a socialist version of Polish national identity that identified the party with the progress of subordinate groups within the nation. He was forced to do this, to some extent, because of the anti-Sovietism that was ingrained in much popular nationalism, and the alternative version of a Polish identity that was articulated by representatives of the Catholic Church.[60] In Hungary, Magyar popular nationalism was infused with continuing resentment against the border changes that followed the First World War, and anger at the treatment of Magyar minorities in neighbouring states, which, in view of its geopolitical position, the Kádár regime found difficult to address. Often the public manifestation of such views attracted the direct attention of the state security agencies.[61]

It was in the multinational states of the region where the relationship between the regime and popular nationalism was at its most oppositional. In Czechoslovakia, de-Stalinization released a torrent of pent-up Slovak anger, particularly among Bratislava intellectuals from 1963, who were incensed at the Czechoslovak party's behaviour over the handling of the rehabilitation of those accused of 'bourgeois nationalism' a decade earlier, and keen to write a more nationalist version of Slovak history. The attempt by intellectuals to shape a distinct Slovak national identity within the socialist Czechoslovak state, as part of a broader political pro-gramme to gain more autonomy, was one of the social pressures that underpinned the Prague Spring.[62] However, it was in multinational Yugoslavia where the greater space for the public expression of national identities was the most difficult for the regime to manage. This was largely because some of those national identities articulated their ideas in opposition to the post-war settlement, seeking redress, as they had perceived themselves to be losers in the institutionalization of Tito's Yugoslavia. This was most notably the case in Croatia, which, in an echo of Croatian complaints against the inter-war Kingdom of Serbs, Croats and Slovenes, saw Tito's Yugoslavia as too Serb-dominated. These complaints crystallized around cultural issues, such as language, with many Croatians regarding Serbo-Croat as little more than 'the Serbian literary language'; economic issues, especially the transfer of resources from Croatia to Belgrade; and Serb hegemony within the security state. These resentments rumbled throughout the 1960s, but as we shall see in chapter 7, they were to come to a dramatic head in 1971.[63] Yet resentment of this kind was not restricted to Croatia. In the autonomous province of Kosovo, with its majority Albanian population, considerable discontent was expressed throughout the 1960s at the way in which the Serbian republican authorities in Belgrade ruled the territory. This discontent led to demonstrations in Kosovo's capital, Priština, in November 1968, when protesters demanded, among other things, an end to 'colonial policy in Kosovo'.[64] These tensions would shape the trajectory of the decay and collapse of socialism in Yugoslavia.

If popular religious opposition gnawed away at the party state's institutional monopoly and popular nationalism provided a destabilizing force that proved powerful over the following decades, then revisionist Marxism within the party provided a more immediately destabilizing force. In many states, particularly in the west of the region, cultural liberalization, de-Stalinization and the influx of the cultural and technical intelligentsia gave an impetus to challenges to the regime from within the ideological framework of Marxian socialism. In Hungary, from 1963, a school of neo-Marxist sociology developed around Rákosi's former prime minister, András Hegedűs, which cautioned against the country turning into a 'technocracy' and argued for a more democratic socialist society. Marxist philosophers around György Lukács, the eminent Communist philosopher, and briefly minister of culture, during the 1956 revolution, articulated demands for radical political reform in the second half of the 1960s.[65] In Poland, the actions of dissident Marxists in the universities, like Leszek Kołakowski, had infused the cat-and-mouse game between intellectuals and the Gomułka regime that shook Poland throughout the mid-1960s.[66] Liberalization in Yugoslavia generated space for the expression of a wide range of neo-Marxist opinions, as groups within Yugoslavia's universities moved to join the debate over the country's future. During the mid-1960s, some of the more radical revisionist Marxists, like those centred on the journal *Praxis*, generated considerable controversy.[67]

Revisionist Marxism played its most central role in the region in the Prague Spring. The action programme of the KSČ, adopted in April 1968, embodied the demands of revisionist Marxists within the party and promised to remake the socialist public sphere. In the words of one of its key authors, Zdeněk Mlynář, the implementation of the programme would create a situation in which 'various societal interests acquired the possibility to express themselves and to try to influence the creation of political decisions by means of freely expressed public opinion, including freedom of the press and via newly formed interest organizations'.[68] The vision that the action programme encapsulated, of a guided, yet democratic socialism, begged a crucial question. It called into doubt the boundaries and limits of the socialist public sphere, established by the late 1960s on the basis of a delicate balance between repression, accommodation, consent and limited opposition. By allowing the relatively free expression of public opinion, it opened up the possibility of the formation of a civil society to replace the socialist public sphere, and one that might have questioned the socialist nature of the Czechoslovak post-war state itself. As the Prague Spring gathered pace, the fear that this would turn fragmented discontent into coherent opposition around a definite political programme motivated the action of the former allies of Novotný within the KSČ leadership and the Soviets. Yet Czechoslovakia's experiment with a more democratic form of socialism was not allowed to continue. In suppressing it, as we shall see in chapter 7, the Soviets, those who worked with them in the Czechoslovak party, and those who accepted the balance of forces that its suppression created were unable to end the experiment without damaging the long-term bases of socialist rule in the region. While the Prague Spring, had it been allowed to continue, might have resulted either in democratization or an early end to the region's socialist dictatorships, its suppression and subsequent normalization set the stage for the decay and eventual collapse of socialist rule in Eastern Europe.

7 Socialism in decay

The Soviet move against the Prague Spring in August 1968 represented a turning point, not only for Czechoslovakia, but in many
respects for the socialist states of the whole region. For those that
remained within the Soviet bloc it underlined the external limits
placed by Moscow on processes such as economic reform and
attempts to incorporate the cultural and technical intelligentsia into
the political system. Change in the early 1970s was driven by
sections of local ruling parties that were always uncomfortable with
the extent to which socialist societies were being remade by the
retreats that accompanied the creation of a social settlement in the
mid-1960s. Even outside the Soviet bloc, in Tito's Yugoslavia, a
similar internal dynamic was observable, as the moves towards
greater cultural and political autonomy in the republics were reined
in from 1971 onwards. The logic of the transformation of the nature
of socialist rule (as the cultural and technical intelligentsia was
incorporated), which had been embodied within the KSČ's action
programme, and the more limited measures of other parties, were
replaced by 'normalization', a term which characterized socialist rule
in the region during the 1970s.

   Normalization is a term that has been used often in a narrow
sense to refer to the period in Czechoslovakia, involving extensive
purges of the party and the intellectual professions, that characterized the consolidation of the rule of Dubček's successor at the helm
of the KSČ, Gustav Husák. Though this chapter analyses the
specifically Czechoslovak process in its own right, it understands
normalization as being a useful term to characterize the pattern of
development of socialist rule in the region more generally during the
early 1970s. In this sense, it refers to the more tense relationship

between the party and the cultural and technical intelligentsia that emerged in the early 1970s, the real retreat from economic reform across the bloc, and the renewed rhetorical emphasis on class struggle and socialist orthodoxy. Yet it also underlines the fact that, real as these shifts were, they did not represent a dismantling of the social settlement that had emerged during the mid-1960s, except in a limited sense. Workerist, class-war rhetoric became increasingly formulaic, as societies continued to evolve in an explicitly con-sumerist direction; often economic reform was suspended rather than reversed. Socialism consequently stagnated, as regimes proved unable to reverse the social settlements that had allowed them to consolidate their rule, yet at the same time were unwilling to allow these social settlements to transform the regimes for fear that such a transformation would lead to their outright collapse. Ideological slogans such as the optimistic references to 'developed socialism', or more conservative notions of 'actually existing socialism' captured the general climate of stagnation that characterized the region during the first half of the 1970s.

The consequences of this normalized climate were to prove disastrous on two counts. The blocking of serious economic reform coincided with the turbulence within the capitalist world economy, on which socialist states depended to some extent. Unwilling and unable to impose the costs of restructuring on populations that were either like the Polish, and thus were unwilling to accept economic sacrifices, or like the Hungarians and Yugoslavs, where legitimation was tied to socialist consumerism, states accumulated a mountain of external debt. By the late 1970s, this debt proved increasingly difficult to finance, particularly as the world economy was hit by shocks at the end of the decade. On the other hand, the visible limits of reform left some social groups and constituencies outside the socialist public sphere and, therefore, the political system as a whole. Motivated in part by opposition to the system, and encouraged by the global discourse of human rights that spread in the region as a result of *détente*, opposition to the regime began to grow, particularly in the westernmost states of the region. By the late 1970s, particularly in Czechoslovakia and Hungary, opposition consisted largely of members of the intelligentsia, while in Poland, intellectual and worker discontent began to coalesce, transcending the divisions that had doomed intellectual protest in 1968. This would explode in August 1980, with the rise of an explicit challenge to the regime, not only from the Church and intellectuals, but also from a working class, disillusioned with the marked gap between the class-war rhetoric of party leaders and the bleak realities of life in Poland during the late 1970s.

As the Soviet invasion of Czechoslovakia marked the turning point that brought the period of consolidation of socialist regimes in the region to an end, events in the country in the years immediately following it set the tone for normalization across the region. The process of normalization in Czechoslovakia, however, was a long and tortuous one; Soviet invasion was launched to coincide with a meeting of the presidium of the KSČ, at which point, it was believed, former supporters of Novotný would be able to count on a majority to topple Dubček. Soviet intervention would thus precipitate a bloodless *coup*, as supporters of the anti-reform faction would be able to mobilize Czechoslovak security forces to secure the country for a change in direction. Yet the plotters failed to mobilize either a majority within the KSČ leadership, which actually used its meeting to condemn the invasion, or the domestic security forces, who failed to secure key buildings in the capital, like that of Radio Prague.[1] This failure was met with widespread resistance to the invasion in both the party and the country. The Fourteenth Congress, originally scheduled for early September, was secretly brought forward to 22 August and met in secret in a factory in the Prague industrial suburb of Vysoćany, where it demanded the 'immediate beginning of the speedy withdrawal of the occupation armies'.[2] From the morning of the invasion, widespread passive resistance in the form of demonstrations convulsed cities across the country, especially Prague. Key reformers in the leadership, including Dubček, were taken captive by the Soviets on the morning of 21 August and transported to Moscow, where they were held for forced negotiations with the Soviet leadership. They were joined later by the rest of the Czechoslovak leadership, and after spirited resistance, Dubček was persuaded to sign a document – the Moscow protocol – on 26 August, in which he agreed to what was ambiguously termed the normalization of Czechoslovakia, something which effectively meant the negation of the Prague Spring.

The autumn of 1968 was characterized by retreat from the liberalizing reforms of April's action programme, as state censorship of the media was restored, organizations independent of those of the party state were again proscribed and it rapidly became clear that Soviet troops would remain on Czechoslovak soil for the foreseeable future. This creeping restoration of order occurred against the backdrop of growing student protest as classes began in the country's universities, culminating in the dramatic suicide of Jan Palach, who set fire to himself in Prague on 16 January 1969 to demand an end to censorship. The impotence of Dubček in the face of the protest that followed Palach's act damaged the cause of reform within the party, whose membership increasingly craved stability in the face of the turbulence of the past six months. During early 1969, Dubček and his supporters found themselves increasingly isolated, while the centre of gravity in the party coalesced around Gustav Husák. The final fall of Dubček was precipitated by a new crisis in March, when the victory of the Czechoslovak ice hockey team over the Soviets provoked riots and anti-Soviet demonstrations across the country, in turn provoking protests and further threats of military intervention by Moscow. Faced with demands for further repressive measures, Dubček resigned in April 1969 and handed over the reins of power to Husák.

Husák moved gradually but resolutely to restore the authority of the party and to eliminate the reform movement. Faced with evidence that party organs were taking a relatively liberal attitude towards continuing student and intellectual opposition, regional and district party organs were vigorously purged during late 1969 and early 1970. From August 1969, the membership of the party was screened to restore political conformity, but also to restore working-class hegemony within the KSČ and to constrain those members from the cultural and technical intelligentsia who, it was assumed, had done so much to undermine Novotný's rule prior to 1967. By December 1970, only 78.3 per cent of the party's pre-screening membership remained within it, yet – in part due to working-class disgust at the suppression of the Prague Spring – the party leadership had failed to restore what it regarded as a 'healthy' class balance; industrial workers only accounted for 26.4 per cent of party members in autumn 1970, while members of the intelligentsia made up as much as 30.9 per cent.[3] The logic of control was extended to the areas like the media, the universities and to literary and cultural production. The extension of state control was accompanied by the extensive removal from white-collar professions of individuals believed to oppose the new order, and their systematic demotion to blue-collar positions. In the words of Milan Simečka, himself expelled from the party, dismissed from a university position, then forced to take a succession of manual jobs, 'the fate of the journalists, who were the first to offer themselves to personnel departments as window-cleaners and boiler-room stokers, was intended as a lesson to the rest: scientists, teachers, civil engineers, theatre personnel, film-makers, television and radio staff'.[4] The purges of those in white-collar occupations created a cycle that generated further pressure for conformity, explicitly squashing the reform movement, but also weakening, in the long-term, the hold of the party over the country's cultural and technical intelligentsia.

The anti-reform backlash that drove Husák's normalization did not stop with restoring political control over the party and silencing critical voices within the cultural and technical intelligentsia. In the economic sphere it resulted in a deep-seated attack on the uneven attempts to reform the Czechoslovak economy that had character-ized policy since the economic recession of 1963. In 1971, Husák's prime minister, Lubomír Štrougal, accused reformers of:

> 'preparing and implementing a transformation of the socialist economy into a system which was meant to deprive the working class and all working people of the revolutionary attainments and of their fundamental economic and political security ... As the most manifest expression of such endeavour, our economy ceased being controlled through a national economic plan.'[5]

While the economic conservatism of the country's normalizers would have debilitating consequences for the Czechoslovak economy over the years to come, this was not immediately obvious. Political passivity was to some extent bought by the Husák regime during the early 1970s, through increasing living standards and the continued promotion of socialist consumerism. Husák himself had claimed that a '... normal person wants to live quietly, without certain groups turning us into a jungle, and therefore we must appeal to people so that they condemn this. This party wants to safeguard a quiet life'.[6] Increasing living standards in a context of privatized depoliticization proved a successful strategy for ensuring political quiescence into the mid-1970s. Privatized consumerism and associated depoliticization led the dissident, Václav Havel – later to become Czechoslovakia's only post-socialist president – to comment on 'the general unwillingness of consumption-oriented people to sacrifice some material certainties for the sake of their own spiritual and moral integrity'.[7]

By the mid-1970s, therefore, Czechoslovakia's normalization regime had been established, based on the suppression of reformist intellectual currents in which a leadership defended an increasingly formalistic notion of socialism, while presiding over a privatized and consumerist society. While Czechoslovakia was an extreme case, largely due to the extent and nature of the political mobilization that had shaken the country's political institutions in 1968, other regimes in the region were characterized by comparable shifts, in part generated by their own domestic pressures, but also by what had occurred in Prague. In Hungary, as we saw in chapter 3, reformist Marxist intellectuals had hoped that economic reform would lead to meaningful reform of the socialist political system in the country, along lines broadly similar to that envisaged in the KSČ's action programme on the other side of the country's northern border. These hopes were dashed when Kádár not only supported Soviet intervention in Czechoslovakia, but also sent Hungarian troops to bolster the invasion. This increasingly strengthened the conviction among such intellectuals that their earlier views about the 'reformability' of the system were untenable, and this set them on a collision course with the country's rulers. Increasingly during the early 1970s, the regime moved to expel critical intellectuals (concentrated in philosophy and sociology) from the party, close down their opportunities for publication and place research institutes under tighter ideological control.[8]

While the attack on reformist Marxism from within the academy, and on student activists like Miklós Haraszti outside it, was marked, it never assumed the proportions of Husák's normalization, modifying rather than reversing the social settlement that emerged in Hungary during the mid-1960s. It was dovetailed with a retreat from economic reform that was not a wholesale reversal of the process, consisting of limited recentralization rather than the restoration of a fully-fledged planned economy. Recentralization, driven by a section of the party apparatus and large industrial enterprises, was justified with reference to the working-class discontent that the early operation of the reform engendered. This logic continued into the mid-1970s, with attacks on white-collar staff and the additional earnings of those who worked on their private plots in agriculture – measures that were designed both to assert central control over the economy and to appease a jealous working class. Yet while the regime deployed egalitarian, workerist rhetoric throughout the early 1970s, it proved to be little more than formalistic. Working-class discontent at the low level of their wages relative to the perceived high prices of consumer goods, their jealousy of other social groups and the perception that extra earnings in the shadow economy were necessary to engage fully with socialist consumerism were never successfully addressed by the regime. One worker in an outlying Budapest suburb complained, in the early 1970s, that 'once I've paid the installment on my loan, what remains of my wages, is needed for food and the household ... If I didn't have the garden, for growing the vegetables, a few other things, a couple of chickens, and that, then my wages wouldn't be enough to feed us'.[9]

Regime workerism in Hungary was able to provide little more than rhetorical compensation for discontent as working-class identity retreated in the face of the privatization that spread along with socialist consumerism and the shadow economy. Workers complained that 'everyone is turning in on themselves. In this factory everyone is busy with thinking about themselves, and they don't deal with each other'.[10] In this climate, workerist rhetoric came to be increasingly formalized and removed from the realities of Hungarian working-class life. By 1974, as far as the party was concerned, improving the role of the working class no longer took the form of wage and social policy measures to cement workers to the state. Instead, the party argued this would be achieved through greater moral rewards for workers, demanding that the working class gain a more prominent place in the media and calling for an increase, from between 12 and 15 to 30 per cent, in the number of state medals given to working-class people.[11]

While Kádár's weak version of normalization paled in comparison with what had occurred under Husák in Czechoslovakia, it nevertheless represented a marked retreat from the culturally liberal climate of the late 1960s. Further north, Poland's different political trajectory produced a comparable shift in the nature of socialist governance in the country during the first half of the 1970s. In 1968, as we saw in chapter 3, Gomułka's regime had beaten back intellectual and student protest through the mobilization of anti-intelligentsia sentiment, only to fall as a consequence of working-class protest in the Baltic ports over price increases immediately prior to Christmas 1970. While potentially dissident sections of the cultural and political intelligentsia were already alienated from the regime as a result of the upheavals of 1968, controlling them was not to represent the most immediate problem that Gomułka's successor, Edward Gierek, faced on assuming office. Instead, he had to cope with the consequences of Gomułka's failure, almost unique in the region, to forge a social settlement with the working class over the course of the 1960s. Rooted in relative poverty by 1970, with stagnant incomes, Polish working-class militancy had taken an organized form unusual in the bloc, using sit-ins and strike committees to maximum effect.[12] With a renewed strike wave in January 1971, which spread beyond the Baltic ports to Łódź's textile plants, Gierek was forced into major concessions, raising wages, pensions and a series of social benefits, while at the same time a two-year price freeze was introduced on foodstuffs.[13] Throughout the 1970s, militant working-class protest, where it erupted, would be dealt with through the judicious deployment of the carrot and stick by the authorities. Strikes were quickly defused through material concessions, but once workers returned to work, militants were dismissed and subjected to intimidation, or worse, by the state security agencies.[14]

Initially, Gierek's policies were characterized by a series of concessions, which were not only made in the sphere of labour and social policy that served to stabilize his rule. A play to national sentiment was made in his declaration of support for the rebuilding of the royal castle in Warsaw, destroyed during the German occupation. In early 1971, the regime also made overtures to the Catholic Church, in the interests of fostering a sense of national unity.[15] Beneath this lay a drive for greater control that was played out initially within the ranks of the PZPR. Potential rivals, most notably, Mieczysław Moczar, who had been, effectively, the second most powerful person in the country under Gomułka, were removed from senior positions. During 1971 and 1972, the party membership itself was subjected to an extensive purge, while greater ideological discipline was enforced within the party through a renewed emphasis on political education.[16] Increasingly, in a Polish variant of the revival of class-based rhetoric on the part of the regimes that characterized Czechoslovakia and Hungary in this period, Gierek became rhetorically aggressive. Official discourse echoed the slogans of the early 1950s that had promised the construction of socialism, though revised them for the different context of the 1970s, instead emphasizing the creation of developed socialism. In 1975, Gierek asserted that 'the construction of the developed socialist society has initiated a gradual transformation of the state of the dictatorship of the proletariat into a general national state, which, under the direction of the working class, embodies the will and interests of the entire nation'.[17]

The assertion that the PZPR, as the vanguard of Poland's working class, was the only legitimate political representative of the entire nation was enshrined in 1976 amendments to Poland's 1952 constitution, which proclaimed that the ruling party was 'the leading political force in society'.[18] This was accompanied by the Gierek regime's promotion of a visibly socialist public culture, through ritual and propaganda, advancing a vision of Poland as a modernizing, industrialized society.[19] Such assertiveness and confidence on the part of the regime were misplaced; its rhetorical assertions were often bitterly contested by the Catholic Church, which challenged, in particular, central passages of the 1976 constitution.[20] Yet it was also ill-judged, given that social stability rested on fragile foundations, as Gierek envisaged stability being achieved through a spectacular gamble on the capacity for growth of the Polish economy. The regime sought to use credit-financed industrial expansion to pay for an increase in real wages of up to 20 per cent between 1971 and 1975, as well as a major increase in the availability of consumer goods. Industrial expansion was spearheaded by prestige projects like the construction of a new steel mill in Gierek's Katowice power base. Meanwhile, new plants were built, producing under Western license, of which the best known was the Fiat Polski factory in Bielsko-Biała, which began producing the Italian-designed cars for sale across the region in 1971.[21] Gierek's gamble was, as we shall see, to fail utterly as the decade wore on.

While Gierek's attempts to identify Poland's socialist regime with the nation proved contentious, raising the ire of substantial constituencies, such as that loyal to the Church, elsewhere the identification of regime and nation could act to legitimate socialist rule. This was most clearly the case in Romania where, as we saw in chapter 3, a national-communist course was successfully attempted, first by Gheorgiu-Dej and then by Ceauşescu, in order to incorporate the cultural and technical intelligentsia into socialist society and thus to legitimate their rule. In 1968, Ceauşescu not only refused to support Soviet intervention in Czechoslovakia, but he explicitly condemned it. This act of defiance, however, was not motivated by sympathy for Dubček's more democratic brand of socialism, but by fear that the Soviet Union would eventually use military force against Ceauşescu's own brand of national communism.[22] One key plank of this had been asserting Romania's foreign policy independence from Moscow, using this as a tool of internal legitimation, extending policies that had begun with Gheorgiu-Dej's negotiated withdrawal of Soviet troops from the country in 1958. Yet the deployment of national sentiment by the regime had not been confined to the sphere of foreign policy alone, but was also directed at Romania's ethnic minorities. Under Gheorgiu-Dej, the separate Hungarian- and Romanian-language universities in the Transylvanian capital, Cluj, were merged in 1959, while the so-called Hungarian Autonomous Region, established in 1952 as a sop to Transylvania's Magyar ethnic minority, was abolished in 1960. Ceauşescu intensified this policy of Romanian nation-building in the country's multi-ethnic regions, identifying those who strove to protect Magyar cultural and political autonomy in Transylvania, for example, as enemies of the regime. In 1971, he warned that 'anybody trying to pursue a policy of national hatred pursues a policy against Socialism and Communism – and must be treated consequently as an enemy of our Socialist nation'.[23]

Notions of the nation and the national were central to both the cultural politics and the ideology of the Romanian regime by the end of the 1960s, which stressed the role of the RCP as the authentic representative of the national tradition. In 1966, one year after taking power, Ceauşescu proclaimed:

'We Communists, consider it is a creditable mission to study, know and honor dutifully all those who contributed to building up our nation, all those who laid down their lives for the Romanian people's national and social freedom ... How would it possible for a party which proposes to lead the people along the road of building a fairer system, the socialist system, not to know the past struggles? ... How could a people feel without knowing its own past, its history, without honoring and appreciating that history'.[24]

Increasingly, as the 1970s progressed, however, the ideological construct of the party as leader and representative of the nation was to shift, as official discourse became increasingly characterized by a 'cult of personality', of both the leader himself and his immediate family. In the increasingly 'dynastic socialism' that had emerged by the end of the 1970s, Ceauşescu was characterized as 'our lay god, the heart of the party and the nation',[25] while his wife, Elena, celebrated by ideologues as an apparently eminent scientist, and his son, Nicu, played increasing roles within the regime propaganda. By the end of the decade, Ceauşescu's own cult of personality had assumed grandiose proportions: as early as 1974, regime propaganda compared him to 'Julius Caesar, Alexander the Great, Pericles, Cromwell, Peter the Great and Napoleon'.[26]

National communism, centred increasingly on a cult of personality, was not only combined with continued repression, but also with an economic policy of centralized, planned economic modernization, which to some extent echoed the one introduced by Gierek in Poland. Industrial production was to be increased and the country's industrial base was to be modernized, through emphasizing investment in sectors like chemicals, as economic planning was deployed in order to drag Romania fully into an era of industrial modernity.[27] The increases in industrial production were underpinned by Ceauşescu's foreign policy measures, which won him considerable plaudits in the West, allowing Romania to join the World Bank, the General Agreement on Tariffs and Trades and the International Monetary Fund during the early 1970s.[28] Romanian diplomacy, particularly in the Middle East, opened markets to

Romanian exports, thus boosting economic growth domestically.[29] As in Poland, this gamble on growth would run into severe problems during the late 1970s, though the nature of Romania's regime would produce a very different response and outcome to the economic crisis to that experienced in the north of the region.

In its combination of national communism with the cult of personality, Albania, albeit outside the Soviet bloc and allied to China until 1978, was the most similar to Ceauşescu's Romania. Enver Hoxha was portrayed, like Ceauşescu, as the wise leader of the nation; in the words of one piece of regime propaganda, Hoxha 'has ensured the consistent, revolutionary implementation of the Marxist-Leninist line and norms of the party, has never allowed it to be diverted on to blind alleys and has brought it triumphant through all the difficult and complicated situations'.[30] Institutionalized paranoia and pervasive restriction and repression within the sphere of everyday life created a culture of deep-seated isolation from the trends visible elsewhere in the region towards export-led modernization and consumerism. Instead, industrialization, supported until 1978 by Chinese advisers, continued to conform to a model reminiscent of that which had been widespread elsewhere during the early 1950s. Poverty and a marked lack of consumer goods led one visitor to comment that in Tirana's main square, in 1971, 'a lonely traffic cop sleeps on his feet, and jumps to attention to greet a car like an old friend if it happens to pass by twice in the same day'.[31] Yet Albania and Romania were both somewhat exceptional. Bulgaria's national-communist undercurrent, at least until the mid-1980s, was less marked, associated with the promotion of national discourses within the sphere of cultural policy under the influence of Liudmila Zhivkova. Politically, Todor Zhivkov remained scrupulously loyal to the foreign policy lines promoted by the Soviet Union. By the 1970s, the regime had begun to stress a limited socialist consumerism,[32] underpinned by rapid economic growth that saw industrial output rise by 9.1 per cent per annum between 1971 and 1975.[33]

While in most of the south-eastern European states, national sentiment helped to bolster socialist regimes, in Yugoslavia, as we saw in chapter 6, cultural liberalization in the late 1960s led to the political articulation of national identities, which threatened the compromise between the republics and the centre that had allowed the second Yugoslavia to emerge and prosper. At the same time, in Serbia, demands for further liberalization and democratization were advanced by members of Serbian party. The pressures generated by the upsurge of national identities in Yugoslavia's republics were to be brought to a head by changes in the leadership of the Croatian party in 1968. A new assertive party leadership demanded that the republic gain more economic autonomy from the centre, while cultural liberalization produced a revival in cultural and political nationalism within Croatia, which generated tension between Zagreb and Belgrade.[34] Against a background of moves to amend the 1963 Federal Constitution in order to accommodate some of the demands that emerged during the 1960s, in-fighting between representatives of the republics and within the party, and growing national mobilization in Croatia itself, during 1971, the party itself began to demand some of the trappings of Croatian statehood, raising the spectre of the collapse of Yugoslavia. As far as Tito was concerned, 'it was 1941 all over again'.[35] Beginning in December 1971, the Croatian leadership was purged and nationalist organizations were banned, as the federal leadership placed limits on liberalization, worried, in Tito's words, that if Croatia were allowed to continue on its pre-December 1971 path 'in six months it would have come to shooting, to a civil war'.[36]

The end of what has been termed the 'Croatian spring' had consequences beyond the republic's borders, leading to the defeat of elements within the party across the federation that had pushed for further political change and the outright democratization of Yugoslav socialism. Purges reached deep into the parties in Macedonia and Slovenia, where Communists had been prominent in demanding greater independence from Belgrade.[37] During the 1972 conference of the League of Communists, the extent to which those arguing for decentralization, democratization and reform had been sidelined was underlined by rhetorical attacks on 'liberals', those in the party who advocated greater independence, student protestors and critical Marxist intellectuals. As in much of the rest of the region, but under the influence of different pressures, moves to restore control and stability replaced the dynamic of reform by the early 1970s.[38] Despite the defeat of radical reform, a new constitution, introduced in 1974, institutionalized much of the decentralization that had taken place from the mid-1960s onwards as far as the republics were concerned, while, much to the consternation of Serb nationalists, it enhanced the status and power of the autonomous provinces of Vojvodina and Kosovo, within Serbia.[39]

For most of the region, the mid-1960s had been characterized by a remaking of patterns of socialist governance as a result of the creation of a social settlement of sorts between regime and people. The early 1970s, by contrast, were characterized by the regime imposing limits on how far social actors would be allowed to reshape the political arrangements in their respective states. Consequently, when compared to the period that immediately preceded it, the first half of the decade seemed to have been a period of restriction and selective repression. It was a period that allowed for the short-term stabilization of socialist rule, but had disastrous medium- and long-term consequences for socialist regimes right across the region.

These problems quickly became clear in the economic and social spheres. The atmosphere of normalized Eastern Europe created a climate that was less than conducive to economic reform. Either, as in Poland, Romania and Bulgaria, developmentalist dreams were pursued in the context of the modified structures of traditional economic planning, or economic reform was reversed, wholesale, as in Czechoslovakia, or partially, as in Hungary, or persisted, but with little further reform, as in Yugoslavia. During the 1960s, financing the region's domestic social contracts had involved expanding the role of the countries of the region within regional and world markets, thus boosting exports. While the East European member states of COMECON (the Soviet bloc's organization for the promotion of economic integration) accounted for 3.8 per cent of world exports in 1950, this figure had reached 5.7 per cent by 1970. Exports to 'developed market economies' represented 26.2 per cent of these countries' exports in the latter year, while 'developing countries' made up another 7.7 per cent, a figure that was dwarfed by trade between these states and each other as well as the Soviet Union, but one that was nevertheless significant.[40] Industrial production was based on low prices for energy, provided to most of the region by the Soviet Union at subsidized prices, and generally unrealistic, administratively determined price levels. Furthermore, economic reform had been attempted, in part, to combat problems in production, which hampered export-oriented policies, as we saw in chapter 3. The suspension of reform in the 1970s was combined with the deterioration of the international economic climate that followed the end of the post-war boom in the capitalist world economy, which was characterized by increasing turbulence by the late 1960s, in turn exacerbated by the energy crises of the early 1970s.[41]

The stagnation of the capitalist world economy and the rise in energy prices caused marked economic turbulence within the region, in part because of the deep recession in Western Europe, but also due to the attempts of the Soviet Union to pass on some of the increases in oil prices to its trading partners in the region. Husák's Czechoslovakia sought to overhaul its industry, importing machinery from the West, but at the same time, recession in Western Europe limited its opportunities to export, resulting in increasing trade deficits with Western states and an external debt which rose from US $0.2 billion in 1971 to US $1.4 billion by 1976.[42] In Poland, Gierek's dash for growth stimulated the economy during the 1970s, generating a socialist consumerism in the country as living standards rose and the ownership of consumer durables spread.[43] Yet much of this increase was financed by debt, while industrialization, driven by the mechanism of the planned economy, had resulted in a marked failure to convert investment into real production. At the same time, recession in the West restricted exports, generating suppressed inflation and a hard-currency debt of US $10.2 billion by 1976.[44] By the late 1970s, Ceauşescu's similar drive for industrial modernization and growth through the structures of the centralized planned economy ran into increasing difficulties, as the operation of the economy became ever more chaotic and the country's external debt burden gradually increased.[45]

Even in the region's reformed economies, the effects of changes in the world economy were felt during the 1970s. Yugoslavia's growth during the decade was largely financed by external borrowing; net foreign debt rose from just under US $6 billion in 1975 to almost US $14 billion four years later – a figure that would rise further until its huge external debt forced it to change policy in 1982.[46] In Hungary, unwillingness to reduce real incomes and the mushrooming of a shadow economy under the pressure of more differentiated consumer demand, as well as the impact of a dialectic of reform followed by recentralization, placed ever greater demands on the economy. These pressures resulted in spiralling state indebtedness, which continued until the point at which the political leadership was threatened with the spectre of outright bankruptcy in the autumn of 1978.[47]

While mushrooming indebtedness was hidden from the populations of the regions by the veil of secrecy thrown over the true economic situation by party leaderships, endemic economic difficulties were experienced by populations in other ways as the decade wore on. In Hungary, for example, where public discussion of social issues was relatively more open that in the rest of the region, inadequate social and health services, endemic corruption, a shadow economy generated by the malfunctioning of state sector services, and poor infrastructure, especially in rural areas, were increasingly discussed throughout the decade.[48] In Poland, growing economic crisis was experienced as a series of increasing shortages, not only in the shops, but also in malfunctioning public services. Consequently, corruption grew throughout the 1970s, leading some social observers to note that economic crisis had:

> given birth to a group of individuals who have a direct interest in seeing that an ailing economy and unhealthy social relations remain untouched. It is a group that by virtue of the functions it performs, 'has access to the second economy' for procuring supplies, housing, health services, and scarce goods.[49]

Shortages and the spread of a shadow economy led a significant proportion of Polish workers – around 40 per cent – to evaluate the improvement in their standard of living negatively over the course of the first eight years of the 1970s, despite the increases in real wages.[50] These perceptions echoed similar discontent in Hungary, described earlier in this chapter, and in Romania, as mentioned in chapter 5.

This lingering discontent, generated by the gap between the promise of socialist consumerism and the frustrating reality of the deterioration of public services, shortages and the spread of the shadow economy, exploded into open working-class discontent in some states when the regime attempted to check the deterioration of the economy by attacking living standards. Such attempts provoked spectacular explosions of working-class protest in Poland and Romania during the late 1970s, but were only met with disgruntled quiescence in Hungary. In June 1976, the Gierek regime in Poland introduced a series of substantial price increases, including a 69 per cent hike in the price of meat. Angered that the Gierek regime was breaking the tacit social contract established after the events of 1970–1, based on increases in working-class living standards, strikes quickly broke out across the country. At the Ursus tractor factory, close to Warsaw, and in the industrial town of Radom, the strikes quickly turned into political demonstrations and rioting; the regime responded with severe repression, as hundreds were arrested and still more lost their jobs.[51] Similar protest was ignited in Romania a year later, when the Ceauşescu regime increased the retirement age for miners, extended the working day and slashed sickness and disability benefits. In the coal mines of southern Transylvania's Jiu Valley, over 30,000 miners responded by stopping work, electing a strike committee and demanding that they negotiate with Ceauşescu personally. Two days into the strike, the Romanian leader met the strikers and ended the protest by agreeing to their demands. Repression was to follow later. By early 1978, 4,000 miners, identified by the *Securitate* as troublemakers, had been forced to move out of the Jiu Valley, dispersed across the country and isolated from the cohesive working-class communities that existed in the mining regions.[52] When the Hungarian regime introduced large price increases in July 1979, as part of an attempt to shift to a policy of austerity in order to rein in its spiralling external debt, working-class discontent was expressed less spectacularly than in either Poland or Romania.[53]

While working-class protest in Poland would produce a major regional crisis at the turn of the 1980s, the late 1970s were also marked by the rise, albeit fragmented, of intellectual opposition to the regime across the region. This stemmed from several pressures. The first of these was that the exclusion of many reform-minded intellectuals from any influence on the political system, and indeed from any form of intellectual employment, as a consequence of the pressures towards normalization, had led them to see the system as 'unreformable'. They had consequently moved to take a stance of outright opposition. Second, the first half of the 1970s had seen a process of *détente* in Europe, between East and West. This had culminated in the signing, in 1975, of the Helsinki Final Act, by both Western and Eastern states. This committed individual states to the protection of basic human rights, including those of freedom of speech, assembly and the protection of ethnic minorities. This led to the spread of the legitimacy of a discourse of human rights in societies across the region, and also gave dissident intellectuals, largely denied these freedoms, a stick with which to beat the regime.

Against the backdrop of these shifts, in Poland it was the regime's use of repression against strikers in 1976 that acted as the major stimulant to oppositional intellectual mobilization. The left among dissident intellectuals founded the Committee for Workers' Defence (*Komitet Obrony Robotników* or KOR) in late summer 1976, in order to provide legal support and advice to workers caught up in the regime's repressive offensive against those who had participated in the June strikes. KOR was the first organization of an oppositional nature to assume organizational form, and was quickly joined by others that mobilized conservative-minded intellectuals and, later, students during 1977.[54] Its long-term significance, however, was that it formed the basis for cooperation between dissident members of the cultural and technical intelligentsia and the working class, which allowed protest in 1980–1 to transcend the divisions between workers and intellectuals that had been exploited by the regime in 1968. In Czechoslovakia, fragmented discontent continued to exist underground throughout the 1970s, surfacing in dramatic fashion in January 1977, with the launch of Charter 77. Charter 77 grew out of attempts to give support to a rock group, The Plastic People of the Universe, who were arrested and tried as the flagship trial in a campaign designed to silence the country's vibrant, underground rock scene.[55] The Charter was a document that drew attention to the discrepancy between the human rights that Czechoslovakia had promised to observe when signing the Helsinki Final Act, and its denial of those rights to large numbers of its citizens. Organized by intellectuals excluded from public life by normalization, like the dissident playwright, Václav Havel, and initially signed by 243 people, the Charter was broadcast by the Voice of America and greeted with hysteria by Husák's regime.[56]

Though Charter 77 never broke out of a restricted area of support, it did serve as a focus for the minority of Czechoslovaks who actively opposed the regime, mobilizing intellectuals and the religious, and laying the foundations for further action, particularly in highlighting the abuse of basic human rights inside the country.[57] It also had an impact beyond the country's borders. Hungary's small, Budapest-based dissident intellectuals, excluded from the ruling party in the early 1970s, responded with a declaration of solidarity with the signatories of the Charter. With the country's nationalist intellectuals largely incorporated into the political system through the liberal cultural policies of the regime, the country's 'democratic opposition' remained small during the late 1970s, though with the onset of austerity after 1979, it increasingly began to mobilize around issues such as poverty, which was a political taboo in Kádár's Hungary.[58] In Romania, the dissident writer, Paul Goma, also expressed his solidarity with Charter signatories, following up this act with a letter to Ceauşescu, protesting human rights abuses in Romania, and a further declaration, signed by Goma and seven supporters, sent to all those states who had signed the Helsinki Final Act. These attempts were greeted with hysteria by the regime, which forced Goma into exile in November 1977.[59] While intellectual opposition continued to exist throughout the 1980s, it did so in a deeply repressive climate. In Bulgaria, dissent was even more fragmented, though declarations demanding that the Zhivkov regime respect basic human rights surfaced sporadically during the late 1970s and early 1980s.[60]

By the end of the 1970s, the social settlements that had allowed socialist regimes to consolidate their rule in the mid-1960s were in an advanced state of decay. Economies were stagnant and struggled under an increasing burden of external debt. Regimes were being forced to turn haltingly to policies of austerity, which transferred the burden of economic failure to the population. The result was increasing discontent and social protest. At the same time, the failure of regimes to renew their systems, and the consequent normalizing tendencies that had emerged from state attempts to rein in those elements among the cultural and technical intelligentsia which they believed threatened their rule, created the space for explicit opposition to develop. While in most countries, intellectual opposition remained small and possessed a highly restricted support base, it was nevertheless a symptom of the erosion of regime legitimacy that had set in through the 1970s. In most states in the region, prior to the 1980s, these trends were experienced as a decay of the socialist system, but in Poland, where the roots of the domestic social settlement between regime and people had been at their weakest during the mid-1960s, they resulted in generalized political crisis.

During the late 1970s, opposition to the Polish regime grew in both strength and confidence, especially following the attempt to jail leading KOR members in May 1977, only to release them a month later in the face of significant international protest. The prestige of the Catholic Church grew with the election of the Archbishop of Kraków, Cardinal Karol Wojtyła, as Pope John Paul II on 16 October 1978. The new Pope's first papal tour of his homeland in June 1979 was a turning point, both in terms of the mass participation of millions of Poles and in the fact that the visit served to open up a public space, independent of the party, through which opposition to the regime could be articulated.[61] Attempts to rein in the opposition with a renewed campaign of repression in the second half of 1979 proved less than effective.[62] Furthermore, the economic situation continued to deteriorate, and in the face of a serious economic crisis, the Gierek regime shifted to pursue a policy of austerity. Political crisis was again sparked by measures related to the supply of meat; attempts to shift a proportion of the supply from state shops to more expensive commercial ones provoked a strike wave which convulsed the country in July 1980. As the month progressed it became clear that the regime's preferred tactic of buying off striking workers on a workplace-by-workplace basis was failing, for as soon as one group of strikers returned to work, strikes spread to other workplaces. It was, however, when the strikes spread to the Lenin Shipyard in Gdańsk, on 14 August, that the strike movement became a much more serious threat to the regime than it had been hitherto.

The specific working-class culture of the Baltic ports, where the workforce was relatively isolated both from its rural roots and the shadow economy, and where local economies were dominated by heavy industrial work in the shipyards, provided fertile ground for working-class militancy. Gdańsk's working class was also able to draw on a rich tradition of popular protest, exhibited in the self-organized strikes in the Baltic ports that had toppled Gomułka in 1970. These traditions were activated as inter-factory strike committees were formed, bridging enterprises in the Baltic ports, which demanded independent trade unions and the right to strike.[63] Within days, the inter-factory strike committee, centred on Gdańsk, demanded negotiations with the government. Backed by a wave of support from other industrial centres, the government was forced to enter serious negotiations with the Gdańsk Inter-Factory Strike Committee, under the leadership of electrician, Lech Wałęsa, which resulted in an agreement on the formation of independent trade unions on 31 August.[64]

The settling of the Gdańsk strike ended Gierek's rule, as the central committee of the PZPR replaced him with Stanisław Kania within days of the agreement. The settlement also set in train a virtual political revolution in the country. Over the course of September, the inter-factory strike committees in the Baltic ports were joined by sympathy strikers across the country, as well as representatives of KOR, to found an independent, national union confederation – Solidarity or *Solidarność*, under the leadership of Wałęsa. Recognized by the constitutional court in November 1980, it began to transform itself into a national organization in the teeth of opposition from the regime. During 1981 it organized outside the factories to bring the peasant population into its ranks, transforming itself into something between a trade union and a focus for opposition to the regime. Throughout the year it moved to become a body that advocated serious political and economic reform; in its programme, *Solidarność* argued that Poland should be transformed into a 'self-managing republic', with greater worker involvement in the management of the economy, as part of a plan to solve the ever deepening economic crisis.

The PZPR was thrown into disarray by the advance of *Solidarność* and its hold over public opinion. Despite the fact that *Solidarność* pursued a strategy that sociologist Jadwiga Staniszkis has described as one of 'a self-limiting revolution',[65] in which the union did not explicitly seek to topple, but merely to transform the socialist regime, many in the PZPR saw the organization as a serious threat to its rule. Furthermore, the Soviet Union became increasingly uneasy at the cultural and political liberalization that *Solidarność* brought in its wake, and increasingly placed pressure on the Polish leadership to rein in the organization. In October 1981, Kania was replaced as first secretary of the PZPR with his prime minister, General Wojciech Jaruzelski, a military figure who combined the posts of first secretary of the PZPR, prime minister and minister of defence. The autumn was characterized by increasing confrontation between *Solidarność* and the state, which culminated in the decision over the weekend of 12–13 December 1981 to declare martial law and suppress *Solidarność*. The declaration was met with an explosion of working-class anger and a strike wave across the country, which it took troops until Christmas to break. During 1982, order was only superficially imposed on a restive society. While Jaruzelski's imposition of martial law signalled a temporary end to Poland's crisis, it marked a further turning point, at which the decay of socialist regimes across the bloc turned into an outright and eventually terminal crisis.

8 The collapse

Poland's declaration of martial law represented an end of sorts to the country's upheavals of 1980–1, yet it also signalled the beginning of the end for socialist regimes in the region as a whole. The terminal crisis of the regimes emerged against the background of chronic indebtedness, which crippled the economies of the region from the beginning of the 1980s. This led to the effective end of the social settlement that had been consolidated in the 1960s, as socialist states were forced to suspend policies based on increasing living standards, and imposed full-blown austerity on their populations. This austerity took different forms in different states, and generated differing forms of protest. While the regime in Poland, established under martial law during early 1982, found austerity most difficult to cope with, in view of its deep-seated lack of legitimacy, opposition to socialist rule spread right across the region, ranging from sporadic explosions of working-class protest to an increasingly broad political mobilization that included youth, intellectuals and the religious. They coexisted with an accelerating withdrawal of trust in the institutions that made up the socialist public sphere as the decade progressed. Furthermore, many of the oppositional tendencies and the views they advanced found resonance within ruling parties, particularly in Hungary, Poland and Yugoslavia.

The arrival in power of Mikhail Gorbachev, in 1985, gradually freed reformists within the ruling parties in Hungary and Poland to begin the struggle to remake their own political institutions, without fear of Soviet intervention. Yugoslav socialism, undermined by economic crises and nationalist mobilization, was in a state of meltdown during the second half of the 1980s. The responses of ruling parties in the various republics shaped the nature of

Yugoslav socialism's collapse and paved the way for the descent into civil war in the early 1990s. Poland and Hungary's own political revolutions, between 1987 and 1989, driven by a reformist, though at times reluctant, party and a confident opposition, provided the spark for revolution elsewhere. Despite the desire of other regimes to resist the tide of reform, by the second half of 1989 they all had to reckon with the mounting crisis. By Christmas, the fate of socialism everywhere in the region, except Albania, was sealed, forcing the countries to engage in the painful reconstruction of their political systems, societies and economies during the 1990s.

As we saw in the previous chapter, the region's economies ran into increasing difficulties during the 1970s. This was because, in order to finance domestic social settlements, they had increased their trade with the West, but had done so without sufficiently reforming their economies to cope with problems of productivity, quality and efficiency. With the end of the post-war boom, East European economies found themselves functioning in a radically different economic climate, as Western states moved into a period of recession, stagnation and then restructuring. Socialist regimes, resting on internal social settlements weakened by the political processes that followed the suppression of the Prague Spring in 1968, proved both unable and unwilling to restructure their own economies – a process that generated spiralling indebtedness.[1] This was exacerbated by a series of international economic shocks and a sharp increase in the cost of borrowing worldwide, initiated by restrictive policies pursued by the United States Federal Reserve from 1979. While in capitalist economies this policy shift generated a severe recession between 1979 and 1982, in Eastern Europe it made the cost of servicing external debt prohibitive to socialist regimes already grappling with increasing economic problems of their own.[2] In Hungary, as we saw in chapter 7, the crunch came just before the worldwide increase in the cost of borrowing in autumn 1978, when the government, faced with the spectre of outright insolvency, turned to a policy of austerity, heralded by cuts in food subsidies and sharp price increases in July 1979. Romania was hit by the effects of recession, which reduced its capacity to export, and the increasing cost of servicing its debt during 1980. Attempts to correct these problems with limited austerity measures failed, and during the first half of 1981 the country's foreign currency reserves fell as it attempted to finance imports, while at the same time banks denied the country further credits. The country's insolvency forced the regime to turn to the IMF, which, in turn, forced Romania's turn towards austerity.[3]

The fiscal crisis of the Polish socialist state unfolded against the background of upheavals of 1980–1. Political transformation was accompanied by deepening economic crisis and mounting external debt, which reached a total of US \$30.2 billion, of which US \$25.5 billion was owed to the West, by 1981. Poland admitted to its financial insolvency when it concluded its first rescheduling agreement with Western banks in March 1981, at the height of political turmoil in the country.[4] Financial insolvency provided the background to developments within the Polish economy throughout the 1980s; the economy remained racked by severe structural crisis, which manifested itself in fluctuating industrial production and further erosions in living standards and the level of public services throughout the middle of the decade.[5] The reluctance of Western lenders to lend to socialist states in the aftermath of financial and then political crisis in Poland generated serious fiscal crisis outside the Soviet bloc, in Yugoslavia, where external debt had reached US \$19 billion by 1981. During 1982, Yugoslavia faced a situation in which Western banks refused to continue to finance its debt, forcing it to turn, like Romania, to the IMF, which granted a debt stabilization package from 1983, in return for Yugoslavia's pursuit of austerity measures.[6] Elsewhere the financial crisis was not so severe in its impact. Though Czechoslovakia's debt rose in the late 1970s, it remained at an estimated US \$3 billion throughout the 1980s. Given the country's dependence on heavy industry, however, its economy was hit by Soviet moves, in 1979–80, to charge more for the oil it exported to the country. While Czechoslovakia was not hit by a fiscal crisis as dramatic as that suffered by Poland, it nevertheless experienced the pressures of the 1980s through creeping economic stagnation.[7] Bulgaria was dogged by economic problems similar to those experienced by other states during the late 1970s, but was not faced with as dramatic a fiscal crisis as that found in Poland, and thus shifted gear, in 1979, towards austerity and greater reform of economic structures.[8]

Given the different nature of the impact of economic crisis on the different states of the region, the responses of the regimes varied, as did the reactions of subject populations. Husák's regime was forced to respond the least to the difficult economic situation, in part, because Czechoslovakia's external debt was the lowest in the region. Economic modernization was pursued through modified rather than reformed economic structures. Yet even here the regime was not able escape the impact on popular morale of stagnating living standards and deteriorating public services, which struggled under increasing shortages. The continuing memory of normalization among the population, and the hegemony of privatized consumerism promoted by the Husák regime, encouraged the privatization of social conflict as Czechs and Slovaks withdrew from activity in the socialist workplace or public sphere, which often manifested itself in the enthusiasm of large sections of the population for consumer goods and weekend houses.[9] In this context, the shadow economy formed a semi-tolerated means of plugging the shortages and gaps in public services that assumed an increasing role throughout the 1980s. As one anonymous Czech philosopher commented, 'people are allowed to better their living standard in illegal ways … Everybody does it, so nobody is clean. This is a more cohesive factor than the secret police – this spread of corruption that unites all Czechs'.[10]

While the Czechoslovak regime tacitly tolerated the spread of the shadow economy to plug the tension generated by economic stagnation, Kádár's regime in Hungary sought to consciously promote and integrate it, as it shifted policy from increasing living standards to austerity. The price hikes in 1979 and the curbs imposed by the regime on growth in working-class incomes produced greater demand among workers for more sources of income outside their main employment, as they continued to focus on their own perceived household needs. This situation produced considerable tension, exacerbating the discontent with incomes that had characterized working-class attitudes during the 1970s. In a meeting of senior party members in the capital in 1981:

> 'Emil Péjak, a major figure in the workers'
> movement … really felt the terrible situation
> which existed in workers' circles … the party had
> to understand that people were increasingly
> dissatisfied … and felt that they just worked and

worked and never got anywhere, and they had no opportunities ...'[11]

Industrial prices were overhauled in 1980; the various exchange rates for the forint were brought more closely into line with world market rates; limited privatization was introduced into the retail sector; major decentralization of the management of enterprises was planned for 1985; and the country joined both the IMF and the World Bank in 1982.[12] In order to buy off worker discontent, the informal economy was institutionalized within state enterprises, with the introduction of the Enterprise Economic Work Partnership in 1982 – a kind of self-managed, private company, which functioned within state enterprises, usually guaranteeing substantial extra earnings to the skilled élite of the working class.[13]

While Hungary responded to its economic downturn and fiscal crisis by renewing economic reform, suspended in the early 1970s, both to improve economic performance and contain political discontent, other states responded by copying the Hungarian model. In 1982, Bulgaria introduced its New Economic Model, copying much of the decentralization of production decisions to enterprises that had been introduced in Hungary 14 years previously.[14] Economic reform, borrowed to some extent from Hungarian models, was implemented by the Jaruzelski regime in Poland, against a background of the consolidation of military rule. More serious, however, was the environment of economic collapse in the country that accompanied the political turmoil of 1980–1; the economy seriously contracted during 1981, with a 12.1 per cent fall in industrial production.[15] Under the cover of the wave of repression that followed the imposition of martial law, Jaruzelski launched a severe austerity package, drastically increasing retail prices and introducing, among other things, a 241 per cent hike in food prices in February 1982.[16] Austerity, combined with liberalization to legalize small-scale private business and to increase the independence of enterprises, succeeded in stabilizing the economy briefly.[17] Though stabilization and reform ended economic crisis, allowing the economy to bottom out during 1983 and grow in 1984, the foundations it established were far from secure. Indebtedness continued to weigh down the economy, with 1985 a year of economic failure.[18] While Polish austerity was harsh, the policies Yugoslavia pursued after the emergence of its severe fiscal crisis were more radical: food subsidies were scrapped, prices of basic consumer goods were increased, the dinar was sharply devalued, while enterprises were instructed to dismiss workers to balance their books. These draconian measures produced stagflation in 1983, as inflation rates rose radically in response to domestic price hikes and devaluation, while the economy contracted and living standards fell dramatically. Austerity in 1982–3 set the tone for the policies pursued during the rest of the decade.[19]

The most radical package of austerity measures was introduced in Romania. In 1981, Ceaușescu reacted to Romania's insolvency by deciding that foreign debt represented a threat to national sovereignty and setting its complete repayment as a central policy goal. Production was directed to export for hard currency in order to finance debt repayment. The structures of economic planning remained unreformed. Between 1982 and 1986, Romania's debt burden was halved, and by 1989 it was almost paid off, but this was done at the cost of isolating the economy completely from outside influence, and generating enormous social tension.[20] The mobilization of the country's resources for the state-led export drive was accompanied by restriction, reminiscent of Albania and the rest of the region during the early 1950s. The state placed considerable controls on private agriculture, restricting the slaughter of livestock and requisitioning agricultural produce. In order to increase the proportion of agricultural goods exported to pay off the debt, the rationing of basic foodstuffs was introduced with the onset of the financial crisis in 1981.[21] The search for food and goods in state shops increasingly resembled the pattern of the early 1950s, described in chapter 5, when endemic shortages dominated the daily lives of the population.[22] Throughout the 1980s, shortages of basic goods, ranging from sugar and cooking oil through to toilet paper, increasingly impinged on the dignity of ordinary Romanians.[23] In this environment, participation in the informal economy became a matter of survival. Given the scope of state restriction and repression, extended kin networks that united town and country were mobilized in order to ensure supplies of food from villages to urban relatives.[24] Added to these measures were the severe restrictions on energy use, which were progressively extended from 1979 onwards, culminating in crisis during the winter of

1984–5, when the homes of many urban Romanians went unheated. Energy consumption fell to one-fifth of its level five years previously, while the use of private cars was banned during the first three months of 1985.[25]

The spread of popular resentment was met with an increase in the scope of repression and an extension of the social role of the *Securitate*. The maintenance of Ceauşescu's cult of personality, discussed in chapter 7, ensured that discontent took a sharply politicized form, though due to the scope of repression it failed to generate organized opposition. The late 1980s demonstrated that privation, particularly in urban centres where the links of the population to rural relatives, and thus to the networks of the informal economy that acted as a safety valve, were non-existent, could lead to spectacular revolt. In Braşov, in 1987, workers at the Red Flag truck plant walked out on strike on the morning of local election day, in response to the attempts of management to impose cuts in wages for failure to make their production targets. Some 350 strikers were joined by another 3,000 people from neighbouring factories, who marched to party headquarters and to the city council buildings, which they stormed and set alight. Repression followed as the state security agencies crushed the uprising, which resulted in 74 demonstrators receiving prison sentences.[26] Though in 1987 protest was unsuccessful, it represented a warning sign to the regime, being strikingly reminiscent of the uprisings that doomed Ceauşescu's regime two years later.

Elsewhere, sporadic working-class protest also marked attacks on living standards. Yugoslavia's post-1983 austerity measures were very different from those in Romania, in that they drove forward a marketization of the economy and represented an attack on working-class living standards. In 1984, 70 per cent of the wages of the lowest paid workers were spent on food, while unemployment and increasing charges for basic services had begun to bite.[27] Continuing austerity and economic reform during the mid-1980s created a climate of deep-seated economic insecurity in the country.[28] By the end of the 1980s, the consensus between party and working class in Yugoslavia had all but collapsed, for while in the 1960s and 1970s the wildcat strike had been a tool within the context of shop-floor bargaining, as we saw in chapter 4, during the late 1980s, workers were 'better organized and ready to take their demands for a living wage and responsible government onto the streets'.[29] Yet workers were politically neutered by the collapse of that consensus, while the middle classes, as one of the bedrocks of the consumerist settlement of the 1960s, were under serious pressure as their incomes fell. Furthermore, political action addressed issues of nationality, while sections of the party, especially in Serbia, moved away from the politics of class towards the politics of nation in order to legitimate their continued rule. In Poland, working-class discontent remained considerable, though it was connected as much to underground resistance to the Jaruzelski regime as it was to explicit protest against austerity measures. Despite the initial wave of repression against *Solidarność* following the imposition of martial law, it continued to exist in underground form throughout the 1980s. In 1983, representatives of the opposition were able to claim that 'Solidarity is alive and cannot be destroyed. It is vigorous and well anchored in the factories'.[30] Yet working-class action suffered, to some extent, from the attempts of ordinary Poles to cope with shortages and the privations generated by economic collapse through the burgeoning informal economy, which, in turn, generated the spread of social privatization during the early 1980s.[31]

The role of working-class identity as a legitimating identity for the regimes and its slow eclipse, together with the spread of consumerism, informal economic activity and then economic crisis, which broke the bargains between regime and working class, contributed to an erosion of working-class identity. This was despite the existence of working-class protest, and represented an Eastern European version of the retreat of the working class visible in the Western half of the continent during the 1970s and 1980s. This was at its most apparent in Hungary, where the tolerated influence of the informal economy and consumerism remained strong during the 1980s. Austerity promoted a sharp de-legitimation of discourses of socialism and class, as workerist rhetoric lost all relevance to ordinary workers. This was observed by Western sociologist Michael Burawoy, who described the resentment of steel workers at participating in increasingly meaningless ideological rituals during the middle of the decade.[32] In the mid-1980s, workers in the industrial Budapest district of Csepel reacted to party references to its past as a cradle of the labour movement with the cynical refrain that 'the only thing that's "red" in Csepel today is the sunset, but even that is darkened by the smog'.[33] These specifically working-class responses formed part of a general de-legitimation of the institutions of the socialist public sphere that set in throughout the mid-1980s. In Hungary, institutions such as the monopoly trade unions lost members throughout the decade,[34] which was in turn underlined by events such as the 1985 multi-candidate parliamentary elections, in which some prominent officials of the regime lost their seats.[35] In Czechoslovakia, secret public opinion surveys, as early as 1986, revealed a widening gulf between party and population over the nature of the political system, underscoring the deep-seated illegitimacy of socialist rule, though this did not take public form prior to the outbreak of unofficial demonstrations on the 20th anniversary of Soviet intervention in August 1988.[36] In Bulgaria, many within the party became increasingly aware of a desire for radical change, as the regime of Todor Zhivkov seemed increasingly out of place in a region characterized by increasing reform.[37] Despite this, in contrast to other states in this region, widespread open political activism did not become marked until Zhivkov had fallen.[38]

Against this backdrop there was a marked increase in social and political activism outside the structures of the socialist public sphere during the second half of the 1980s. The older intellectual opposition of the 1970s, produced by reform and then the normalizing pressures of the early part of the decade, remained a thorn in the side of the regimes. It was joined by a new opposition, consisting of a new, younger generation. The 1980s produced a realignment in the concerns of the older opposition, varying from country to country, which occurred in response to events of regional significance like the Polish crisis of 1980–1, but also to domestic upheaval. The most exceptional course pursued by an intellectual opposition was the Yugoslav one, where, particularly in Serbia, it embraced nationalism, which it deployed to challenge the post-war Yugoslav settlement.

The gradual 'nationalization' of Serbia's intellectual opposition began at the end of the 1960s, when the writer Dobrica Ćosić publicly complained at the consequences of the decentralization of the Yugoslav state for Serbia. Protesting autonomy for Kosovo and Vojvodina, he had asked: 'Will the Sava and the Danube indeed be for our generation the border between Belgrade and Novi Sad,

Mačva and Srem, Banat and Danubia?', thus raising the issue of the 'survival' of the 'Serb nation'.[39] The turn towards nationalism spread during the 1970s, but gathered pace during the early 1980s, following Tito's death in 1980, when economic crisis combined with political upheaval in Kosovo. In March 1981, student demonstrations at the University of Priština ignited significant protests across Kosovo, which demanded that the territory be upgraded from the status of an autonomous province within Serbia to a full republic within the Yugoslav federation. The demonstrations were only suppressed by the use of extraordinary force by the state security services.[40] Far from triggering liberalization, the political upheavals of 1981 accelerated conflict between Serbs and Albanians within Yugoslavia over the future of Kosovo, as Serbian intellectuals proved determined to resist what they regarded as any further threat to the integrity of their republic. The gradual hegemony of nationalism among Serbian intellectuals was underscored in 1986, when formerly revisionist Marxist philosophers associated with the journal *Praxis*, discussed in chapter 6, signed a petition warning of 'genocide' against Kosovo's Serbs and protesting what it saw as the Serb authorities' 'gradual surrender of Kosovo and Metohija – to Albania: the unsigned capitulation which leads to a politics of national treason'.[41] While Croatia was not marked during the 1980s by similar nationalist intellectual mobilizations, in part because of the impact of the purges that had followed the suppression of the 'Croatian spring' in 1972, growing Serb intellectual nationalism met with a reaction in Slovenia, although this was tied to the new rather than the old opposition.[42]

The pattern of Yugoslav evolution was exceptional and was closely tied to the distinctive trajectory of the crisis of the country's socialism during the 1980s, which was marked by the growing political salience of nationalism. Elsewhere the declaration of martial law in Poland provided a context to which the old intellectual opposition of the 1970s had to respond, and thus provided an impetus for their realignment. Polish intellectuals joined and committed themselves to the development of an underground opposition in the aftermath of Jaruzelski's turn to martial law. Yet in a network of opposition groups, which included the remnants of *Solidarność*, religious and other civil organizations, intellectuals were only one of many voices; the crisis of 1980–1 and the experience of martial law broadened the opposition movement.[43] Czechoslovakia's intellectual and religious opposition continued to advocate the protection of human rights throughout the 1980s. They were joined by groups, like Revolutionary Action, which sought, with little success, to organize the working class in Czech lands.[44] Hungary's 'democratic opposition' responded to the rise of *Solidarność* with the publication of its own, illegal samizdat periodical, *Beszélő*, in 1981, but the imposition of martial law in Poland was met with a loss of direction. By the middle of the decade, as Hungary's crisis deepened, Budapest intellectuals began to find common cause with nationalist intellectuals, who had been courted previously by the regime. A joint meeting in the town of Monor, in 1985, briefly signalled a sense of common purpose among intellectuals of different political and cultural traditions to articulate demands for radical change.[45] Intellectual opposition in Romania and Bulgaria remained weak in comparison to that in the western-most states of the region.

In Poland, Hungary, Czechoslovakia and, to some extent, Slovenia, the political programmes of the old intellectual opposition evolved beyond their original concerns with the non-observance of human rights. Across the western part of the region, stimulated by the Polish example, first, of *Solidarność* and, then, the underground that arose in opposition to Jaruzelski, oppositional intellectuals became increasingly interested in promoting and defending forms of political and social activism, independent of the state and the formal public sphere. This enabled previously isolated intellectual oppositions in Hungary and Czechoslovakia to build links to other tendencies, among others, those interested in the nationality issues, such as Slovakia's Magyars, and the religious, who sought to practice beyond the eyes of the state. It also allowed them to forge links with a newer opposition of environmentalists, peace activists, youth organizations, feminists and activists for gay and lesbian rights. This allowed them to slowly construct an embryonic 'civil society', a concept from political theory, which denotes a public sphere whose independence is legally guaranteed. Increasingly, intellectuals became interested in securing such a sphere, which entailed their gradual conversion to political liberalism as the decade pro-gressed.[46] Together with this developed an intellectual challenge to the cold-war geopolitical divide in Europe, as oppositional intellectuals in the west of the region reacted against the influence of the Soviet Union and its brand of socialism. They began to explore the cultural and historical roots of their own societies that bound them to Western European states, resulting in the articulation of a concept of 'Central Europe'.[47] Outside the Soviet bloc, it had more local meanings to Slovenian intellectuals, for whom notions of Central Europe could be used to distance themselves from both socialism in Belgrade and increasingly strident Serb nationalism.[48]

Programmes organized around civil society and Central Europe allowed an old intellectual opposition to coalesce with a new opposition, based on young people, who were frustrated by the pervasive economic and political restrictions in the western states of the region during the 1980s, the sense of endemic economic and social decay, and their exclusion from the European mainstream, which they saw as represented by the capitalist West. In Czechoslovakia, when the young participated in opposition activity, they tended to be more militant than an older generation who had experienced the full force of Husák's normalization.[49] Youth militancy was combined with oppositional activity based on new and imaginative cultural forms of expressing dissent. This was particularly marked in Slovene social activism, which spread through the early 1980s, manifesting itself in the increasing popularity of punk music in youth culture in the Yugoslav republic. This evolved into explicitly political popular music, generated by groups like Laibach, who used the symbols of fascist and communist regimes to attack official Yugoslav socialist culture. Artists, like the collective *Neue Slowenische Kunst*, sought to emphasize Slovenia's links to Central Europe and provoke the leadership in Belgrade. Joined by gay and lesbian activism, a peace movement and environmentalists, Slovenia's alternative public sphere became increasingly political as the decade progressed.[50]

The alternative forms of social activism that so marked the activities of the new opposition in Slovenia were also visible elsewhere in the westernmost states of the region. Padraic Kenney has documented the range and variety of the Polish new opposition's activism in the city of Wrocław, over the course of the 1980s. Ranging from cultural activists who styled themselves as 'socialist surrealists', to teenagers who organized students in the city's schools against the socialist state, new opposition took a variety of forms that chipped away at the authority of the regime at the local level.[51] In Czechoslovakia, popular music was a battleground between the regime and the young, in a comparable way to the 1960s and 1970s; by the 1980s, punk, though largely forbidden by the authorities, had come to enjoy a large following.[52] In more liberal Hungary, a sizeable alternative music scene existed, augmented by fragmented environmental activism and a small peace movement, which gathered force.[53]

Growing opposition, together with economic decline, provided the background to the collapse, but it was the attempts of some, though not all, of the ruling parties of the region to seek new bases for their rule, in the context of the bankruptcy of the post-war East European settlement, that provided the collapse with its initial dynamic. Yugoslavia's rulers had to face a growing crisis, while after the elevation of Mikhail Gorbachev, in 1985, it became increasingly difficult for the leaders of Soviet-bloc states to avoid reshaping their social settlements. Hungary's MSZMP, shocked by its unexpected reverses in some constituencies in the 1985 parliamentary elections, and consisting of a younger, better educated membership, frustrated at the hold of an older generation on leadership, looked to political change during the late 1980s. With persisting economic problems in the country and Kádár beginning to ail, groupings within the party began to manoeuvre to secure the succession. Furthermore, reformers within the party leadership, most notably Imre Pozsgay, looked to recast the MSZMP's governing formula.[54] Pozsgay's solution was to base future socialist rule on an alliance with nationalist sections of the cultural and technical intelligentsia. Pozsgay responded to the growing unity of the opposition, which manifested itself in events like the Monor meeting, by encouraging nationalist intellectuals to found their own political organization, thus breaking the monopoly of the state and the socialist public sphere over political organization. This led to the foundation, in September 1987, of the Hungarian Democratic Foundation (*Magyar Demokrata Fórum* or MDF) on the initiative of the writer, Sándor Lezsák, in the small provincial town of Lakitelek.

Against the background of manoeuvring in the MSZMP over the succession to Kádár and persistent frustration in the country, the founding of the MDF opened the door to the creation of other organizations that defined themselves as in opposition to the

MSZMP during 1988. They were met with increasingly ineffective police harassment, which gradually abated as the crisis of socialist rule advanced. The 'democratic opposition' responded to the launch of the MDF with the creation of their own Network of Free Initiatives, which in November 1988 transformed itself into the Alliance of Free Democrats (*Szabad Demokráták Szövetsége* or SZDSZ). Free trade unions were founded in the universities during spring 1988, while a small group of students at Budapest's Karl Marx Economics' University challenged the official youth organization by forming their own anti-communist alternative, the Alliance of Young Democrats (*Fiatal Demokráták Szövetsége* or FIDESZ). New organizations emerged and older parties, like the Smallholders and Social Democrats, from the pre-socialist period, were refounded.[55]

A visibly ailing Kádár was removed from party leadership, after almost 32 years in office, at the MSZMP's party congress in May 1988, electing the prime minister, Károly Grósz, as his replacement. Grósz intended to promote reform only in so far as it renewed and strengthened socialist dictatorship; however, his position was weakened by the situation in the country and the advance of radical reformism within the party. His eventual successor as prime minister, Miklós Németh, pushed for an economic reform package that effectively implied the dismantling of the socialist economic system, in that he sought to overcome economic crisis through explicitly neo-liberal policies of deregulation and privatization. With Pozsgay's position within the leadership strengthened, he used his influence to force through measures of cultural and political democratization. The splits in the leadership of the MSZMP were replicated, as sections of the membership organized themselves into 'reform circles' to fight their corners within the party.[56]

As the party split from top to bottom, Imre Pozsgay broke the ultimate political taboo in January 1989, when he exposed the founding myth of the Kádár regime, that the events of 1956 constituted a 'counter-revolution'. By labelling 1956 a 'popular uprising' he shook the foundations of socialist rule, and in doing so he defined the regime, based on the suppression of the revolution, as illegitimate. Within a month, the party accepted the need to shift towards a multi-party system and, eventually, free elections. The growing opposition was able to bring 150,000 onto the streets of Budapest on 15 March 1989, the anniversary of the outbreak of the 1848 revolution. This militancy was accompanied by a sense of growing unity, as the diverse opposition cooperated in order to avert the use of divide-and-rule tactics by the party, forming an opposition round table and demanding that the party negotiate the political future of the country with them. The convening of a 'national round table' in June 1989, between the MSZMP, the remnants of the organizations that had formed the socialist public sphere and the opposition, to discuss a political transition to a multi-party democratic system marked a new stage, though by no means the end of Hungary's revolution.[57]

Hungary was not the only country where pressures within the ruling party interacted with opposition and growing discontent to produce change by the end of the decade. Yugoslavia was in a serious crisis by the mid-1980s. With the death of Tito in May 1980, the state had lost a figure of stature and authority, and it failed to find a replacement. The position of the leadership of the state was filled by a rotating collective presidency. The debt crisis brought austerity packages, imposed by the federal government in Belgrade, which resulted in high unemployment and declining real incomes. Increasingly, the republics began to assert their autonomy from the centre, as dominant national identities revived in each republic. The final act in the existence of Yugoslav socialism began with the capture of the leadership of the League of Communists, in both Serbia and Slovenia, by individuals and groups sympathetic to the national mobilizations under way in each republic.

As we saw above, during the 1980s, the issue of Kosovo, an autonomous province within the republic, provided the focus for increasingly broad, popular, nationalist mobilization in Serbia, which unified many of the divergent strands within the opposition.[58] Against this mobilization, the Serbian Communists, under Ivan Stambolić, adopted a politically ambiguous position, attempting to argue for revision to Yugoslavia's constitution in order to placate nationalism, while condemning the nationalist opposition. In 1985, Stambolić encapsulated this line in the statement that 'nationalist views and action must be beaten everywhere and at all times. We have realistically grasped this danger and have tried to examine its roots and causes'.[59] Stambolić's ally and protégé within the party, Slobodan Milošević, moved to use nationalism, rather than appease it, both to win power among the Serbian Communists and to generate a new basis of legitimacy for the regime in society, through shifting the party's stance to a national-communist one.

This began when Milošević was dispatched by Stambolić to Kosovo Polje, in April 1987, to meet Serbs who were furious at what they saw as their marginalization in a province they regarded as an integral part of Serbia. While Milošević conducted one meeting inside the local House of Culture, a violent demonstration of local Serbs degenerated into a fight with the police, forcing Milošević to leave his meeting to calm the crowd. After one demonstrator interrupted him to complain that the ethnically Albanian police had beaten him, Milošević replied, 'no one should dare to beat you again'.[60] The demonstration in Kosovo Polje represented a turning point, as Milošević turned to nationalism to advance his position. He became increasingly assertive, sidelining Stambolić, who resigned as Serbia's president in December 1987. Milošević moved quickly to extend his influence over the Serbian Communists, and used increasingly violent tactics to reverse forcibly the autonomy granted to Serbia's provinces in the 1970s. In October 1988, large demonstrations in Novi Sad forced out Vojvodina's government in an event that later came to be known as the 'yoghurt revolution', leaving the province firmly under Milošević's control. The government in the neighbouring republic of Montenegro followed two days later, while Kosovo was placed under the control of Belgrade in March 1989, when the province's assembly voted itself out of existence, threatened by the extraordinary presence of the Yugoslav army.

Slovenia's leadership moved towards a very different strategy of recasting its legitimacy, arguing first for autonomy and then for a degree of separation from Belgrade, after the elevation of Milan Kučan to head the republic's League of Communists in 1986. Slowly the new leadership began to accept the emergence of vibrant civil society in Slovenia, at the time when the ties that bound Yugoslavia were falling apart and Milošević's emergent nationalism placed the federation under increasing strain. In 1988, allegations in the Slovene press about corruption in the Yugoslav army provoked political crisis. The federal government retaliated by convening a military court to try those responsible, which found the defendants guilty after a trial which contravened local law. The crisis generated a broad popular movement, organized by human rights activists. The popular movement led directly to the foundation of political parties outside the framework of the League of Communists, and the latter's transformation into a democratic political party in its own right. Serb nationalist mobilization and direct threats to Slovenia's independence were made by Belgrade in 1989, after protest from Slovenes at Milošević's dismantling of Kosovo's autonomy. This acted as a catalyst for talks between Kučan and the opposition to pave the way for a transition to democracy.[61] Increasing fear of Milošević and the democratization of Slovenia affected other republics. In Croatia, parliament asserted its sovereignty, while new political parties formed during the first half of 1989, as cultural and political liberalization swept the republic.[62]

The other state where the party was forced to respond to a mounting challenge from below, prior to autumn 1989, was Poland, where the strength of opposition was at its greatest. Poland's martial law regime was characterized by the spread of a large underground opposition and attempts by the state to impose austerity on the Polish population. After the suspension of martial law and the Jaruzelski regime's attempts to consolidate its rule, the situation in the country remained deeply tense. Events like the murder of the popular pro-opposition priest, Father Jerzy Popiełuszko, in October 1984, contributed to this climate. The PZPR remained deeply split, while the economy continued to perform poorly. Jaruzelski turned towards reform, by granting a full amnesty to political prisoners in September 1986, and prepared a reform package to be put to the population in a two-question referendum in November 1987. As a result of low turnout, the two propositions – one on political, the other on economic reform – failed to gain the support of the required 50 per cent of the total electorate for the referendum to stand. Despite rejection at the ballot box, the government persevered with renewed austerity into 1988, raising prices, which was met by a strike wave in May and then a further outbreak of industrial disruption in August, as workers demanded compensation.[63]

Industrial unrest in August 1988 prompted the PZPR to inch towards negotiations with the opposition, including *Solidarność*. These culminated in the beginning of round-table negotiations between government and opposition in February 1989, which sat until April and set the ground rules for Poland's transition. While *Solidarność* was legalized, political transition was based on a compromise between the PZPR and the opposition. Jaruzelski remained president, but all the seats in the Senate and 35 per cent of the seats in the *Sejm*, the lower house of parliament, would be elected on a competitive, democratic basis. In the June 1989 elections, which took place over two rounds, opposition candidates standing for *Solidarność* won a landslide, with 65 per cent of the vote and 99 of the 100 Senate seats. In elections to the *Sejm*, they won all the 161 seats they contested. After protracted attempts to form a government, *Solidarność* demanded the position of prime minister. In August 1989, Tadeuz Mazowiecki emerged as the first non-communist head of government in over 40 years, leading a coalition government, which included PZPR nominees at the ministries of Interior and Defence.[64]

By summer 1989, it had become obvious that the political map of Europe would be redrawn as a result of the developing revolutions in Hungary, Poland and Yugoslavia, as well as statements from Moscow that the Soviet Union would not stand in the way of radical political developments in the countries within the Soviet sphere of influence. The summer also marked the beginning of a new phase in the unfolding crisis of socialist regimes. In May 1989, Hungary dismantled the guard posts and removed the barbed wire that had marked the country's border with Austria, which ended a process of liberalization that had seen the lifting of many restrictions on Hungarians travelling to the West, introduced in 1988. With the arrival of summer holidays in the German Democratic Republic, large numbers of East German citizens travelled to Hungary in order to use the relatively open border to escape to West Germany, despite the fact that the border was only legally open to Hungarians. The summer was marked by East German tourists illegally crossing Hungary's Austrian border, most dramatically underlined during the events of the Pan-European Picnic, when several hundred East Germans used the occasion of a demonstration by the Hungarian opposition on the border near Sopron to force their way into the West. As East Germans surrounded the West German embassy and congregated close to the road border in September, the Hungarian government opened its western border to them. The crisis ignited popular opposition in the German Democratic Republic itself, leading to the implosion of the socialist regime throughout the autumn, and, most dramatically, the opening of the land border of the state in Berlin in November 1989 – the fall of the Berlin wall – an event which later symbolized the political changes under way in the region during the second half of the year.[65]

As a consequence of the crisis of the GDR's regime, the revolutionary wave accelerated in countries like Hungary and Yugoslavia, while it spread to states like Bulgaria, Czechoslovakia and Romania, whose rulers were instinctively opposed to reform. The day after the opening of the GDR's western borders, on 10 November 1989, reformers within the Bulgarian party, organized by the foreign minister, Petûr Mladenov, ousted Todor Zhivkov from office, allowing Mladenov to become president.[66] The final years of Zhivkov's rule had been marked, not by reform, but by an increasingly assertive and extreme variant of national communism directed at the country's sizeable Turkish minority. In 1984, the regime had begun a policy of overt assimilation of ethnic Turks, demanding, among other things, that those who had names which were judged to be 'insufficiently Slavic' change them. These attempts led to violent demonstrations, culminating in large and violent protests in May 1989, which were met with repression and the pursuit of an effective expulsion policy, in which over 300,000 Turks left the country, stopped by Turkey closing the border in August 1989.[67] Despite this, intellectual opposition remained fragmented and small; its most significant movement, the environmentalist Eco-Glasnost, was formed only in October 1989, days before the change of leadership. Its ability to organize demonstrations, most notably when 5,000 took to the streets of Sofia on 3 November, showed dramatically that Bulgaria could not be insulated from the changes elsewhere in the region. This turmoil provided the background to the moves of party reformers against Zhivkov. With the fall of Zhivkov, opposition organizations snowballed, with the new parties coalescing into a broad anti-regime alliance, the Union of Democratic Forces (*Sayuz na Demokratichni Sili* or SDS), which demanded further changes. The dynamic of revolutionary change was one of pressure from below and liberalization from above, culminating in the abolition of the party's leading role and the opening of round-table talks with the opposition in January 1990.

The crisis of the GDR regime affected Czechoslovakia directly, despite the fact that Miloš Jakeš, who replaced Husák (who remained president) as secretary of the KSČ in December 1987, had set his face firmly against reform. The collapse of socialist regimes around them left many Czechoslovaks feeling that they were trapped in a state reluctant to move with the times. Mounting crisis was also driven by Czechoslovak youth's increasing restiveness; major demonstrations, with students at their centre, were held in Prague in August 1988, on the 20th anniversary of the Soviet intervention.[68] During autumn 1989, as regimes collapsed around them, Prague students became increasingly bold, while sections of the party leadership began to consider dialogue with the opposition as a way out of the mounting crisis. The dam broke when 15,000 students gathered for a demonstration in Prague, to mark the 50th anniversary of Hitler's suppression of student opposition to the German occupation and dismemberment of Czechoslovakia on 17 November 1989. The commemoration quickly turned into explicit political protest and violent confrontation with the police. The demonstrations ended in excessive violence as the police broke up the protest; the popular anger that violence had ignited was exacerbated by rumours of the killing of one student by the police.

Student protest quickly spread and was joined by Prague's actors, who began a strike in support of the students that spread quickly beyond the capital. During the weekend following 17 November, the capital was convulsed by protest, while the regime reacted to popular mobilization with mounting panic. Major demonstrations on 20 November in Prague, Ostrava, Brno and Bratislava demanded political change, while the Czech opposition organized itself, founding Civic Forum (*Občanske forum* or OF), which unified an older generation of the opposition, consisting, among others, of Charter 77 signatories like Václav Havel, along with younger activists. In Slovakia, the opposition formed a parallel organization, Public Against Violence (*Veřejnost Proti Násilí* or VPN). Over the course of the following week, the KSČ lost control of the country as it was convulsed by ever larger non-violent protests, as students and dissident intellectuals like Havel were joined by veterans of the Prague Spring, most notably Dubček, and by a large section of the population, including many from the industrial working class, frustrated at the stagnation and decay of the 1980s. The spread of revolution to the factories, the collapse of party control of the media and the unwillingness and inability of the party to resort to military force, provoked the resignation of the party leadership at the end of the week. The new secretary of the KSČ, Karel Urbánek, lacked authority and it was left to the prime minister, Ladislav Adamec, to conduct negotiations with the opposition. Negotiations over the composition of a new government became mired in disputes over its composition, as the KSČ attempted to cling to power and the OF transformed itself into a political party. Adamec, unwilling to concede power in coalition negotiations, resigned, and the task of forming a government that involved the OF and VPN fell to Slovak communist, Marian Čalfa. With a new government in place committed to a democratic transition, Husák left the stage, paving the way for Václav Havel, key mover behind Charter 77, to become president.

The wave of change left only one socialist dictatorship still firmly in place within the Soviet bloc by mid-December 1989. During the late 1980s, many within Romania's Communist Party and within the state grew increasingly frustrated with both the country's economic situation and Ceauşescu's increasingly bizarre cult of personality. Such murmurings rarely reached the public; one notable exception was in 1987, when disgraced former senior Communist, Ion Iliescu, called in an article in the party daily for an 'unhampered spreading and circulation of knowledge'.[69] Further-more, events like the demonstration in Braşov in 1987, discussed above, underlined the deep-seated discontent that existed in Romanian society, and, despite the state's repressive nature, the violent forms that change might take. Popular revolt started in the city of Timişoara, after the *Securitate* moved in to arrest and remove a troublesome Hungarian Protestant minister, László Tőkes, on 14 December 1989. In an unprecedented act of protest, members of his congregation defended their minister, initially surrounding his house. Soon protests began outside the local headquarters of the RCP, which were broken up by the army and security services, who, on the orders of Ceauşescu, fired on demonstrators. Events in Timişoara provoked two processes that together combined to produce revolution. Large sections of the army, together with elements within the RCP leadership, started to lay plans to remove Ceauşescu, while at the same time, the news of events in Timişoara provoked widespread popular revulsion, which paved the way for outright revolt. When Ceauşescu was shouted down at a mass rally in Bucharest on 21 December, which he himself had called, revolution broke out. Popular demonstrations were fired on by representatives of the *Securitate*. The regime lost control of the country as the army sided with the demonstrators, and the revolution rapidly spread beyond Bucharest to major provincial population centres. The following day, Ceauşescu fled the capital, only to be captured by the army, while a new organization, calling itself the National Salvation Front (*Frontul Salvárii Nationale* or FSN), headed by Iliescu, seized power. Heavy fighting followed between the army, alongside demonstrators, and the *Securitate*, until the new government executed Nicolae and Elena Ceauşescu on Christmas Day 1989, and broadcast the execution on television, thus ensuring the victory of Romania's violent revolution.

The events of the autumn had a radicalizing effect on the revolutions already under way elsewhere. In Hungary, they ended any chance that either the ruling party or Imre Pozsgay would emerge in real positions of power as a result of the revolutionary changes taking place in the country. In September, against the background of the opening of Hungary's western border to East Germans, an increasingly impotent MSZMP voted to reconstitute itself as the Hungarian Socialist Party (*Magyar Szocialista Párt* or MSZP), committed to a social democratic programme. As factions on both ultra-reformist and hardline wings of the MSZMP refused to join the new party, this reconstitution set in train a fragmentation of Hungary's left. In the same month, the national round table achieved partial agreement on arrangements for political transition, allowing Hungary to transform itself from a people's republic to a democratic republic on 23 October – the 33rd anniversary of the outbreak of the 1956 revolution. However, the disputed clauses in the agreement, including provisions for a directly elected president, which were believed to help Imre Pozsgay take the post, were the subject of a referendum, forced by a number of parties, led by the liberal and increasingly anti-communist SZDSZ. Held in November, on the weekend following Jakeš's resignation in Czechoslovakia, the SZDSZ and their allies emerged triumphant, effectively winning the case that Hungary should be a parliamentary and not a presidential republic, thus blocking Pozsgay's attempts to win for himself a key position in the new political system. The November referendum, and ensuing scandals over the bugging of opposition politicians' telephones by state security agencies, effectively destroyed the chances of the MSZP in the forthcoming elections, set for spring 1990. These events thus ensured that Hungary's transition would mark a clean break with socialist rule.

The acceleration of revolutionary pressure impacted upon Yugoslavia too, but there it was tied to the disintegration of the state as political leaderships sought to reconstruct their authority. While the transformation of the state in the post-revolutionary era represented a major challenge for all Eastern Europe states, as we shall see in the final chapter, in Yugoslavia it was tied to the dynamic of the collapse of the multinational south Slav state, as the leaders of its major republics came to emphasize nation-building at the turn of the 1990s. Political transition led inexorably to the outbreak of a series of interconnected civil wars that rumbled throughout the 1990s, on the territory of what would soon be the former Yugoslavia.

9 After socialism

It is too soon to say what the long-term significance of the revolutions of 1989 will be, as their consequences continue to unfold. Some commentators regarded them as representing 'the end of history',[1] a judgment that seems premature given the upheavals that have shaken the region and the world since. Others have spoken of a 'rebirth of history',[2] a phrase which conjures an image of change sweeping away an era that was static – an impression not ultimately compatible with the analysis presented in the preceding chapters of this book. On the basis of an analysis of the decade that separated the revolutions from the end of the century, some of the initial assessments that stressed the transformative role of 'civil society' and placed weight on the democratization of the political systems are in need of some qualification. While the events of 1989 triggered the end of socialism and thus drew a line under the region's post-war settlement, the construction of an alternative post-socialist order during the 1990s was an uneven, conflict-ridden process, which frustrated as many of the hopes of those who had supported the changes of 1989 as it realized.

By the mid-1990s, after Albania's collapse in 1992, all the states in the region had attempted to legitimate themselves through building institutions that enabled governments to be selected through competitive election, though the degrees to which different states resembled liberal democracies of the Western European kind varied widely. The transformation of socialist into post-socialist states proved to be a difficult process, unleashing some of the forces suppressed by the socialist, post-war settlement, and taking some of the tendencies visible during the period of collapse to their logical conclusions. Building post-socialist political orders was most

painful in the former Yugoslavia, where it resulted in the fragmentation and disappearance of the south Slav state. This in turn led to a
series of tragic and bloody conflicts, which shocked European
opinion and cast their shadow over the region for most of the 1990s.
While tension and political mobilizations around national identities
shaped the politics of other states in the region, and in the case of
Czechoslovakia led to its peaceful break-up, these did not have the
same tragic consequences as in the former Yugoslavia.

In the rest of the region, while some semblance of democracy
was established in all countries by the end of the decade, post-
socialism took directions not envisaged in 1989. The impetus to
build on the revolutions and cement a clear, long-term break with
socialist regimes was never fully realized, while vibrant civil societies
found it difficult to take root and transform social behaviour.
Continuing economic crisis and the response of post-socialist
governments, usually inspired by neo-liberal prescriptions of cuts in
subsidies, budget cuts and privatization, forced the region's full
integration into the capitalist world economy. Rather than generate
widespread prosperity, states found themselves on the periphery of
the European economy, as sharp differences opened up between
them, with states like Hungary, Poland and Slovenia able to attract
sizeable amounts of foreign capital, while others, like Romania and
Bulgaria, could not. While sections of the population benefited from
economic transformation – sections that, in states like Hungary,
could be substantial – everywhere, changes generated social
polarization, as sharp differences opened up between rich and poor.
Socialism's societies organized around productive labour dissolved,
as a new élite emerged, some of whose members had connections to
the old élite, while working-class and rural incomes declined as
unemployment and job insecurity spread.

The revolutions of 1989, outside Czechoslovakia, were
characterized by deep ambiguity in that ruling parties voluntarily
handed over power as the opposition mobilized. Except in the Czech
Republic and Slovakia, this enabled ruling parties that reconstituted
themselves as social democrats to argue that they were a legitimate
part of the post-socialist political system. Successor parties were
able to muster considerable popular support by the mid-1990s, as
many looked back to the relative material security of the 1960s and
1970s, given the harsh and uncertain economic climate.

Representatives of the opposition bitterly contested the legitimacy of these parties, ensuring that politics was characterized by growing polarization by the end of the decade. At the heart of this polarization lay a struggle over the meaning of the events of 1989, and whether parties that had conceded power through reform, however belatedly, had a right to claim a role in the post-socialist political system. Political polarization in many states, the continuing dissatisfaction with their material circumstances of large sections of the population and the aftershocks of conflict in the former Yugoslavia all posed different, but in some ways related, challenges to the post-socialist order at the end of the decade.

At the turn of 1990, the region turned from the task of overthrowing its old order to constructing a new one. It was in Yugoslavia where this led to bloody and tragic conflict that made this state exceptional within the region. As socialism collapsed from below in the republics, particularly Croatia, Serbia and Slovenia, the federal government attempted to impose its authority on the situation, through pursuing an economic stabilization package after nearly seven years of austerity and drift. These reforms were championed by Ante Marković, who took over the federal premiership in March 1989. Circumventing many of the labyrinthine structures of decision-making in post-Tito Yugoslavia, Marković pushed through his plan, which linked the dinar to the Deutschmark and brought the federal budget into balance in order to curb inflation, in the teeth of opposition from Milošević. The Serbian leader was able to use this to cement his alliance to those within the federal bureaucracy and the army who were concerned to defend as much of Yugoslav socialism and Yugoslavia as possible from imminent destruction. The creation of an alliance between Serbian nationalism and pro-Yugoslav sentiment within the state apparatus, with Milošević at its centre, was fundamental to the launching of war in Slovenia and, more crucially, in Croatia in 1991.

While Marković's stabilization package was fatally undermined by the Serbian regime in 1990, his attempt to reconstruct the authority of the federal state through the pursuit of explicitly neo-liberal policies occurred when many of the other institutions that bound Yugoslavia together were in a state of all but total collapse. The army, alarmed at the dynamic of collapse, urged the League of Communists to convene a congress in January 1990, in the belief that this would reverse, or at least slow, the country's outright disintegration. Instead the congress resulted in a split, based on a dispute between those, like Bosnia-Hercegovina, Croatia, Slovenia and Macedonia, that sought differing degrees of decentralization, and Serbia and Montenegro, which argued for continued centralization.[3] While the fiasco of the 1990 congress drove the army further into the arms of Milošević, it also strengthened the dynamic of break-up. Slovenia held its first post-socialist elections in April 1990; Kučan successfully reconfigured the base of his power, being elected president. However, his allies did not emerge as the victors in the parliamentary election held on the same day, as a coalition of opposition parties won a clear majority and began to lay plans for eventual independence.[4] Croatia, initially a latecomer in the process of democratization among Yugoslav republics, was not far behind. In December 1989, the republic's League of Communists elected Ivica Račan as their leader; he transformed the party and called multi-party elections for the following year. When elections were held in April 1990, the nationalist Croatian Democratic Union (*Hrvatska Demokratska Zajednica* or HDZ), which had only been founded in 1989, triumphed. It benefited from its good organization, its ability to mobilize the financial resources of the global Croatian diaspora, the charisma of its leader, Franjo Tudjman, and its ability to cast itself as the defender of Croatian national identity and sovereignty in a climate of growing inter-republican tension within Yugoslavia.[5]

While Slovenia was relatively ethnically homogeneous and, therefore, its moves for independence were never seriously contested inside the republic, Croatia was an entirely different proposition. In the 1991 census, 12.2 per cent of Croatia's population identified themselves as ethnically Serb.[6] Among this minority there were many who feared Tudjman's nationalism and the republic's drive toward independence, in part because of the value they placed on living in a common state with other Serbs, but also due to the memory of the Ustaša genocide, between 1941 and 1945, which had marred Croatia's previous experience of independent statehood. The rise of the HDZ was met by political mobilization among the Serb minority. While many had voted in April 1990 for Račan's former communists, in order to stop Tudjman, after the elections many turned to the small nationalist Serbian Democratic Party (*Srpska Demokratska Stranka* or SDS), founded in 1990. The aggressive nationalism of the new government in Zagreb, and its new constitution, which replaced earlier references to the republic as 'the national state of the Croatian nation and the state of the Serbian nation in Croatia', with a statement that the new Croatia was a national state for Croats alone, provoked Serbian outrage.[7] This was exacerbated, in turn, by Tudjman's decision to reorganize the police, in which Croatia's Serbs were over-represented, which provoked open revolt, centred on the town of Knin. Yet in the face of ethnic tension, Tudjman pushed ahead with plans for independence, procuring arms abroad to defend Croatia against any threat from Belgrade.

Milošević, meanwhile, had reconstituted Serbia's Communists as the Serbian Socialist Party (*Socijalisticka Partija Srbije* or SPS), as the opposition in the republic organized itself into political parties, in response to the revolutions under way elsewhere and the collapse of the League of Communists in 1990. He cemented his power in a new multi-party political system, winning a landslide victory in presidential and parliamentary elections in December 1990. Serbia's opposition responded by unifying against Milošević, taking their campaign against him to the streets in March 1991, only to fragment into impotent disunity when faced with repression and internal fragmentation between nationalists and liberals, as the Serbian president again deployed nationalism, threatening Croatia with support for its internal Serb revolt if the Tudjman government pressed ahead with its plans for independence.[8] At the same time, Milošević aligned himself with sections of the Yugoslav army leadership, determined to resist the destruction of the state, while simultaneously encouraging the formation of nationalist paramilitary groups inside Serbia, and moved to organize Serb minorities in Bosnia in the event that drives for independence should spread beyond Croatia and Slovenia.

Slovenia's and Croatia's eventual secessions were both greeted with military intervention when they occurred in June 1991. In Slovenia, where the Yugoslav army intervened directly to prevent the republic from declaring independence, resistance was swift and well organized, while international opinion was able to force the army into withdrawal in exchange for the face-saving concession that Slovenia would suspend its independence for three months. Croatia's secession occurred against the background of increasing violence between Croats and Serbs in the republic, sparked by fighting, after leaders of the growing Serb rebellion against the Tudjman government set up the Serbian Autonomous Region of the Krajina, declaring independence from Croatia and voting to remain part of Yugoslavia, as the rest of the republic voted for statehood in May 1991. As the Yugoslav army moved to defend the unity of the Yugoslav state, through the 'intensive organization and preparation of Serbian rebels in Croatia ... to defeat the Croatian army',[9] it began, paradoxically, to reinforce the logic of Yugoslavia's destruction. Violence spread quickly from beyond the Krajina to eastern Slavonia, as Serbian paramilitaries, organized by Belgrade, made their first appearance in the theatre of conflict. As Croatia declared its independence, local Serb rebels and Serb nationalist militias were joined by the Yugoslav army, which sided with the Serb insurgents. They pressed forward with a programme of using war to create ethnically pure Serbian regions that could be joined to Belgrade. For those in the army, this represented the abandonment of any meaningful notion of defending a vision of Yugoslavia as anything other than a greater Serb state. The war in Croatia, which raged for the second half of 1991, was a bloody and brutal affair. The Slavonian city of Vukovar was subjected to a bloody siege, in which the town was flattened and starved into submission, and Dubrovnik, on the Adriatic coast, was shelled. The war was accompanied by atrocities against civilians that were reminiscent of the brutality of the Second World War in the region, as Serb paramilitaries introduced a reign of terror against populations that stood in their way. Furthermore, in an attack on the Slavonian village of Ćelje in July 1991, Serb insurgents forcibly expelled the local Croatian population, setting the village alight. This heralded what would later be euphemistically termed 'ethnic cleansing', as Serb insurgents forced Croatian populations out of homes in the territories they intended to conquer and incorporate into their greater Serbia.

The 1991 war, in which Croatia lost one-third of its pre-war territory, ended in January 1992, with a ceasefire and recognition of the new state by the European Community. It sealed the fate of Yugoslavia, hastening the centrifugal tendencies which were pulling the state apart, as Macedonia declared its independence in November 1991. Macedonia, despite a multi-ethnic population and a furious campaign against it waged by Greece, which believed the existence of the independent republic represented a threat to its sovereignty, managed a relatively peaceful transition to statehood.[10] The same could not be said of Bosnia-Hercegovina, plunged into a conflict in April 1992 of even more tragic proportions than that experienced by Croatia. Bosnia-Hercegovina was a multi-ethnic society with no hegemonic nationality; the Bošniaks – those defined as Muslim by nationality – represented 44 per cent of the population in 1991, with Serbs accounting for another 31 per cent and Croats making up a further 17 per cent.[11] Democratization began in early 1990, after the collapse of the League of Communists, with Bosnia's local party legalizing opposition parties provided that they were not based on principles of ethnic exclusivity. Once the republic's constitutional court ruled this provision illegal,[12] in the face of escalating ethnic tension as Yugoslavia disintegrated, ethnic identities within Bosnia formed the basis of political mobilization, as the republic's civil society fractured. The extent of this was revealed in the December 1990 elections, which were won by the Party of Democratic Action (*Stranka Demokratse Akcije* or SDA), which represented Bosnia's Muslims and was led by their most prominent dissident, Alija Izetbegović, jailed in 1983 on trumped-up charges connected with his advocacy of the development of a Muslim identity in Bosnia. Nationalist parties won by far the most votes among the republic's other ethnic groups; the Serbian Democratic Party, or SDS, led by Radovan Karadžić, polled most votes among Serbs, while the Bosnian wing of Tudjman's HDZ won among Croats in Hercegovina.[13]

During 1991, the mounting Serb rebellion in Croatia affected Bosnia as the creation of the Serbian Autonomous Region of the Krajina led members of the Bosnian SDS to advocate the creation of similar autonomous regions within areas of Bosnia, where the Serbs constituted a majority. With Milošević's move to a policy of reconstituting Yugoslavia as a greater Serb state in the first half of 1991, Belgrade, with the cooperation of the Yugoslav army, began to arm Karadžić and the Bosnian Serbs, in order to create the autonomous Serb territories necessary to realize this aim. After war was launched in Croatia in June, Serb autonomous regions were formed in Bosnia with the protection of the Yugoslav army, while Karadžić withdrew from the republic's parliament in Sarajevo in October 1991, in order to lay the foundations for a unified Bosnian Serb state. This, in turn, provoked the government in Sarajevo to seek independence from Yugoslavia, calling a referendum over two days in February and March 1992. Despite the organization of a boycott by Karadžić and the Bosnian Serbs, the referendum resulted in an endorsement of independence, which led to a further escalation of tension in the republic. Violence spread throughout the republic during March, as armed Bosnian Serbs, supported by units of the Yugoslav army and the Serb nationalist paramilitaries that had been active in Croatia the previous autumn, consolidated their hold over parts of the republic.

The Bosnian Serbs responded to the European Community's recognition of Bosnia-Hercegovina's independence, on 6 April 1992, by launching an all-out war, signalled by Bosnian Serb gunmen firing from Sarajevo's Holiday Inn on a peace demonstration assembled outside. This precipitated the siege of Sarajevo, which lasted for well over three years. It also launched open war in the rest of Bosnia-Hercegovina, as Karadžić's Bosnian Serb forces, commanded by the former Yugoslav army officer, Ratko Mladić, moved to create a viable Bosnian Serb state that could serve as a bridge between the Krajina and Serbia proper, by unifying areas of western Bosnia adjacent to the Krajina with those in the east of the country that bordered on Serbia. This was achieved by tactics of ethnic cleansing, accompanied by rape, murder and internment, that had been introduced in Croatia in late 1991. In Bosnia they were deployed on a far greater scale, as the Bosnian Serb forces, in cooperation with paramilitaries from Serbia proper, removed Bošniaks and Croats from the villages of the regions they intended to conquer. Many of their aims had been achieved in rural areas by the end of 1992; however, urban centres like Srebrenica, Goražde and the capital, Sarajevo, proved much more difficult to overcome, setting the stage for an increasingly bloody stalemate over the two and a half years that followed. Sarajevo, in particular, swelled by an influx of Bošniak refugees from the rest of the country, resisted, bolstered by international humanitarian aid and black-market trade throughout the war. Meanwhile, Croatian forces, with the tacit support of Zagreb, began to pursue the consolidation of Croatian-dominated territories in Hercegovina, launching their own offensives, which, in some cities, like Mostar, degenerated into three-way battles over centres of population.

The costs of financing the Serb Autonomous Regions in Croatia and the bloody stalemate in Bosnia-Hercegovina were borne by Belgrade, as hyperinflation rocketed and the economy descended into crisis, exacerbated by an increasingly leaky regime of international sanctions. As the domestic situation worsened, Milošević sought a way out of the crisis by engaging with ineffective attempts by the Western powers to secure a peace deal. As a consequence, Milošević abandoned ultra-nationalist allies, like Vojislav Šešelj, inside Serbia, while splits increasingly opened up between Belgrade and its Bosnian and Croatian clients.[14] By 1995, despite an international arms embargo, Zagreb had managed to strengthen its armed forces and had increased its diplomatic leverage with the West, by pressuring Croats in Bosnia to end their own grab for territory and form a political union with the Bošniaks. In May, it used its position to overrun western Slavonia, beginning the violent reverse of the Serbs' victory in the war of 1991.[15] The same month saw increasing Western intervention in Bosnia, with NATO using air strikes against those bombarding Sarajevo, resulting in the Bosnian Serbs taking UN personnel hostage. The growing will of Western powers to resolve the situation in Bosnia was strengthened by the fall of the Bošniak enclave of Srebrenica to Bosnian Serb forces in July, which resulted in Serb retribution against the civilian population, including the massacre of around 4,000 of the city's male residents.[16] It was the growing spectre of military defeat that forced Serbs to the negotiating table. Croatia's successful invasion of the Krajina in August 1995 underlined this, severely weakening the Serbs in western Bosnia. With Milošević increasingly desperate to settle a conflict that threatened his own position, and with signs that diplomatic failure would bring outright Western military intervention, the parties agreed to a constitutional settlement for Bosnia-Hercegovina that enshrined the territorial integrity of the republic, while granting the Serbs autonomy, signed at Dayton in the United States in November 1995.

If the bloody wars that shook the former Yugoslavia seemed to confirm pessimistic diagnoses about post-socialist Eastern Europe becoming a region characterized by instability, ethnic nationalism and a revival of ghosts supposedly laid to rest at the end of the Second World War, the rest of the region, to some extent, confounded them. In most of the region, elections between 1990 and 1992, of varying degrees of fairness and with diverse outcomes, marked the end of the revolutionary upheavals of the late 1980s and early 1990s. While the Yugoslav tragedy was replicated nowhere else, some of the tendencies that had marked Yugoslavia's descent were visible elsewhere. As we saw in chapters 2 and 6, the region's post-war political and social settlements had rested on particular constellations of ethnic and national identities within and between states. Indeed, Yugoslavia's wars were caused fundamentally by the unravelling of a flexible settlement first developed in 1946 and revised throughout the socialist regime's existence. Occasionally, clashes based on issues of national identity erupted into violence, though outside Yugoslavia inter-communal violence was exceptional, occurring only in areas of ethnic tension. In Transylvania, where Romanian nation-building had been promoted by the Ceauşescu regime, democratization produced mobilization around issues of nationality, both Magyar and Romanian. Political conflict promoted by this pattern of democratization spilled over into several days of riots in the city of Tirgu Mureş in March 1990, when representatives of a Romanian nationalist group lay siege to the offices of the political party of the region's Magyars.[17]

Despite the persistence of considerable ethnic tension in Transylvania throughout the 1990s, the region remained largely peaceful. Furthermore, the only change in state boundaries stimulated by the unmaking of the post-war political settlement outside Yugoslavia was achieved entirely without bloodshed. Despite its existence between 1918 and 1992, Czechoslovakia was founded on an uneasy union between the Czech lands and Slovakia, as we saw in chapter 1. Even after its reincorporation into Czechoslovakia after the Second World War, Slovakia's political culture differed radically from that of the Czech lands, while liberalization in Bratislava during the 1960s, as discussed in chapter 6, generated demands for recognition of the distinctiveness of Slovakia's national culture. The split between the two component parts of Czechoslovakia emerged rapidly after the revolution, as political representatives, elected in Slovakia during Czechoslovakia's first post-socialist parliamentary elections in June 1990, demanded greater recognition of Slovak national identity within the state.[18] While OF had won the elections in the Czech lands, VPN emerged triumphant in Slovakia. There were deep-seated differences between the two organizations, which emerged over the issue of economic reform during 1991 and 1992, but which reflected marked differences between the two components of the state. These intensified as the two umbrella organizations fragmented, with OF splitting between social and economic liberals, with the latter forming the centre-right Civic Democratic Party (*Občanská demokratická strana* or ODS) around the Czechoslovak finance minister, Václav Klaus. In Slovakia, the prime minister, Vladimír Mečiar, split VPN, forming the Movement for a Democratic Slovakia (*Hnutie za Demokratické Slovensko* or HZDS). While Mečiar was removed as prime minister of Slovakia, he continued to be a powerful political figure, as early elections, necessitated by the break-up of the revolutionary movements in both parts of the country, drew near.

The elections held in June 1992 revealed the depth of division between the Czech lands and Slovakia, as Klaus and the ODS advocated neo-liberalism in order to transform the economy, while Mečiar called for statist solutions to the country's economic ills. The ODS polled 33.9 per cent in the Czech lands, while the HZDS topped the poll with 33.53 per cent in Slovakia.[19] With no viable coalition possible and the two parts of the country moving in diametrically opposed directions, Klaus and Mečiar dissolved the federation, with the Czech Republic and Slovakia becoming independent states on 1 January 1993. While the Czech Republic moved towards a relatively stable political system, with Klaus remaining prime minister until his final exit from office in 1997, Slovakia developed a political system dominated by the powerful personality of Mečiar, who governed, with the exception of a brief pause in 1994, when he was ousted by his coalition partners and a split in his own party, until 1998. Mečiar's regime, particularly following its reconstitution after his success in the October 1994 elections, was characterized by policies of authoritarian nation-building, punctuated by bouts of undemocratic behaviour directed at political opponents. Nation-building was underlined by the making of Slovak the sole official language of state in 1995, and moves in the same year to make the instruction of Slovak compulsory in schools attended by the Magyar minority.[20]

Slovak nationalism could not but surface as one of the central legitimating planks of the new regime in Bratislava, based as it was on the restoration of a Slovak sovereign state that had only previously existed under the sponsorship of Berlin between 1939 and 1944. Yet Mečiar's authoritarian behaviour polarized opinion and paved the way for his removal in the 1998 elections. In wartime and post-war Croatia, Franjo Tudjman's regime cast itself as the only authentic representative of the nation. Drawing on national identities suppressed during the years of Tito's Yugoslavia, Franjo Tudjman proclaimed that the aim of his regime was to realize the 'thousand-year-old dream' of Croatian statehood.[21] Nationalism was used, as in Slovakia, as a cover for authoritarianism, a phenomenon intensified by the tension generated by the civil wars after 1991. It was also strengthened by the widespread perception that Croatia had emerged the winner of war in 1995, which was taken by the Tudjman government as a vindication, further encouraging it to cast itself as the sole authentic representative of the nation. Yet by the end of the 1990s, opposition victories in local elections in major cities reflected growing disquiet among urban Croats with the authoritarian policies of Tudjman.[22] It was not only in new states, like Croatia and Slovakia, where national identities proscribed under socialism were used by governments to legitimate their rule. In Hungary, the first post-socialist elections, held over two rounds in March and April 1990, resulted in a victory for a three-party centre-right coalition government led by the MDF, which had transformed itself from its origins as a grouping of nationalist intellectuals into a mainstream conservative political party. The new prime minister, József Antall, drew on the political saliency of the memory of the Treaty of Trianon, and the related issue of the situation of Magyar minorities living beyond the country's borders, to declare that he wished to be the prime minister of 'fifteen million Hungarians', and not only the ten million inhabitants of Hungary.

While anti-communist political leaders like Antall and Tudjman used previously oppositional national identities to legitimate their rule, there were others, who came from the ranks of the leaders of the outgoing regimes, who used nationalism to legitimate their rule, as Milošević had done in Serbia. During the initial phases of Romania's post-revolutionary regime, the country's president, Ion Iliescu, and others within his government were not averse to reviving elements of Ceaușescu's national communism in order to deflect attacks from an insurgent opposition. His regime sought to build its legitimacy on the deployment of national symbols, while attacks that questioned the loyalty of members of certain ethnic minorities to the Romanian state were used to rally support against forces that argued for greater democracy. Unlike Milošević, however, Iliescu was not prepared to take the manipulation of nationalism to its logical conclusion, and as his presidency matured, his deployment of it became less strident.[23] It was also in Romania, perhaps due to the effect of Ceauşescu's national communism on the ruling élite of the socialist era, where actors from that era attempted to enter the stage as political players, deploying nationalist ideologies, perhaps to the greatest extent outside the former Yugoslavia. Sections of the security services, the army and the government in Bucharest during the early 1990s gave considerable material assistance to ultra-nationalist organizations and parties, as part of a campaign to ward off democratic challenge. It was in multi-ethnic Transylvania, where ethnic tension translated into support for ultra-nationalist parties, where they performed most creditably. Their crowning moment came in 1992, with the election of ultra-nationalist Gheorge Funar as Mayor of Cluj, Transylvania's capital.[24] Yet while ultra-nationalism formed an important element within post-socialist Romanian political culture for the whole of the decade, it failed to enter the political mainstream after 1992. Bound to the Iliescu government between 1992 and 1996, it was then isolated after the victory of the anti-socialist opposition in 1996, to be sidelined by Iliescu following his re-election in 2000. Extreme right-wing activity elsewhere, embodied in organizations like Hungary's Hungarian Justice and Life Party (*Magyar Igazság és Élet Pártja* or MIÉP), had some influence on the political system, but its impact was limited. In the three parliamentary elections since its foundation in 1993, MIÉP only once gained sufficient support to enter parliament, in 1998, and then barely surmounted the 5 per cent hurdle for entry.

While in much of the former Yugoslavia, the politics of nationalism overwhelmed pressures for democratization and the politics of anti-socialism, in the rest of the region, precisely the reverse occurred. National identities and their deployment by political actors continued to be important to rulers, though in different ways to those prior to 1989. The pressures for greater anti-socialist democratization released in the late 1980s proved more decisive in shaping post-socialist states. This was particularly the case where the events of 1989 had led to a partial survival of forces associated with the socialist regime, even if they had survived only in the context of compromises with the opposition, as in Poland, or in reconstituted form, as in Bulgaria and Romania. In Bulgaria, the Communists reconstituted themselves as the Bulgarian Socialist Party (*Bulgarska Sotsialisticheska Partiya* or BSP), to face the challenge from an opposition that had united, as we saw in chapter 8, as the SDS in late 1989. The BSP won the first free election in 1990, taking 47.15 per cent to the 36.2 per cent polled by the SDS; the new BSP government, however, was weak, while the SDS refused to lend its support. This situation generated political polarization between government and opposition, characterized by revelations about Mladenov's support for the armed suppression of opposition demonstrations the previous autumn. This forced the BSP to concede the presidency to the SDS candidate, former dissident, Zheliu Zhelev. Mounting economic crisis and spreading popular protest forced the BSP to relinquish control to a broad coalition government, while new elections in October 1991 led to a narrow victory for the UDF, able to form a coalition government in partnership with the party of the country's Turkish minority.[25]

If the continuing dynamic of revolutionary change into the post-socialist era accelerated political change in Bulgaria, the spread of the revolutionary wave to Albania, after 1989, marked its own political transition. In view of Albania's isolation under Enver Hoxha, who died in 1985, to be replaced with Ramiz Alija, the country's late response to transformation elsewhere was unsurprising. The first opposition party, the Democratic Party, was founded in December 1990, as demonstrations spread across the country, demanding an end to socialist rule. Elections, called in the previous year, prior to the development of opposition, were held in March 1991, and resulted in victory for Alija's Party of Labour. Yet, as in Bulgaria, demonstrations continued, demanding political change, eventually leading Alija to concede rule through coalition between the two main parties, and then, in March 1992, elections, which the Democratic Party won convincingly.[26]

With the collapse of socialism elsewhere in the region, Poland's historic compromise between regime and opposition, which had sealed the country's political transition in 1989, looked outmoded a year later. Lech Wałęsa, using his position at the head of *Solidarność*'s trade union arm, launched calls for Jaruzelski's resignation in April 1990, arguing for the need to complete Poland's political transition. The run-up to the presidential election in November represented the end of the period of transitional compromise and also of *Solidarność* as a unified political actor, as it split into factions, one supporting Wałęsa's candidacy and the other supporting that of Prime Minister Mazowiecki. Wałęsa was easily elected, with Mazowiecki taking third position in the second round of polls, with an unknown *émigré* businessman, Stanisław Tymiński, claiming second place. A new government came to office, while the 1989 parliament continued until the fragmentation of *Solidarność* eventually made new elections unavoidable, which, in turn, resulted in a highly fragmented legislature, presided over by a series of shifting coalition governments.[27]

In Romania, however, initial pressures from the opposition for further change after the initial period of revolutionary transition were frustrated, at least prior to the eventual victory of the opposition in the 1996 elections. The FSN, which came to power as a result of the 1989 revolution, was able to cast itself as the defender of the goals of the revolution and mobilize rural support with a redistribution of some agricultural land to peasants. This allowed it to win a convincing victory, with 66.31 per cent of the votes in elections in May 1990, though the elections were marred by allegations of fraud and other irregularities.[28] Amid mounting economic crisis, the Iliescu government was shaken by growing challenges mounted by the opposition on the streets, similar in nature to those experienced in Bulgaria, following the elections. Iliescu was able to use his majority in parliament, showing both a willingness to use repressive methods against opposition demonstrations and an ability to manipulate national sentiment to divide a fragmented opposition, in order to overcome the crisis. When the FSN split in March 1992, Iliescu's faction, which was eventually to be renamed the Social Democratic Party of Romania (*Partidul Democraţiei Sociale din România* or PDSR), was able to achieve a plurality of the vote in September 1992, and ruled in cooperation with ultra-nationalist parties until its defeat in 1996.[29]

Even in Romania, where former communists had managed more successfully than anywhere else in the region to reconstitute their hold on power after the revolutionary wave, the legacy of the revolution was bitterly contested. Those who participated placed pressure on the Romanian state for the actions of the security services in December 1989 to be investigated, and those found guilty of crimes to be bought to trial, though they would have to wait until Iliescu was defeated by Emil Constantinescu in the 1996 elections for these demands to be heard.[30] Demands for 'historical justice', however, were not only heard in states like Romania, where the eventual political outcome of the 1989 revolutions had been ambiguous, but were articulated across the region. Organizations of political prisoners or the formerly persecuted demanded that the state not only investigate the crimes of employees of the state security agencies against them and their families, but that the perpetrators, and those politically responsible for their actions, be brought to justice. Such mobilizations also created demands, partially met in acts of parliament, like Hungary's 'agents' law', passed in 1994 and implemented during the late 1990s, that those implicated in the activities of the socialist-era state security agencies, be barred from public office or have to face full public disclosure of what they had done. Measures to institute historical justice, in order to emphasize that post-socialist states had broken with the practice of their socialist predecessors, went furthest in Czechoslovakia prior to its break-up. The so-called 'lustration act', passed in October 1991, gave the Interior Ministry the power to dismiss or demote those determined to have worked for the state security services of the socialist regime. The measure was unevenly applied and partially reversed by Czechoslovakia's successor states, but nevertheless was far more radical than anything attempted elsewhere.[31]

Post-socialist states distanced themselves from their socialist predecessors not only through limited and uneven policies of retribution, but also through processes of restitution and compensation. Anti-socialist parties, particularly those that claimed to represent an agrarian population dispossessed by collectivization, like Hungary's resurrected Smallholders, placed property restitution at the heart of their political programme in 1989 and 1990.[32] Generalized restitution was introduced by states like Czechoslovakia, which, prior to its collapse in June 1991, ensured that political prisoners would be rehabilitated and given entitlements to compensation.[33] Policies of restitution played central roles in policies of the distribution and privatization of state property, as well as bolstering the anti-socialist credentials of the early post-socialist states of the region. They had the greatest effect in agriculture, where they spearheaded a process of generalized post-socialist land reform that differed in its radicalism and its extent across the region. It also merged with the generalized conflict over the reshaping of property rights that the reintroduction of the region into the capitalist world market after socialism entailed, provoking both support and opposition.[34]

The remaking of property relations formed a plank in a process that led to the integration of the region into the global capitalist market during the 1990s. Oppositions and reformist groups within the ruling parties had invested in a 'market utopianism' by the end of the 1980s, through which the introduction of market mechanisms was advocated as a generalized solution to the 'failures' of socialist economies.[35] Furthermore, Western Europe's relative prosperity seemed to add weight to popular sentiment that the development of capitalism would lead to the evolution of fully-fledged, Western-style consumer societies in the region. Finally, the discovery of political liberalism by large sections of the opposition assisted those seeking to import into Eastern Europe the neo-liberal policy prescriptions implemented by Western leaders, like the United Kingdom's Margaret Thatcher. This strengthened international organizations, like the IMF, which sought the implementation of packages of economic stabilization in the region as part of the solution to its economic ills. Poland's 1990 stabilization package, termed 'shock therapy' by many commentators, freed prices, slashed state subsidies, made the currency convertible, cut state spending and held down wages.[36] While most other new governments in the region balked at such radical policies, given the likely social and political consequences, all were to some extent forced to adopt neo-liberal strategies of transformation by the mid-1990s. In part, this was because all inherited crisis-ridden economies, as a consequence of the economic decay and collapse of socialism that had unfolded since the late 1970s, and required Western financial assistance, which in turn forced them to pursue neo-liberal policies. It was also driven forward by the unfolding dynamic of post-socialist economic collapse.

Inherited economic difficulties and mounting political turmoil led to further budgetary restrictions, exacerbated by the collapse of trade within the economic space shared by the Soviet Union and

Eastern Europe, which was brought on by revolution and then by the Soviet Union's own terminal crisis in 1991. Added to this was deepening recession in Western Europe during the early 1990s, which exacerbated the problems that bedevilled the region during its transformation. The early 1990s saw dramatic falls in the gross domestic product of countries right across the region; in 1991, Hungary's GDP fell by 21.5 per cent, Czechoslovakia's by 24.7 per cent and Poland's by 11.9 per cent.[37] Further east, Romania's GDP fell by 12.9 per cent in same year,[38] while Bulgaria's was reduced by 11.7 per cent.[39] Economic contraction generated increasing social strain, which combined with persistent budget deficits as state revenues fell, and the economies of the region stagnated during the mid-1990s, producing fiscal crises which post-socialist states were forced to address. Hungary's March 1995 austerity package, associated with the socialist finance minister, Lajos Bokros, which imposed deep cuts in social welfare budgets, was forced on the country by a currency crisis, generated by the state's persistent fiscal difficulties.[40]

The politics of stabilization through monetary and budgetary restriction were combined with measures that opened up the region's economies to multinational capital and launched policies of privatization to transform the Eastern European economy. While policies of privatization were associated with the influx of multinational capital into the region's economies, privatization was intended by many post-socialist governments as an instrument of economic and social policy. While private ownership, it was believed, would transform moribund, bureaucratically run state enterprises, it was also intended as a tool of post-socialist social engineering, leading to the creation of a class of domestic capitalists. With this in mind, early post-socialist governments pursued a bewildering array of privatization strategies, which ranged from the sale of businesses to foreign multinationals to policies of restitution. Some states, particularly Poland and Hungary, designed privatiza-tion policies to encourage foreign direct investment in the country, despite controversy provoked by many on the political right, who argued against foreign ownership. Other governments, like that of Czechoslovakia prior to its break-up, attempted to encourage wide share-ownership, by granting vouchers to the population that could be exchanged for shares in newly privatized companies. Even those states which moved most slowly towards the global market, like

Iliescu's Romania, made concessions in the direction of the privatization of their economies.[41] The dismantling of the region's state sectors continued apace, driven, by the mid-1990s, as much by the fiscal crisis of post-socialist states as governments divested themselves of public utilities and physical infrastructure, such as the state-constructed housing that dominated the outskirts of many of the region's cities. Under pressure from international financial institutions, and in some cases willingly, governments offered tax and other concessions to foreign multinationals to persuade them to invest in the region's economies.

Despite the severity of the initial post-socialist recessions and the fiscal crisis of the state, which persisted into the mid-1990s, by the end of the decade there was a gradual, although uneven, economic recovery. By 2000, Hungarian average living standards had recovered to their level of the late 1980s, after severe falls between 1988 and 1996. Recovery across the region was not uniform, aided by its integration into the global economy and largely underpinned by foreign direct investment. With a much lower standard of living, and consequently lower labour costs than in Western Europe, investment in Eastern European states was attractive to global multinationals, especially in a climate of trade liberalization, as the region's economies opened themselves to foreign competition and the European Union began to prepare actively for the admission of the western states of the region as members. Yet not all states benefited equally from growth based on the region's integration into a global market on the semi-periphery of the European economy. Foreign direct investment in manufacturing was concentrated close to the post-1995 external borders of the European Union in the Czech Republic, Hungary, Poland and Slovenia. Budapest benefited from Hungary's liberal attitude to foreign investment and its location, becoming a regional financial centre by the end of the decade. Investors were reluctant to move into Slovakia prior to 1998, given their disquiet over the policies of Mečiar, while Bulgaria and Romania suffered from poor infrastructure and remained too distant from core European markets.[42]

As the region moved from post-socialist recession to semi-peripheral growth close to the European Union's borders, and peripheral stagnation further away from them, social relations were remade. Considerable social polarization resulted, with the development of new economic élites, which were able to accumulate wealth to an extent that had not been tolerated in the socialist era. In contrast to the expectations of early post-socialist governments, this new élite was made up of younger members of the former state and enterprise apparatus, who quickly gained senior managerial positions in a new economic environment.[43] While in countries like Hungary, where by the end of the decade a new middle class had emerged, employed in the foreign-owned service sector, most of the population experienced sharp declines in real incomes, as insecurity spread, unemployment became pervasive and successive budget cuts removed large sections of the social safety net of the socialist era, without putting anything in its place. Fear of crime and discontent at endemic corruption became pervasive, while social tension frequently found an outlet in popular racism, directed at the Roma population. The most notorious, but by no means the only manifestation of this came in 1999, in the Czech Republic, when the city council in the Bohemian town of Ústí nad Labem erected a wall around the local Roma community, in response to complaints from residents about a crime wave, which they blamed on the local Roma.

Under the pressure of economic restructuring, the socialist society based on productive labour dissolved, as unemployment became a fact of life in many rural and working-class communities, and participation in the shadow economy, necessary in the socialist era to procure products in short supply, became, for many, a matter of survival. With the costs of creating Eastern Europe's new peripheral capitalism borne by its working class, after a few years of post-socialist government, they began to look back with a degree of nostalgia to socialism's society organized around productive labour. Anthropologist David Kideckel reported that significant numbers of Romanian industrial workers displayed 'portraits of Ceauşescu on lathes, lockers and workbenches'.[44] Economic transformation's devaluation of the social value of manual labour produced a marked reaction in those of the region's factories that survived the implementation of bankruptcy laws, rooted in a desire to return to some of the material security of a recent past – a complaint underpinned by the widespread nostalgia in Hungary for the socialist consumerism of the 1970s, which was marked by the mid-1990s.[45]

As burgeoning inequality, insecurity and declining real incomes undercut support for the anti-socialist dynamic that had characterized politics after 1989, the successor organizations of the ruling parties of the socialist regimes profited politically, at least outside the Czech Republic and Slovakia. Romania, where the left remained in power after 1990 until eventual defeat in 1996, also formed a partial exception to this rule. Such parties had suffered in 1989 because of their ambiguous role, in that they defended the old order, yet to some extent launched the process of reform that led to revolution. Half a decade later they were able to profit from it, exploiting discontent among the working class, the unemployed and the new rural poor with the social costs of economic restructuring, and pointing to their reformist credentials to assuage the fears of middle-class voters that they were intent on a restoration of the socialist system.

The political return of the former communist parties was heralded by the Polish left's victory in the September 1993 parliamentary elections, when the Alliance of the Democratic Left (*Sojusz Lewicy Demokratycznej* or SLD) – the successor of the PZPR – won a plurality with 20.41 per cent of the vote, and proved able to form a left-wing coalition government. It cemented this success in November 1995, when the SLD's leading light, Aleksander Kwaśniewski, defeated Lech Wałęsa in presidential elections.[46] In Hungary, the MSZP, led by the last foreign minister of the pre-1989 regime, Gyula Horn, built an impressive base of popular support as the country's first MDF-led centre-right coalition failed spectacularly to consolidate its authority. In May 1994, after an election campaign chiefly fought on the issue of the MSZP's links to socialist dictatorship, it won a landslide victory, with 32.99 per cent of the vote and an absolute parliamentary majority. After the divisive campaign, the MSZP formed a coalition with the second-placed SZDSZ, in an attempt to create a historic compromise with the former opposition. However, this paved the way for further polarization and not reconciliation.[47] In December 1994, after their ejection from office four years previously, Bulgaria's BSP returned to power as the dominant partner in a left-wing coalition, which decisively ejected the SDS.[48]

The return of reconstituted ruling parties was limited, however. In Slovakia, the left was weak and split, as politics polarized between supporters and opponents of Mečiar, a division that transcended the conventional cleavages of left and right. In the Czech Republic, the

Communists remained isolated, albeit attracting the votes of a stable minority, while the Social Democrats (*Česká strana sociálně demokratická* or CSSD) attracted the votes of those discontented with social polarization, winning 28.44 per cent of the vote in the 1996 elections, eventually capturing power and then becoming the country's largest political force in 1998.[49] Furthermore, the successor parties in government proved incapable of reversing the patterns of social polarization, declining levels of welfare provision or job security. Gyula Horn's government in Hungary intensified neoliberal restructuring of the economy, privatizing public utilities, slashing state spending and introducing means-tested, targeted welfare benefits to replace the universal entitlements of the socialist years. While these policies underpinned renewed economic growth, and a consumer boom centred on the emergent middle classes by the end of the government's term of office, they provoked enormous discontent from among its natural constituency, which paved the way for its ejection from office in 1998.[50] In Bulgaria, the new BSP-led administration proved incapable of dealing with the country's economic difficulties, and consequently presided over a mounting a crisis during 1996 that eventually destroyed the government.[51]

The demonstration during the mid-1990s that reformed ruling parties could command a broad base of popular support came as a shock to many members of the anti-socialist opposition that had emerged in power as a result of the revolutions of 1989. It convinced many that the anti-socialist agenda of removing the influence of former ruling parties over their populations had not been carried far enough, and that the opposition would have to realign to complete the task begun in the 1980s. In Hungary, it was the most senior political representative of the new opposition that had emerged in the 1980s, Viktor Orbán, co-founder of FIDESZ in 1988, who moved to rally the right, especially in view of the fact that members of the old opposition in the SZDSZ had formed a coalition with the Socialists. During the late 1990s, he built a coalition which united the centre-right to defeat the MSZP in the 1998 elections. In government, he further unified the right into an anti-socialist bloc, yet his divisive style generated further polarization, especially following the narrow defeat of his government by the MSZP in the 2002 elections.[52] In Poland, Kwaśniewski's 1995 victory over Wałęsa persuaded the *Solidarność* trade union that it needed to field a united list of candidates in the September 1997 parliamentary elections if it were to prevent SLD hegemony. This list formed the fulcrum of a centre-right coalition after the 1997 elections. Poland's right lacked a politician of the ability of Orbán, who could build a permanent right-wing alliance, and the coalition collapsed. It failed to prevent Kwaśniewski's re-election as president in 2000, and its own electoral humiliation at the hands of the SLD in September 2001.[53]

The polarization produced by the emergence of the successor organizations of the ruling parties of the socialist era manifested itself most dramatically in Bulgaria, where it combined with an unfolding economic crisis. When the opposition candidate, Petûr Stoianov, won the presidential election in November 1996, political crisis ensued. The BSP government collapsed, while the new president sought to force the reluctant BSP majority in parliament to face early elections. This resulted in widespread street protest in support of Stoianov's position, and the eventual invasion of parliament by protestors. Elections, held against the background of economic crisis, resulted in defeat for the BSP and victory for the SDS.[54] Polarization and violence, this time directed against a government of the opposition, which benefited a successor party, occurred in Albania in 1997, paving the way for the final crisis to shake Eastern Europe during the twentieth century.

The victory of the Democratic Party in the 1992 elections had resulted in the election of Sali Berisha as the new president of Albania. Chronic unemployment, poverty and flawed attempts at economic transformation resulted in social unrest, which developed during 1993. Berisha responded to growing protest in an authoritarian manner, arresting and jailing his political opponents, most notably the leader of the Socialist Party, the successor organization of Hoxha and Alija's Party of Labour, Fatos Nano.[55] The situation worsened, culminating in the last-minute decision of the opposition to boycott the May 1996 elections. To this fragile situation was added a mounting crisis over so-called 'pyramid schemes', a form of investment scam, which attracted savings by promising quick returns, which could only be guaranteed by attracting new savers. When these schemes collapsed during late 1996 and early 1997, many Albanians, who had lost all their savings, took to the streets, blaming Berisha, whose party, it was believed, had profited from the schemes. Outright revolution ensued, centred on the south of the country, as power in many towns was seized by demonstrators, prisons were emptied and insurgents quickly disarmed the police and security forces, arming themselves. The popular uprising destroyed Berisha's regime, forcing elections, which resulted in the election of a newly freed Fatos Nano as the country's prime minister in June 1997, though much of the north of the country, where Berisha's support had been strongest, was far from reconciled to this outcome.

Instability in Albania affected the neighbouring province of Kosovo, incorporated into Milošević's Serbia in 1989. The Albanian majority in the province opposed direct rule from Belgrade through policies of civil disobedience during the 1990s, fearful that armed resistance would result in the Serb leadership unleashing the violence that it had in Bosnia and Croatia. Supplies of arms entered the province from northern Albania, which the government in Tirana still did not fully control after the upheavals of 1997. This was combined with the perceived weakening of Milošević's grip, following the peace settlement at Dayton. These factors led to the spread of an armed uprising against Serb rule in the province during 1998. As Serb security forces responded with violence, the Western powers intervened to impose a peace settlement in early 1999. Milošević responded by mobilizing Serb security forces and paramilitaries against the Albanian population, in tactics reminiscent of those pursued earlier in the decade in Bosnia and Croatia. NATO, in turn, responded with military action, launching a bombing campaign against Yugoslavia in March 1999. While Belgrade initially responded with escalation, moving to expel the whole of the Albanian population from Kosovo, this hardened opinion in Western Europe and North America. In June, Milošević was forced to accept United Nations supervision of Kosovo – though it remained part of Yugoslavia – in exchange for an end to the NATO bombing of Yugoslav cities.

Defeat in Kosovo represented the beginning of the end for Milošević. Though after Dayton he had reconstituted his authority, moving from the Serbian presidency to the Yugoslav one in 1997, this had only been achieved against a background of growing opposition mobilization, following demonstrations in late 1996 and early 1997 over Milošević's refusal to allow opposition victories in local elections in Serbia's major cities to stand. After 1999, his situation was even more serious; faced with the consequences of military defeat and economic penury, he moved to strengthen his authority, as violence increasingly characterized Serbian politics during early 2000. In order to strengthen his position, Milošević called direct elections for the Yugoslav presidency in September 2000, in which the opposition united behind the candidacy of Vojislav Koštunica. While Koštunica won the popular vote, Milošević's allies in the electoral commission and the courts moved to prevent him being declared the winner. The result was a series of strikes and demonstrations that toppled Milošević on 5 October.

With Milošević's fall and the death of Tudjman in late 1999, and the subsequent transfer of power in Zagreb in early 2000, an era had ended in the former Yugoslavia. Bloody conflict had been replaced by an unstable peace, maintained only with the support of international organizations and the Western powers in Bosnia-Hercegovina and Kosovo. Especially in Yugoslavia, soon to be renamed Serbia-Montenegro, those seeking to build a viable post-Milošević political order faced a formidable task, given the legacy of internecine ethnic conflict and the shattered economy he left the country. The revolution that overthrew Milošević in October 2000 echoed, to some extent, those that had destroyed socialist regimes 11 years earlier, yet it also underlined the limits of revolutionary change in the region.

In Yugoslavia, the centrifugal forces unleashed by the politics of national identity overwhelmed those pushing for a peaceful, democratic transition, thus ensuring that the revolutionary wave of 1989 in the multinational south Slav state led inexorably to civil war and state break-up. Fortunately, however, in this respect, the territories of the former Yugoslavia were exceptional; though the politics of most post-socialist states had been marked to varying degrees by the politics of nation and ethnic conflict, during the 11 years following 1989, these were contained. The revolutions of 1989 were successful to the extent that across the region, with different degrees of success, functioning democratic political systems were established that relied on political pluralism and competitive elections. By the end of the century, the calls of revolutionaries for their societies to join the mainstream of European development had received a partial answer from the policy-makers of the European Union, who promised gradual enlargement during the first decade of the twenty-first century.

Yet as the economic crisis of the socialist regimes that began during the 1970s unfolded in the post-socialist context of the 1990s, Eastern Europe was integrated into the global capitalist market on the periphery of the European economy. While its westernmost states prospered, to some extent, as a result of companies operating inside the European Union exporting capital to states with lower labour costs in order to maintain profitability, this led to the opening up of a divide between the economies of the region. The internal social polarization that the creation of peripheral capitalism generated during the 1990s bred resentment and a turn away from political participation or towards the political extremes. The deterioration of the position of the working class and the rural poor, relative to their position during the socialist era, also bred social tension. At the same time, many of post-socialism's losers turned towards nostalgia for the social settlement of the 1960s, underlining the limits of the revolutionary wave of 1989. As former oppositions responded to evidence of growing support for the successor organizations to former ruling parties, they mobilized to demand further anti-socialist change. Thus, at the end of the twentieth century, the political conflicts that emerged through revolutionary change in 1989 seemed set to characterize politics during the opening years of the twenty-first century.

Notes

Introduction

[1] Quoted in D. Reynolds, *One World Divisible. A Global History since 1945* (Harmondsworth, 2000), p. 29.

[2] S. Drakulič, 'Who is Afraid of Europe?', *East European Politics and Societies*, 15 (1), 2001, p. 2.

[3] *Népszabadság*, 21 August 1989; http://sopron.hu/paneu-piknik/piktort.htm

[4] P. Kenney, *Carnival. Central Europe, 1989* (Princeton, NJ, 2002).

[5] T. Garton Ash, *The Uses of Adversity: Essays on the Fate of Central Europe* (Cambridge and Harmondsworth, 1991), pp. 161–70.

[6] Quoted in M. Mazower, *The Balkans* (London, 2000), p. 128.

[7] Adapted from L.R. Johnson, *Central Europe: Enemies, Neighbors, Friends* (New York, 1996), p. 285.

[8] D. Fishburn and S. Green (eds.), *The World in 2003* (London, 2002), p. 95.

[9] *Enlarging the European Union* (Luxembourg, 2003).

[10] D. Ugrešič, *The Culture of Lies. Antipolitical Essays*, trans. C. Hawkesworth (London, 1998), p. 237.

[11] J. Böröcz, 'The fox and the raven: the European Union and Hungary renegotiate the margins of "Europe"', *Comparative Studies in Society and History*, 42 (4), 2001, p. 847.

[12] Ibid., p. 869.

[13] E. Pargeter, *The Coast of Bohemia*, with an introduction by T. Meagher (Pleasantville, NY, 2001), p. 4.

[14] *Komárom-Esztergom Vármegyei Dolgozók Lapja*, 25 April 1948.

[15] L. Woolf, *Inventing Eastern Europe: The Map of Civilization on the Mind of the Enlightenment* (Stanford, CA, 1994).

[16] S. Woolf, 'The construction of a European world-view in the revolutionary Napoleonic years', *Past & Present*, 137, 1992, p. 90.

[17] T. Kaiser, 'The evil empire? The debate on Turkish despotism in eighteenth-century French political culture', *The Journal of Modern History*, 72 (1), 2000, pp. 6–34.

[18] I.B. Neumann, *Uses of the Other: The East in European Identity Formation* (Manchester, 1999), pp. 65–112.

[19] L. Woolf, *Inventing Eastern Europe*, pp. 1–16.

[20] I.T. Berend, *Decades of Crisis: Central and Eastern Europe before World War II* (Berkeley, CA, 1998), pp. 3–23.

[21] J. Breuilly, *Nationalism and the State* (Manchester, 1993), 2nd edition.

[22] P.J. Bowler, *The Invention of Progress: The Victorians and the Past* (Oxford, 1989).

[23] M. Hroch, 'From national movement to the fully-formed nation: the nation-building process in Europe' in G. Balakrishnan (ed.), *Mapping the Nation* (London, 1996), pp. 78–97.

[24] M. Glenny, *The Balkans, 1804–1999. Nationalism, War and the Great Powers* (London, 1999), pp. 249–392.

[25] R. West, *Black Lamb and Grey Falcon: A Journey through Yugoslavia*, with an introduction by T. Royle (Edinburgh, 1993), p. 21.

[26] Z.K. Brzezinski, *The Soviet Bloc: Unity and Conflict* (Cambridge, MA, 1967), revised and enlarged edition; E. Hankiss, *East European Alternatives* (Oxford, 1990); I. Szelényi, *Socialist Entrepreneurs. Embourgeoisiement in Rural Hungary* (Oxford, 1988); Á. Róna-Tas, *The Great Surprise of the Small Transformation. The Demise of Communism and the Rise of the Private Sector in Hungary* (Ann Arbor, MI, 1997).

[27] P.M. Johnson, 'Changing Social Structure and the Political Role of Manual Workers' in J.F. Triska and C. Gati (eds.), *Blue-Collar Workers in Eastern Europe* (London, 1981), pp. 29–42.

[28] R. Bessel and R. Jessen (eds.), *Die Grenzen der Diktatur: Staat und Gesellschaft in der DDR* (Göttingen, 1996).

Chapter 1

[1] J. Gross, 'War as Revolution' in N. Naimark and L. Gibianski (eds.), *The Establishment of Communist Regimes in Eastern Europe* (Boulder, CO, 1997), p. 34.

[2] I.T. Berend, *The Crisis Zone of Europe* (Cambridge, 1986).

[3] I. Livezeanu, *Cultural Politics in Greater Romania: Regionalism, Nation Building and Ethnic Struggle* (Ithaca, NY, 1995).

4 D. Sayer, *The Coasts of Bohemia: A Czech History* (Princeton, NJ, 1998), p. 168.

5 A.B. Wachtel, *Making a Nation, Breaking a Nation: Literature and Cultural Politics in Yugoslavia* (Stanford, CA, 1998), pp. 67–127.

6 S.B. Várdy, 'The Impact of Trianon upon the Hungarian Mind: Irredentism and Hungary's Path to War' in N. Dreisziger (ed.), *Hungary in the Age of Total War (1938–1948)* (Boulder, CO, 1998), pp. 27–48.

7 N.F. Dreisziger, 'The Dimensions of Total War in East Central Europe' in B.K. Király and N.F. Dreisziger (eds.), *East Central European Society in World War I* (Boulder, CO, 1985), pp. 3–23.

8 B.K. Király, 'Red Wave in Central Europe: A Repercussion of a Total War' in I. Banac (ed.), *The Effects of World War I: The Class War after the Great War: The Rise of Communist Parties in East Central Europe, 1918–1921* (Boulder, CO, 1983), pp. ix–xv.

9 E.A. Radice, 'General Characteristics of the Region between the Wars' in M.C. Kaser and E.A. Radice (eds.), *The Economic History of Eastern Europe 1919–1975. Volume 1: Economic Structure and Performance between the Two Wars* (Oxford, 1985), pp. 23–65.

10 A. Teichova, *The Czechoslovak Economy 1918–1980* (London, 1988), p. 9.

11 E.A. Radice, 'General Characteristics of the Region', p. 31.

12 R. Daskalov and H. Sundhaussen, 'Modernisierungsansätze' in M. Hatschikjan and S. Troebst (eds.), *Südosteuropa: Gesellschaft, Politik, Wirtschaft, Kultur: Ein Hanbuch* (München, 1999), pp. 123–5; I.T. Berend, *Decades of Crisis: Central and Eastern Europe before World War II* (Berkeley, CA, 1998), pp. 253–65.

13 D.E. Kaiser, *Economic Diplomacy and the Origins of the Second World War: Germany, Britain, France and Eastern Europe, 1930–1939* (Princeton, NJ, 1980), p. 165.

14 V. Tismaneanu and D. Pavel, 'Romania's Mystical Revolutionaries: The Generation of Angst and Adventure Revisited', *East European Politics and Societies*, 8 (3), 1994, pp. 419–20.

15 M. Lackó, *Nyilasok, Nemzetiszocialisták 1935–1944* (Budapest, 1966).

16 Z. Barbu, 'Psycho-Historical and Sociological Perspectives on the Iron Guard, the Fascist Movement of Romania' in S.U. Larsen, B. Hagtvet and J.P. Myklebust (eds.), *Who Were the Fascists? Social Roots of European Fascism* (Bergen, 1980), pp. 379–94.

[17] K. Hitchins, *Romania 1866–1947* (Oxford, 1994), pp. 418–25.

[18] M. Lackó, 'The Social Roots of Hungarian Fascism: the Arrow Cross' in Larsen, Hagtvet and Myklebust (eds.), *Who Were the Fascists?*, pp. 395–400.

[19] V. Mastny, *The Czechs under Nazi Rule. The Failure of National Resistance, 1939–1942* (New York, 1971), pp. 45–64.

[20] Y. Jelinek, *The Parish Republic: Hlinka's Slovak People's Party 1939–1945* (Boulder, CO, 1976).

[21] M. Vrzgulová, 'Jewish Tradesmen and Craftsmen during the Slovak Republic Period, 1939–1945' in G. Kiliánová and E. Riečanská (eds.), *Identity of Ethnic Groups and Communities: The Results of Slovak Ethnological Research* (Bratislava, 2000), p. 110.

[22] I. Pintér, 'A Kényszerpályára Szavazó Ország – 1939' in G. Földes and L. Hubai (eds.), *Parlamenti Választászok Magyarországon 1920–1998* (Budapest, 1999), pp. 197–203.

[23] L. Kürti, *The Remote Borderland: Transylvania in the Hungarian Imagination* (Albany, NY, 2001), p. 34.

[24] Mastny, *The Czechs under Nazi Rule*, pp. 74–80.

[25] I.T. Berend and G. Ránki, *Magyarország gyáripara a második világháború elött és a háború időszakában, 1933–1944* (Budapest, 1958).

[26] D. Turnock, *The Romanian Economy in the Twentieth Century* (London, 1986), pp. 59–60.

[27] Hitchins, *Romania*, p. 483.

[28] Y. Don, 'Economic Implications of Anti-Jewish Legislation in Hungary' in D. Cesarani (ed.), *Genocide and Rescue: The Holocaust in Hungary 1944* (Oxford, 1997), pp. 47–76.

[29] J.T. Gross, *Revolution from Abroad: The Soviet Conquest of Poland's Western Ukraine and Western Belorussia* (Princeton, NJ, 1988).

[30] I. Kershaw, *Hitler 1936–1945: Nemesis* (Harmondsworth, 2000), p. 239.

[31] G. Aly and S. Heim, *Architects of Annihilation: Auschwitz and the Logic of Destruction*, trans. A.G. Blunden (London, 2002), p. 73.

[32] G. Aly, *Final Solution: Nazi Population Policy and the Murder of the European Jews*, trans. B. Cooper and A. Brown (London, 1999), pp. 33–58.

[33] Kershaw, *Hitler*, pp. 250–2.

[34] A. Paczkowski, *Fél Évszázad Lengyelország Történetéből, 1939–1989*, trans. L. Pálfalvi (Budapest, 1997), p. 25.

35 G. Aly, *Final Solution*, p. 37.

36 M. Burleigh, *The Third Reich: A New History* (London, 2001), pp. 593–4.

37 Quoted in Kershaw, *Hitler*, p. 245.

38 Paczkowski, *Fél Évszázad*, p. 26.

39 J.T. Gross, *Polish Society under German Occupation: The Generalgovernement, 1939–1944* (Princeton, NJ, 1979), p. 78.

40 Quoted in Z. Landau and J. Tomaszewski, *The Polish Economy in the Twentieth Century*, trans. W. Roszkowski (London, 1985), p. 157.

41 E.A. Radice, 'The Development of Industry' in M.C. Kaser and E.A. Radice (eds.), *The Economic History of Eastern Europe 1919–1975. Volume II: Interwar Policy, the War and Reconstruction* (Oxford, 1986), p. 431.

42 Landau and Tomaszewski, *The Polish Economy*, p. 164.

43 Gross, *Polish Society*, pp. 97–8.

44 E.A. Radice, 'Agriculture and Food' in Kaser and Radice, *Economic History of Eastern Europe. Volume II*, p. 396.

45 J. Coutovidis and J. Reynolds, *Poland 1939–1947* (Leicester, 1986), p. 37.

46 Paczkowski, *Fél Évszázad*, p. 26.

47 Gross, *Polish Society*, pp. 213–58.

48 Burleigh, *The Third Reich*, p. 587.

49 Mastny, *The Czechs under Nazi Rule*, pp. 184–94.

50 Quoted in C. Bryant, 'Either Czech or German: Fixing Nationality in Bohemia and Moravia, 1939–1946', *Slavic Review*, 61 (4), 2002, p. 692.

51 Quoted in J. Connelly, 'Nazis and Slavs: From Racial Theory to Racist Practice', *Central European History*, 32 (1), 1999, p. 8.

52 M. Hauner, 'Military Budgets and the Armaments Industry' in Kaser and Radice, *Economic History of Eastern Europe. Volume II*, pp. 80–1.

53 Mastny, *The Czechs under Nazi Rule*, pp. 80–2.

54 E.A. Radice, 'Territorial Changes, Population Movements and Labour Supplies' in Kaser and Radice, *Economic History of Eastern Europe. Volume II*, pp. 320–1.

55 C. Rogel, 'In the Beginning: The Slovenes from the Seventh Century to 1945' in J. Benderly and E. Kraft (eds.), *Independent Slovenia: Origins, Movements, Prospects* (Basingstoke, 1997), p. 18.

[56] S.K. Pavlowitch, *Yugoslavia* (London, 1971), p. 109.

[57] M. Vickers, *The Albanians: A Modern History* (London, 1999), p. 139.

[58] S. Troebst, 'Yugoslav Macedonia, 1943–1953: Building the Party, the State, and the Nation' in M.K. Bokovoy, J.A. Irvine and C.S. Lilly (eds.), *State–Society Relations in Yugoslavia 1945–1992* (New York, 1997), pp. 244–5.

[59] A. Djilas, *The Contested Country: Yugoslav Unity and Communist Revolution 1919–1953* (Cambridge, MA, 1991), p. 110.

[60] M. Glenny, *The Balkans, 1804–1999: Nationalism, War and the Great Powers* (London, 1999), p. 499.

[61] Quoted in M. Tanner, *Croatia: A Nation Forged in War* (New Haven, 1997), p. 145.

[62] N. Malcom, *Bosnia: A Short History* (London, 1994), p. 175.

[63] Quoted in Djilas, *The Contested Country*, p. 120.

[64] Tanner, *Croatia*, p. 151.

[65] Djilas, *The Contested Country*, pp. 120–1.

[66] Pavlowitch, *Yugoslavia*, p. 115.

[67] I. Winner, *A Slovenian Village: Žerovina* (Providence, 1971), pp. 46–7.

[68] J. Walston, 'History and Memory of the Italian Concentration Camps', *Historical Journal*, 40 (1), 1997, p. 176.

[69] Malcom, *Bosnia*, pp. 178–83.

[70] Pavlowitch, *Yugoslavia*, p. 128.

[71] Jelinek, *The Parish Republic*, p. 91.

[72] M. Myant, *Socialism and Democracy in Czechoslovakia 1945–1948* (Cambridge, 1981), p. 27.

[73] I.T. Berend, 'The Composition and Position of the Working Class during the War' in G. Lengyel (ed.), *Hungarian Economy and Society during World War II*, trans J. Pokoly (Boulder, CO, 1993), pp. 151–68.

[74] G. Erdmann, *Begyűjtés, Beszolgáltatás Magyarországon 1945–1956* (Gyula, 1992), pp. 7–13.

[75] J.R. Lampe, *The Bulgarian Economy in the Twentieth Century* (London, 1986), pp. 114–15.

[76] Quoted in Bryant, 'Either Czech or German', p. 697.

[77] Myant, *Socialism and Democracy*, pp. 28–9.

[78] Coutovidis and Reynolds, *Poland*, p. 84.

[79] Jelinek, *The Parish Republic*, p. 125.

[80] P. Sipos, *Legális és Illegális Munkásmozgalom (1919–1944)* (Budapest, 1988), pp. 209–309.

[81] Hitchins, *Romania*, pp. 490–1.

[82] R.J. Crampton, *A Short History of Modern Bulgaria* (Cambridge, 1987), p. 129.

[83] Hitchins, *Romania*, pp. 493–500.

[84] C.B. Eby, *Hungary at War: Citizens and Soldiers in World War II* (University Park, PA, 1998); R.L. Braham, *The Politics of Genocide: the Holocaust in Hungary* (Detroit, MI, 2000), p. 153.

[85] Jelinek, *The Parish Republic*, pp. 125–31.

[86] Coutovidis and Reynolds, *Poland*, pp. 113–69.

[87] Burleigh, *The Third Reich*, pp. 754–5.

[88] M. Pittaway, 'The Politics of Legitimacy and Hungary's Post-war Transition' (manuscript, 2002), p. 21.

[89] A. Pető, 'Stimmen des Schweigens: Erinnerungen an Vergewaltigungen in den Hauptstädten des "ersten Opfers" (Wien) und des "letzten Verbündeten" Hitlers (Budapest) 1945', *Zeitschrift für Geschictswissenschaft*, 47 (10), 1999, pp. 892–913.

[90] P. Biddiscombe, 'Prodding the Russian Bear: Pro-German Resistance in Romania, 1944–5', *European History Quarterly*, 23 (2), 1993, pp. 210–11.

[91] G. Zielbauer, 'Magyar polgári lakosok deportálása és hadifogsága (1945–1948)', *Történelmi Szemle*, 3–4, 1992, pp. 270–91.

[92] E. Völkl, 'Abrechnungsfuror in Kroatien' in K-D. Henke and H. Woller (eds.), *Politische Säuberung in Europa: Die Abrechnung mit Faschismus und Kollaboration nach dem Zweiten Weltkrieg* (München, 1991), pp. 366–70.

[93] P. Ther, *Deutsche und polnische Vertriebene: Gesellschaft und Vertriebenenpolitik in der SBZ und in Polen 1945–1956* (Göttingen, 1998), p. 55.

[94] Quoted in N. Naimark, *Fires of Hatred: Ethnic Cleansing in Twentieth-Century Europe* (Cambridge, MA, 2001), p. 127.

[95] E. Glassheim, 'National Mythologies and Ethnic Cleansing: The Expulsion of Czechoslovak Germans in 1945', *Central European History*, 33 (4), 2000, pp. 475–7.

[96] P. Corner, *History in Exile: Memory and Identity at the Borders of the Balkans* (Princeton, NJ, 2003), p. 193.

[97] K. Brown, *The Past in Question: Modern Macedonia and the Uncertainties of Nation* (Princeton, NJ, 2003), pp. 119–22.

98 E.A. Radice, 'The Collapse of German Hegemony and its Economic Consequences' in Kaser and Radice, *Economic History of Eastern Europe. Volume II*, p. 496.

99 Naimark, *Fires of Hatred*, p. 132; P. Apor, 'A népi demokrácia építése: Kunmadaras, 1946', *Századok*, 132 (3), 1998, pp. 601–32.

100 I. Márkus, 'Urak Futása' in I. Márkus, *Az Ismeretlen Főszereplő: Tanulmányok* (Budapest, 1991), p. 87.

101 J. Bloomfield, *Passive Revolution: Politics and the Czechoslovak Working Class, 1945–1948* (London, 1979), pp. 66–7; Pittaway, 'The Politics of Legitimacy', pp. 18–25.

102 I.T. Berend, *Central and Eastern Europe 1944–1993: Detour from the Periphery to the Periphery* (Cambridge, 1996), p. 6.

103 S. Siebel-Achenbach, *Lower Silesia from Nazi Germany to Communist Poland, 1942–49* (Basingstoke, 1994), p. 179.

104 Pittaway, 'The Politics of Legitimacy', p. 26.

105 B.Y. Berry, *Romanian Diaries 1944–1947*, ed. C. Bodea (Iaşi, 2000), p. 168.

106 B.F. Abrams, 'The Second World War and the East European Revolution', *East European Politics and Societies*, 16 (3), 2002, p. 631.

Chapter 2

1 Quoted in M. Mevius, 'Agents of Moscow: The Hungarian Communist Party and the Origins of Socialist Patriotism, 1941–1953' (D.Phil. thesis, University of Oxford, 2002), p. 36.

2 Quoted in Z. Brzezinski, *The Soviet Bloc: Unity and Conflict* (Cambridge, MA, 1967), p. 27.

3 M. Rákosi, 'Mi a Magyar Demokrácia?' in M. Rákosi, *Válogatott Beszédek és Cikkek* (Budapest, 1950), p. 47.

4 Vickers, *The Albanians*, pp. 163–4.

5 J.R. Lampe, *Yugoslavia as History: Twice There was a Country* (Cambridge, 1996), p. 234.

6 Crampton, *A Short History of Modern Bulgaria*, pp. 145–53.

7 Hitchins, *Romania*, pp. 501–17.

8 Pittaway, 'The Politics of Legitimacy', pp. 18–45.

9 Coutovidis and Reynolds, *Poland*, pp. 198–228.

10 Myant, *Socialism and Democracy*, pp. 25–52.

11 I. Lukes, 'The Czech Road to Communism' in Naimark and Gibianski (eds.), *The Establishment of Communist Regimes*, pp. 252–3.

12 J. Micgiel, ' "Bandits and Reactionaries": The Suppression of the Opposition in Poland, 1944–1946' in Naimark and Gibianski (eds.), *The Establishment of Communist Regimes*, pp. 91–102.
13 Pittaway, 'The Politics of Legitimacy', p. 28.
14 D. Deletant, *Communist Terror in Romania: Gheorghiu-Dej and the Police State 1948–1965* (London, 1999), pp. 114–17.
15 Crampton, *Short History of Modern Bulgaria*, pp. 145–7.
16 Quoted in D. Rusinow, *The Yugoslav Experiment 1948–1974* (London, 1977), p. 15.
17 Quoted in Lampe, *Yugoslavia as History*, p. 238.
18 I. Blumi, 'The Politics of Culture and Power: The Roots of Hoxha's Post-war State', *East European Quarterly*, 31 (3), 1997, p. 396n.
19 H. Hamm, *Albania: China's Beachhead in Europe* (London, 1963), p. 53.
20 Völkl, 'Abrechnungsfuror', p. 386.
21 Pavlowitch, *Yugoslavia*, pp. 181–2.
22 C.S. Lilly, *Power and Persuasion: Ideology and Rhetoric in Communist Yugoslavia 1944–1953* (Boulder, CO, 2001), p. 87.
23 D. Roksandic, 'Shifting References: Celebrations of Uprisings in Croatia, 1945–1991', *East European Politics and Societies*, 9 (2), 1995, pp. 256–71.
24 Quoted in B.R. Frommer, 'Retribution against Nazi Collaborators in Post-war Czechoslovakia' (Ph.D. thesis, Harvard University, 1999), p. 81.
25 Crampton, *History of Modern Bulgaria*, pp. 145–7.
26 L. Karsai, 'The People's Courts and Revolutionary Justice in Hungary, 1945–46' in I. Deák, J.T. Gross and T. Judt (eds.), *The Politics of Retribution in Europe: World War II and its Aftermath* (Princeton, NJ, 2000), p. 237.
27 Pittaway, 'The Politics of Legitimacy', pp. 40–1.
28 Ibid., pp. 40–5.
29 Frommer, 'Retribution against Nazi Collaborators', p. 2.
30 B. Abrams, 'The Politics of Retribution: The Trial of Jozef Tiso', *East European Politics and Societies*, 10 (2), 1996, pp. 255–92.
31 Quoted in Frommer, 'Retribution against Nazi Collaborators', pp. 95–6.
32 Quoted in J. King, *Budweisers into Czechs and Germans: A Local History of Bohemian Politics, 1848–1948* (Princeton, NJ, 2002), p. 192.

33 Quoted in B. Frommer, 'To Prosecute or to Expel? Czechoslovak Retribution and the "Transfer" of Sudeten Germans' in P. Ther and A. Siljak (eds.), *Redrawing Nations: Ethnic Cleansing in East Central Europe, 1944–1949* (Lanham, 2001), p. 226.

34 N. Spulber, *The Economics of Communist Eastern Europe* (New York and London, 1957), p. 32.

35 Ther, *Deutsche und Polnische Vertriebene*, p. 59.

36 Stanislaw Jankowiak, ' "Cleansing" Poland of Germans: the Province of Pomerania, 1945–1949' in Ther and Siljak (eds.), *Redrawing Nations*, p. 98.

37 Spulber, *The Economics of Communist Eastern Europe*, pp. 30–1.

38 Ther, *Deutsche und Polnische Vertriebene*, p. 53.

39 Spulber, *The Economics of Communist Eastern Europe*, p. 31.

40 M.K. Bokovoy, *Peasants and Communists: Politics and Ideology in the Yugoslav Countryside 1941–1953* (Pittsburgh, PA, 1998), p. 50.

41 A. Tóth, *Migrationen in Ungarn 1945–1948: Vertreibung der Ungarndeutschen, Binnenwanderungen und Slowakisch-Ungarischer Bevölkerungsaustausch*, trans. R. Fejér (München, 2001), pp. 177–208.

42 Public Records Office (PRO) Foreign Office (FO) 371/71352, 'Confidential Report, British Embassy, Prague, 5th August 1948', p. 1.

43 Z. Radvanovský, 'The Social and Economic Consequences of Resettling Czechs into Northwestern Bohemia, 1945–1947' in Ther and Siljak (eds.), *Redrawing Nations*, p. 243.

44 Siebel-Achenbach, *Lower Silesia*, p. 196.

45 Quoted in P. Kenney, *Rebuilding Poland: Workers and Communists, 1945–1950* (Ithaca, NY, 1997), pp. 137–8.

46 Blumi, 'The Politics of Culture and Power'.

47 Wachtel, *Making a Nation, Breaking a Nation*, p. 131.

48 Quoted in Djilas, *The Contested Country*, p. 162.

49 Quoted in Wachtel, *Making a Nation, Breaking a Nation*, p. 137.

50 Troebst, 'Yugoslav Macedonia, 1949–1953', pp. 250–5.

51 Mevius, 'Agents of Moscow', p. 117.

52 Quoted in Bloomfield, *Passive Revolution*, p. 98.

53 A. Mód, 'Az üzemi bizottságok és az újjáépités', *Szakszervezeti Közlöny* (1 June 1945), pp. 4–5.

54 Quoted in Kenney, *Rebuilding Poland*, p. 78.

55 Pittaway, 'The Politics of Legitimacy', pp. 57–63.

56 Kenney, *Rebuilding Poland*, pp. 74–134.

[57] Myant, *Socialism and Democracy*, p. 125.
[58] Abrams, 'The Politics of Retribution', pp. 258–66.
[59] Pittaway, 'The Politics of Legitimacy', pp. 45–66.
[60] Hitchins, *Romania*, p. 533.
[61] Crampton, *A Short History of Modern Bulgaria*, p. 155.
[62] Coutovidis and Reynolds, *Poland*, pp. 229–310.
[63] Brzezinski, *The Soviet Bloc*, pp. 3–64; H.R. Seton-Watson, *The East European Revolution* (London, 1961).
[64] C. Gati, *Hungary and the Soviet Bloc* (Durham, NC, 1986), pp. 13–123.
[65] Myant, *Socialism and Democracy*, p. 140.
[66] K. Kaplan, *The Short March: The Communist Takeover in Czechoslovakia 1945–1948* (London, 1987), pp. 148–9.
[67] PRO FO 371/71264, 'Czechoslovakia: Weekly Information Summary, 20th February–3rd March 1948', p. 1.
[68] É. Standeisky, G. Kozák, G. Pataki and J.M. Rainer (eds.), *A fordulat évei, 1947–1949. Politika-Képzőművészet-Építészet* (Budapest, 1998).
[69] Kenney, *Rebuilding Poland*, pp. 189–236.
[70] R.R. King, *History of the Romanian Communist Party* (Stanford, CA, 1980), pp. 72–3.
[71] Lampe, *Yugoslavia*, pp. 241–9.
[72] Pavlowitch, *Yugoslavia*, p. 211.
[73] Wachtel, *Making a Nation, Breaking a Nation*, pp. 132–3.
[74] Vickers, *The Albanians*, pp. 173–5.
[75] M. Ormos et al., *Törvénytelen Szocializmus. A Tényfeltáró Bizottság Jelentése* (Budapest, 1991), pp. 64–8.
[76] Deletant, *Communist Terror*, pp. 118–26.
[77] *News From Behind the Iron Curtain*, 1 (1), 1952, pp. 13–14.
[78] Pavlowitch, *Yugoslavia*, pp. 214–15.
[79] PRO FO 371/71265, 'Czechoslovakia: Weekly Information Summary, 24th–30th September 1948', p. 1.
[80] Crampton, *A Short History of Modern Bulgaria*, pp. 160–6.
[81] PRO FO 371/71264, 'Czechoslovakia: Weekly Information Summary, 20th February–3rd March 1948', p. 2.
[82] Z. Kádár, 'A szociáldemokraták üldözése és diszkriminálása' in L. Varga (ed.), *A Magyar Szociáldemokrácia Kézikönyve* (Budapest, 1999), pp. 163–9.
[83] G.H. Hodos, *Schauprozesse: Stalinistische Säuberungen in Osteuropa 1948–54* (Frankfurt-am-Main, 1988), pp. 28–35.

[84] T. Zinner, *Adalékok a magyarországi koncepciós perekhez* (Székesfehérvár, 1988).
[85] Crampton, *A Short History of Modern Bulgaria*, p. 171.
[86] Pavlowitch, *Yugoslavia*, p. 214.
[87] J. Pelikán (ed.), *The Czechoslovak Political Trials, 1950–1954: The Suppressed Report of the Dubček Government's Commission of Inquiry, 1968* (London, 1971), pp. 101–14.
[88] Magyar Országos Levéltár (Hungarian National Archive, hereafter MOL), M-Bp.-95f.3/69ö.e., pp. 120–1a.
[89] PRO FO 371/77248, 'Weekly Information Summary for the period 30th June–6th July', p. 2.
[90] D. Jarosz, 'Polish Peasants versus Stalinism' in A. Kemp-Welch (ed.), *Stalinism in Poland, 1944–1956: Selected Papers from the Fifth World Congress of Central and Eastern European Studies, Warsaw, 1995* (Basingstoke, 1999), pp. 70–1.
[91] S. Alexander, *Church and State in Yugoslavia since 1945* (Cambridge, 1979), pp. 53–94.
[92] S. Skendi, *Albania* (London, 1956), pp. 294–9.
[93] Deletant, *Communist Terror in Romania*, pp. 89–103.
[94] Alexander, *Church and State*, pp. 196–201.
[95] Deletant, *Communist Terror in Romania*, pp. 90–1.
[96] J. Gergely, *A Politikai Katolicizmus Magyarországon 1890–1950* (Budapest, 1977), p. 275.
[97] K. Kersten, 'The Terror, 1949–1954' in Kemp-Welch (ed.), *Stalinism in Poland*, pp. 84–9.
[98] Kenney, *Rebuilding Poland*, pp. 192–8.
[99] PRO FO 371/71264, 'Czechoslovakia: Weekly Information Summary, 1st–7th January 1948', p. 1.
[100] L. Srágli, 'A Dunántúli Olajbányászat Hároméves Terve (Adatok a MAORT történetéhez, 1947–1949)', *Zalai Gyűtemény*, 25, 1986, pp. 295–307.
[101] W. Brus, '1950 to 1953: The Peak of Stalinism' in M.C. Kaser (ed.), *The Economic History of Eastern Europe 1919–1975. Volume III: Institutional Change within a Planned Economy* (Oxford, 1986), p. 8.
[102] Quoted in A.L. Cartwright, *The Return of the Peasant: Land Reform in Post-Communist Romania* (London, 2001), p. 67.
[103] Quoted in Bokovoy, *Peasants and Communists*, p. 90.
[104] Open Society Archives (OSA) 300/40/4/22, Item No. 3242/54, p. 1.

[105] 'Some Place to Hide', *News From Behind the Iron Curtain*, 2 (12), 1953, pp. 20–1.

[106] Jarosz, 'Polish Peasants versus Stalinism', pp. 64–5.

[107] 'Peasant Rebellion Reported', *News From Behind the Iron Curtain*, 1 (1), 1952, p. 17.

[108] Bokovoy, *Peasants and Communists*, pp. 136–7.

[109] Zala Megyei Levéltár (Zala County Archive, hereafter ZML) 57f.1/17ö.e.

[110] Deletant, *Communist Terror in Romania*, p. 142.

[111] T. Dessewffy and A. Szántó, *'Kitörő Éberséggel' A budapesti kitelepítések hiteles története* (Budapest, 1989).

[112] J. Keane, *Václav Havel: A Political Tragedy in Six Acts* (London, 2000), p. 88.

[113] J. Mark, 'Prospering through Discrimination and Manufacturing New Identities: How the Middle Class Survived the Stalinist State in Hungary' (paper presented at BASEES annual conference, Cambridge, 2003), p. 1.

[114] J. Connelly, *Captive University: the Sovietization of East German, Czech and Polish Higher Education, 1945–1956* (Chapel Hill, NC, 2000), p. 266.

[115] Mark, 'Prospering through Discrimination'.

[116] Connelly, *Captive University*, p. 239.

[117] Spulber, *The Economics of Communist Eastern Europe*, p. 280.

[118] M. Pittaway, 'The Social Limits of State Control: Time, the Industrial Wage Relation and Social Identity in Stalinist Hungary, 1948–1953', *Journal of Historical Sociology*, 12 (3), 1999, pp. 271–301.

[119] S. Satjukow and R. Gries (eds.), *Sozialistische Helden: Eine Kulturgeschichte von Propagandafiguren in Osteuropa und der DDR* (Berlin, 2002).

[120] Quoted in Kenney, *Rebuilding Poland*, p. 252.

[121] Pittaway, 'The Social Limits of State Control'.

[122] Spulber, *The Economics of Communist Eastern Europe*, p. 386.

[123] I. Birta, 'A szocialista iparositási politika néhány kérdése az első ötéves terv időszakában', *Párttörténeti Közlemények* (3), 1970, pp. 125–8.

[124] 'Men at Work', *News From Behind the Iron Curtain*, 2 (1), 1953, p. 19.

[125] Pittaway, 'The Social Limits of State Control'.

126 P. Heumos, 'Aspekte des Sozialen Milieus der Industriear-
beiterschaft in der Tscheschoslowakei vom Ende des Zweiten
Weltkrieges biz zur Reformbewegung der Sechziger Jahre',
Bohemia, 42 (2), 2001, p. 349.

127 M. Pittaway, 'Industrial Workers, Socialist Industrialisation and
the State in Hungary, 1948–1958' (Ph.D. thesis, University of
Liverpool, 1998), p. 225.

128 M. Pittaway, 'The Education of Dissent: the Reception of the
Voice of Free Hungary, 1951–1956', *Cold War History*, 4 (1), 2003,
p. 109.

129 'The Czechoslovak Currency Reform: A Survey of its Background,
Provisions and Popular Reaction', *News From Behind the Iron
Curtain*, 2 (7), 1953, p. 20.

130 PRO FO 371/77264, 'British Consulate, Bratislava, 10th January
1949', p. 1.

131 'Persistent Shortage of Consumer Goods', *News From Behind the
Iron Curtain*, 1 (1), 1952, p. 16.

132 'Black Market Operations', *News From Behind the Iron Curtain*, 1
(12), 1952, p. 31.

133 Pelikán (ed.), *The Czechoslovak Political Trials*, p. 56.

134 O. Ulc, 'Pilsen: the unknown revolt', *Problems of Communism*, 14
(3), 1965, pp. 46–9.

Chapter 3

1 Quoted in M. Myant, *The Czechoslovak Economy: The Battle for
Economic Reform* (Cambridge, 1988), p. 72.

2 Deletant, *Communist Terror in Romania*, p. 220.

3 Hodos, *Schauprozesse*, pp. 140–3.

4 Magyar Országos Levéltár (Hungarian National Archive, hereafter MOL) M-Bp.-176f.2/154ö.e., p. 275.

5 Quoted in F. Lewis, *The Polish Volcano: A Case History of Hope*
(London, 1959), p. 146.

6 Quoted in A. Kemp-Welch, 'Khrushchev's "Secret Speech" and
Polish Politics: The Spring of 1956', *Europe-Asia Studies*, 48 (2),
1998, p. 194.

7 J. Granville, 'From the Archives of Warsaw and Budapest: A
Comparison of the Events of 1956', *East European Politics and
Societies*, 16 (2), 2002, pp. 526–33.

8 MOL M-Bp.-176f.2/154ö.e., p. 274.

9 G. Litván et al., *The Hungarian Revolution of 1956: Reform, Revolt and Repression 1953–1963* (Harlow, 1996), pp. 143–4.

10 G. Földes, 'A Kádár-rendszer és a munkásság', *Eszmélet*, 18–19, 1993, pp. 57–73.

11 M. Pittaway, 'Industrial Workers, Socialist Industrialisation and the State in Hungary, 1948–1958' (Ph.D. thesis, University of Liverpool, 1998), pp. 359–68.

12 Lewis, *The Polish Volcano*, pp. 256–7.

13 G. Kolankiewicz, 'The Polish Industrial Manual Working Class' in D. Lane and G. Kolankiewicz (eds.), *Social Groups in Polish Society* (London, 1973), p. 120.

14 'Decree Punishing Absenteeism Revoked', *News From Behind the Iron Curtain*, 2 (8), 1953, p. 11.

15 J. Mašata, 'Der Kreisgewerkschaft in Ostrau und die Entwicklung der Lohnsysteme 1949–1959', *Bohemia*, 42 (2), 2001, p. 317.

16 Heumos, 'Aspekte des sozialen Milieus', p. 352.

17 I. Kemény, 'Kompromisszumok egyezség nélkül' in I. Kemény, *Szociológiai Írások* (Szeged, 1992), p. 208.

18 I. Kemény and G. Kozák, *A Csepel Vas-és Fémművek Munkásai* (Budapest, 1971).

19 Myant, *The Czechoslovak Economy*, p. 139.

20 Kolankiewicz, 'The Polish Industrial Working Class', pp. 96–7.

21 Myant, *The Czechoslovak Economy*, p. 136.

22 L. Héthy and C. Makó, *Munkásmagatartások és gazdasági szervezet* (Budapest, 1972), pp. 85–106.

23 Bokovoy, *Peasants and Communists*, pp. 149–52.

24 J.B. Allcock, *Explaining Yugoslavia* (London, 2000), pp. 132–3.

25 P.G. Lewis, 'The Peasantry' in Lane and Kolankiewicz (eds.), *Social Groups in Polish Society*, p. 56.

26 Quoted in Derek Hall, *Albania and the Albanians* (London, 1994), p. 121.

27 Cartwright, *The Return of the Peasant*, p. 81.

28 M. Draganova, 'Senses of the Private when Working in the Collectives in Socialist Bulgaria' (manuscripts, Sofia, 2003), p. 6.

29 Myant, *The Czechoslovak Economy*, p. 93.

30 S. Orbán, *Két Agrárforradalom Magyarországon: Demokratikus és szocialista agrárátalakulás 1945–1961* (Budapest, 1972), p. 218.

31 N. Swain, 'A framework for comparing social change in the post-socialist countryside', *East European Countryside*, 4, 1998, pp. 5–19.

[32] D.A. Kideckel, *The Solitude of Collectivism: Romanian Villagers to the Revolution and Beyond* (Ithaca, NY, 1993), pp. 105–8.

[33] Quoted in Hall, *Albania and the Albanians*, p. 121.

[34] Draganova, 'Senses of the Private', p. 16.

[35] Z. Varga, *Politika, paraszti érdekérvényesítés és a termelőszövetkezetek Magyarországon, 1956–1967* (Budapest, 2001).

[36] I. Kemény, 'A nem regisztrált gazdaság Magyarországon' in Kemény, *Szociológiai Irások*, pp. 219–44; S. Sampson, 'The Informal Sector in Eastern Europe', *Telos*, 66, 1986, pp. 44–66.

[37] Lewis, 'The Peasantry', p. 52.

[38] K. Fazekas and J. Köllő, *Munkaerőpiac Tőkepiac Nélkül* (Budapest, 1990), p. 95.

[39] Quoted in D. Petrescu, 'Workers and Peasant-Workers in a Working Class "Paradise": Patterns of Working Class Protest and Co-optation in Communist Romania' (manuscripts, Bucharest, 2003), p. 6.

[40] Myant, *The Czechoslovak Economy*, p. 68.

[41] D. Crowley, 'Warsaw's Shops, Stalinism and the Thaw' in S.E. Reid and D. Crowley (eds.), *Style and Socialism: Modernity and Material Culture in Post-war Eastern Europe* (Oxford, 2000), pp. 25–47.

[42] M. Pittaway, 'Towards a Social History of Socialist Consumerism in Hungary, 1953–1968' (manuscripts, Milton Keynes, 2000).

[43] M. Szántó, *Életmód, Művelődés, Szabadidő* (Budapest, 1967), pp. 78–80.

[44] Héthy and Makó, *Munkásmagatartások és gazdasági szervezet*, p. 144.

[45] 'Az MSZMP Központi Bizottsága Politikai Bizottságának Állásfoglalása a Munkásosztály Helyzetéről Szóló 1958-as KB-Határozat Végrehajtásáról, a Munkásosztály Jelenlegi Helyzetéről. 1970. január 10' in H. Vass (ed.), *A Magyar Szocialista Munkáspárt Határozatai és Dokumentumai 1967–1970* (Budapest, 1974), p. 468.

[46] P.H. Patterson, 'The New Class: Consumer Culture under Socialism and the Unmaking of the Yugoslav Dream, 1945–1991' (Ph.D. dissertation, University of Michigan, 2001), pp. 74–84.

[47] P.H. Patterson, 'An Everyday for Everyman (and Everywoman Too): Consumer Culture, the New "New Class", and the Making of the Yugoslav Dream, 1950–1965' (manuscripts, San Diego, 2003).

48 Rusinow, *The Yugoslav Experiment*, p. 251.
49 L.M. Lees, *Keeping Tito Afloat: the United States, Yugoslavia and the Cold War* (University Park, PA, 1997), pp. 43–119.
50 S.L. Woodward, *Socialist Unemployment: The Political Economy of Yugoslavia, 1945–1991* (Princeton, NJ, 1995), pp. 164–73.
51 Rusinow, *The Yugoslav Experiment*, pp. 138–41.
52 Woodward, *Socialist Unemployment*, p. 193.
53 Allcock, *Explaining Yugoslavia*, p. 83.
54 Lampe, *Yugoslavia as History*, pp. 286–9.
55 B.D. Denitch, *The Legitimation of a Revolution: The Yugoslav Case* (New Haven, 1976), p. 167.
56 Rusinow, *The Yugoslav Experiment*, p. 202.
57 G. Hunya, 'Ceauşescu-korszak gazdasága' in G. Hunya (ed.), *Románia 1944–1990: Gazdaság-és Politikatörténet* (Budapest, 1990), p. 58.
58 Myant, *The Czechoslovak Economy*, pp. 90–106.
59 G. Földes, *Az Eladósodás Politikatörténete 1957–1986* (Budapest, 1995), pp. 21–38.
60 I. Pető and S. Szakács, *A hazai gazdaság négy évtizedének története 1945–1985 I. Az újjáépités és a tervutasitásos irányitás időszaka* (Budapest, 1985), pp. 651–68.
61 J. Keep, *A History of the Soviet Union 1945–1991: Last of the Empires* (Oxford, 1995), p. 91.
62 Myant, *The Czechoslovak Economy*, pp. 121–56.
63 N. Swain, *Hungary: the Rise and Fall of Feasible Socialism* (London, 1992), pp. 99–107.
64 'Az MSZMP Központi Bizottsága Politikai Bizottságának Állásfoglalása', p. 464.
65 M. Pittaway, 'Workers, Industrial Conflict and the State in Socialist Hungary, 1948–1989' (manuscripts, Milton Keynes, 2003), p. 41.
66 K.A. Soós, 'Béralku és "sérelmi politika": Adalékok a mechanizmusreform 1969. évi első megtorpanásának magyarázatához' in T. Miklós (ed.), *Magyar gazdaság és szociológia a 80-as években* (Budapest, 1988), pp. 89–110.
67 Landau and Tomaszewski, *The Polish Economy*, p. 257.
68 Kolankiewicz, 'The Polish Industrial Manual Working Class', p. 130; Z.A. Pełczyński, 'The Downfall of Gomułka' in A. Bromke and J.W. Strong (eds.), *Gierek's Poland* (New York, 1973), p. 5.
69 M. Myant, *Poland: A Crisis for Socialism* (London, 1982), p. 60.

70 M.F. Rakowski, 'December 1970: The Turning Point' in Bromke and Strong (eds.), *Gierek's Poland*, p. 124.

71 D. Lane, 'Structural and Social Change in Poland' in Lane and Kolankiewicz (eds.), *Social Groups in Polish Society*, p. 17.

72 J. Kepecs and A. Klinger, 'A felsőfokú végzettségűek demográfiai adatai' in T. Huzsár (ed.), *Értelmiségiek, diplomások, szellemi munkások: Szociológiai tanulmányok* (Budapest, 1978), p. 273.

73 N. Tilkidjiev, 'Social Stratification' in N. Genov and A. Krasteva (eds.), *Recent Social Trends in Bulgaria 1960–1985* (Montreal, 2001), p. 189.

74 G. Kolankiewicz, 'The Technical Intelligentsia' in Lane and Kolankiewicz (eds.), *Social Groups in Polish Society*, p. 203.

75 L. Haney, *Inventing the Needy: Gender and the Politics of Welfare in Hungary* (Berkeley, CA, 2002), pp. 93–7.

76 Patterson, 'The New Class', pp. 100–93.

77 Denitch, *The Legitimation of a Revolution*, p. 77.

78 Kolankiewicz, 'The Polish Industrial Manual Working Class', p. 129.

79 R. Andorka, 'Az értelmiség társadalmi mobilitásának történeti alakulása' in Huzsár (ed.), *Értelmiségiek, diplomások, szellemi munkások*, p. 82.

80 H.G. Skilling, *Czechoslovakia's Interrupted Revolution* (Princeton, NJ, 1976), p. 75.

81 A. White, *De-Stalinization and the House of Culture: Declining State Control over Leisure in the USSR, Poland and Hungary, 1953–89* (London, 1990), pp. 31–68.

82 Vickers, *The Albanians*, pp. 188–201.

83 S. Verona, *Military Occupation and Diplomacy: Soviet Troops in Romania, 1944–1958* (Duke, NC, 1992).

84 D. Deletant, *Ceauşescu and the Securitate: Coercion and Dissent in Romania, 1965–1989* (London, 1995), pp. 107–234.

85 K. Verdery, *National Ideology under Socialism: Identity and Cultural Politics in Ceauşescu's Romania* (Berkeley, CA, 1991).

86 Crampton, *A Short History of Modern Bulgaria*, p. 183.

87 A. Heller, '1968' in S. Révész (ed.), *Beszélő évek 1957–1968: A Kádár-korszak története I rész* (Budapest, 2000), p. 557.

88 E. Csizmadia, *A Magyar Demokratikus Ellenzék (1968–1988): Monográfia* (Budapest, 1995), pp. 17–37.

89 G. Gömöri, 'The Cultural Intelligentsia: The Writers' in Lane and Kolankiewicz (eds.), *Social Groups in Polish Society*, pp. 173–6.

90 J. Eisler, 'March 1968 in Poland' in C. Fink, P. Gassert and D. Junker (eds.), *1968: The World Transformed* (New York, 1998).
91 Quoted in Paczkowski, *Fél Évszázad*, p. 245.
92 A. Domány, 'Fajvédő kommunizmus Lengyelországban' in Révész (ed.), *Beszélő évek*, p. 572.
93 Allcock, *Explaining Yugoslavia*, p. 273.
94 Rusinow, *The Yugoslav Experiment*, p. 233.
95 Skilling, *Czechoslovakia's Interrupted Revolution*, pp. 45–89.
96 W. Shawcross, *Dubcek: Dubcek and Czechoslovakia 1918–1990* (London, 1990), pp. 104–14.
97 K. Williams, *The Prague Spring and its Aftermath: Czechoslovak Politics 1968–1970* (Cambridge, 1997), pp. 3–28.
98 Skilling, *Czechoslovakia's Interrupted Revolution*, pp. 493–613.
99 Shawcross, *Dubcek*, pp. 126–8.
100 Quoted in J. Suri, *Power and Protest: Global Revolution and the Rise of Détente* (Cambridge, MA, 2003), p. 199.
101 Williams, *The Prague Spring and its Aftermath*, pp. 112–25.

Chapter 4

1 *A Dolgozó Nép Alkotmánya – A Magyar Népköztársaság Alkotmánya* (Budapest, 1949), p. 37.
2 Quoted in Berend, *Central and Eastern Europe*, p. 51.
3 Quoted in 'Labor Discipline and Control', *News From Behind the Iron Curtain*, 1 (1), 1952, p. 18.
4 J. Aulich and M. Sylvestrová, *Political Posters in Central and Eastern Europe 1945–95: Signs of the Times* (Manchester, 1999), pp. 136–7.
5 P. Kenney, 'The Gender of Resistance in Communist Poland', *American Historical Review*, 104 (2), 1999, pp. 403–4.
6 'Men, Money and Machines', *News From Behind the Iron Curtain*, 1 (3), 1952, p. 17.
7 T. Smidt, 'Über die Geschichte eines Bildmotivs: Der polnische Arbeitsheld im Spiegel der Kunst' in Satjukow and Gries (eds.), *Sozialistische Helden*, p. 184.
8 Spulber, *The Economics of Communist Eastern Europe*, pp. 385–6.
9 Petrescu, 'Workers and Peasant-Workers in a Working Class "Paradise"', p. 4.
10 W. Höpken, 'Sonderfall Jugoslawien? Arbeiter im jugoslawischen Selbstverwaltungssozialismus: Abstract' (manuscripts, Leipzig, 2003), p. 2; Allcock, *Explaining Yugoslavia*, p. 58.

11 P. Heumos, 'Die Arbeiterschaft in der Ersten Tschechoslowakischen Republik: Elemente der Sozialstruktur, organisatorischen Verfassung und politischen Kultur', *Bohemia*, 29 (1), 1988, pp. 50–72.

12 Pittaway, 'Workers, Industrial Conflict and the State in Socialist Hungary', p. 5.

13 Kenney, *Rebuilding Poland*, pp. 85–111.

14 Pittaway, 'The Social Limits of State Control'.

15 S. Satjukow and R. Gries, 'Zur konstruktion des "sozialistischen Helden": Geschichte und Bedeutung' in Satjukow and Gries (eds.), *Sozialistische Helden*, p. 26.

16 M. Pittaway, 'The Reproduction of Hierarchy: Skill, Working-Class Culture and the State in Early Socialist Hungary', *The Journal of Modern History*, 74 (4), 2002, pp. 737–69.

17 'Men at Work', *News From Behind the Iron Curtain*, 2 (1), 1953, p. 22.

18 C. Brenner and P. Heumos, 'Eine Heldentypologie der Tschechoslowakei: Zur Einführung' in Satjukow and Gries (eds.), *Sozialistische Helden*, pp. 240–1.

19 D. Janák, 'Zur Sozialen Lage der Bergarbeiter im Ostrau-Karwiner Revier 1945–1955', *Bohemia*, 42 (2), 2002, pp. 290–306.

20 Kenney, *Rebuilding Poland*, pp. 135–85.

21 Pittaway, 'The Reproduction of Hierarchy'.

22 Quoted in Spulber, *The Economics of Communist Eastern Europe*, p. 390n.

23 'Handmaidens of Communism: Women in a New Dimension', *News From Behind the Iron Curtain*, 2 (4), 1953, p. 31.

24 MOL M-KS-276f.116/43ö.e., pp. 15–17.

25 Quoted in 'Handmaidens of Communism', p. 33.

26 Ibid., p. 32.

27 Spulber, *The Economics of Communist Eastern Europe*, p. 391.

28 S. Zimmermann, 'A szabad munkaerő nyomában, "Utolérő" fejlődés és női munka Magyarországon', *Eszmélet*, 25, 1995, pp. 166–83.

29 Heumos, 'Aspekte des sozialen Milieus', p. 326.

30 Pittaway, 'The Reproduction of Hierarchy', p. 648.

31 Petrescu, 'Workers and Peasant-Workers in a Working Class "Paradise" ', p. 4.

32 'Men, Money and Machines', p. 18.

33 Pittaway, 'The Reproduction of Hierarchy', pp. 745–51.

34 Heumos, 'Aspekte des sozialen Milieus', pp. 345–8.

35 Myant, *The Czechoslovak Economy*, pp. 133–43.
36 J. Kulpinska and M. Jaroskinska, 'A Munkásosztály Helyzete Lengyelországban' in F. Kovács (ed.), *A Munkásosztály Fejlődése a Szocialista Országokban 1945–1975: Tanulmányok* (Budapest, 1981), p. 78.
37 Kolankiewicz, 'The Polish Industrial Working Class', p. 133.
38 Kulpinska and Jaroskinska, 'A Munkásosztály Helyzete Lengyelországban', p. 79.
39 *1970 év Népszámlalási adatok. Foglalkozási adatok I.* (Budapest, 1973), p. 20.
40 Pittaway, 'Workers, Industrial Conflict and the State in Socialist Hungary', p. 33.
41 Petrescu, 'Workers and Peasant-Workers in a Working Class "Paradise" ', p. 3.
42 V. Ivanov, K. Petkov, K. Misev and L. Szpaszovszka, 'A Bolgár Munkásosztály a Fejlett Szocialista Társadalom Épitésében' in Kovács (ed.), *A Munkásosztály Fejlődése a Szocialista Országokban*, p. 6.
43 Denitch, *The Legitimation of a Revolution*, p. 64.
44 Petrescu, 'Workers and Peasant-Workers in a Working Class "Paradise" ', p. 6.
45 Ivanov, Petkov, Misev and Szpaszovszka, 'A Bolgár Munkásosztály', p. 23.
46 Höpken, 'Sonderfall Jugoslawien?', pp. 3–4.
47 I. Georgiev, 'Die Arbeiter als Modernisierungsbremse im real-sozialistischen Bulgarien?' (manuscripts, Berlin, 2003), p. 5.
48 Petrescu, 'Workers and Peasant-Workers in a Working Class "Paradise" ', pp. 7–8.
49 Radice, 'General Characteristics of the Region between the Wars', p. 31.
50 I.T. Berend, 'Agriculture' in Kaser and Radice, *Economic History of Eastern Europe. Volume I*, p. 154.
51 N. Swain, 'Czechoslovak Agriculture Prior to System Change' (University of Liverpool, Centre for Central and East European Studies, Rural Transition Series, Working Paper no. 28, Liverpool, 1994), p. 11.
52 N. Swain, 'Polish Agriculture Prior to System Change' (University of Liverpool, Centre for Central and East European Studies, Rural Transition Series, Working Paper no. 27, Liverpool, 1994), p. 8.

53 Allcock, *Explaining Yugoslavia*, pp. 126–7.
54 F. Donáth, *Demokratikus földreform Magyarországon, 1945–1947* (Budapest, 1969), pp. 124–5.
55 Cartwright, *The Return of the Peasant*, pp. 55–7.
56 Allcock, *Explaining Yugoslavia*, pp. 126–7.
57 Spulber, *The Economics of Communist Eastern Europe*, p. 242.
58 Pittaway, 'The Politics of Legitimacy', p. 65.
59 Kideckel, *The Solitude of Collectivism*, p. 80.
60 Bokovoy, *Peasants and Communists*, p. 89.
61 Cartwright, *The Return of the Peasant*, p. 68.
62 Spulber, *The Economics of Communist Eastern Europe*, pp. 248–53.
63 N. Swain, 'Collective farms as sources of stability and decay in the centrally planned economies of East Central Europe' (University of Liverpool, Centre for Central and East European Studies, Rural Transition Series, Working Paper no. 30, Liverpool, 1994), p. 6.
64 Cartwright, *The Return of the Peasant*, p. 74.
65 Pető and Szakács, *A hazai gazdaság*, p. 181.
66 Quoted in G.W. Creed, *Domesticating Revolution: From Socialist Reform to Ambivalent Transition in a Bulgarian Village* (University Park, PA, 1998), p. 56.
67 Á. Balázs, *A Lenin Tsz Tiszaföldváron* (Szolnok, 1970), pp. 57–8.
68 'Letters from Poland', *News From Behind the Iron Curtain*, 1 (1), 1952, p. 35.
69 'Agriculture and Collectivization', *News From Behind the Iron Curtain*, 1 (1), 1952, p. 16.
70 Draganova, 'Senses of the Private', p. 6.
71 Swain, 'Czechoslovak Agriculture Prior to System Change', pp. 16–18.
72 G. Hunya, 'Az Élelmezési Válság Okai' in Hunya (ed.), *Románia 1944–1990*, pp. 96–7.
73 M. Lampland, *The Object of Labor: Commodification in Socialist Hungary* (Chicago, 1995), pp. 176–80.
74 Swain, 'Collective farms as sources of stability and decay', p. 6.
75 Swain, 'Czechoslovak Agriculture Prior to System Change', p. 9.
76 Quoted in Creed, *Domesticating Revolution*, p. 70.
77 Z. Varga, 'The Transformation of Labor in Hungary's Collectivized Agriculture' (manuscripts, Budapest, 2003), p. 13.
78 Creed, *Domesticating Revolution*, pp. 79–82; Lampland, *The Object of Labor*, pp. 200–7.

79 Swain, 'Collective farms as sources of stability and decay', pp. 10–11.

80 Hunya, 'Az Élelmezési Válság Okai', p. 97.

81 Kideckel, *The Solitude of Collectivism*, p. 106.

82 D.A. Kideckel, 'The Social Organization of Production on a Romanian Cooperative Farm', *Dialectical Anthropology*, 1 (2), 1976, p. 274.

83 Varga, 'The Transformation of Labor', p. 11.

84 Lampland, *The Object of Labor*, p. 231.

85 Swain, 'Collective farms as sources of stability and decay', p. 10.

86 Hunya, 'Az Élelmezési Válság Okai', p. 113.

87 Draganova, 'Senses of the Private', p. 18.

88 Creed, *Domesticating Revolution*, p. 95.

89 N. Swain, *Collective Farms Which Work?* (Cambridge, 1985), p. 67.

90 Swain, 'Collective farms as sources of stability and decay', pp. 13–14.

91 Quoted in Spulber, *The Economics of Communist Eastern Europe*, p. 400.

92 Pittaway, 'The Reproduction of Hierarchy', p. 755.

93 'Public Health', *News From Behind the Iron Curtain*, 1 (6), 1952, p. 45.

94 Spulber, *The Economics of Communist Eastern Europe*, pp. 396–7.

95 Quoted in Connelly, *Captive University*, p. 63.

96 'Political Education in Communist Europe', *News From Behind the Iron Curtain*, 1 (2), 1952, p. 23.

97 Connelly, *Captive University*, p. 136.

98 'Political Education in Communist Europe', p. 23.

99 Lilly, *Power and Persuasion*, pp. 94–9.

100 Pittaway, 'The Education of Dissent', pp. 102–3.

101 G. Péteri, 'Introduction. Intellectual Life and the First Crisis of State Socialism in East Central Europe, 1953–6' in G. Péteri (ed.), *Intellectual Life and the First Crisis of State Socialism in East Central Europe* (Trondheim, 2001), p. 12.

102 P. György, 'The Mirror of Everyday Life, or the Will to a Period Style' in P. György and H. Turai (eds.), *Art and Society in the Age of Stalin* (Budapest, 1992), pp. 15–26.

103 M. Svašek, 'Contacts: Social Dynamics in the Czechoslovak State-Socialist Art World', *Contemporary European History*, 11 (1), 2002, pp. 72–6.

[104] OSA RFE Magyar Gy. 6/ Item No. 673/57, pp. 1–2.
[105] G. Péteri, 'New Course Economics: The Field of Economic Research after Stalin, 1953–6' in Péteri (ed.), *Intellectual Life and the First Crisis of State Socialism*, pp. 47–79.
[106] P. Machewicz, 'Intellectuals and Mass Movements: The Study of Political Dissent in Poland in 1956' in Péteri (ed.), *Intellectual Life and the First Crisis of State Socialism*, pp. 120–1.
[107] J.M. Rainer, *Az Író Helye: Viták a magyar irodalmi sajtóban 1953–1956* (Budapest, 1990).
[108] É. Standeiszky, *Az Írók és a Hatalom, 1956–1963* (Budapest, 1996).
[109] Gömöri, 'The Cultural Intelligentsia: the Writers'.

Chapter 5

[1] Fejér Megyei Levéltár Magyar Szocialista Munkáspárt Fejér Megyei Bizottság archivium iratai (Fejér County Archive, Papers of the Fejér County Committee of the Hungarian Socialist Workers' Party, hereafter MSZMP FMBA), ir. 9f.1/46ö.e.; *Statisztikai Össeszitő (kerület, járás, város, nagyüzem részére): Fejér megyei összesitő 1952 I. hó.*
[2] Quoted in B. Janus, 'Labor's Paradise: Family, Work and Home in Nowa Huta, Poland, 1950–1960', *East European Quarterly*, 23 (4), 2000, p. 454.
[3] A. Sándor, *Híradás a Pusztáról 1945–1950*, (Budapest, 1951), p. 213.
[4] M. Pittaway, 'Creating and Domesticating Hungary's Socialist Industrial Landscape: from Dunapentele to Sztálinváros, 1950–1958' (manuscripts, Milton Keynes, 2003), pp. 12–13.
[5] D. Crowley, 'Warsaw Interiors: The Public Life of Private Spaces, 1949–1965' in D. Crowley and S.E. Reid (eds.), *Socialist Spaces: Sites of Everyday Life in the Eastern Bloc* (Oxford, 2002), p. 190.
[6] S. Horváth, 'A parasztság életmódváltozása Sztálinvárosban', *Mozgó Vílág*, 26 (6), 2000, pp. 30–40.
[7] Spulber, *The Economics of Communist Eastern Europe*, p. 385.
[8] Pető, 'Stimmen des Schweigens'.
[9] A. Milić, 'Women and Nationalism in the Former Yugoslavia' in N. Funk and M. Mueller (eds.), *Gender Politics and Post-Communism: Reflections from Eastern Europe and the Former Soviet Union* (London, 1993), p. 111.

10 J. Benderly, 'Feminist Movements in Yugoslavia, 1978–1992' in M.K. Bokovoy, J.A. Irvine and C.S. Lilly (eds.), *State–Society Relations in Yugoslavia 1945–1995* (New York, 1997), p. 185.

11 A. Pető, *Nőhistóriák: A politizáló Magyar nők történetéből 1945–1951* (Budapest, 1998), pp. 88–121.

12 A. Heitlinger, *Women and State Socialism: Sex Inequality in the Soviet Union and Czechoslovakia* (London, 1979), p. 136.

13 Haney, *Inventing the Needy*, pp. 28–30.

14 G. Kligman, *The Politics of Duplicity: Controlling Reproduction in Ceausescu's Romania* (Berkeley, CA, 1998), p. 47.

15 Haney, *Inventing the Needy*, p. 32.

16 M. Fuszara, 'Abortion and the Formation of the Public Sphere in Poland' in Funk and Mueller (eds.), *Gender Politics and Post-Communism*, pp. 241–2.

17 M. Pittaway, 'Retreat from Collective Protest: Household, Gender, Work and Popular Opposition in Stalinist Hungary' in J. Kok (ed.), *Rebellious Families: Household Strategies and Collective Action in the Nineteenth and Twentieth Centuries* (New York, 2002), pp. 199–229.

18 M. Lampland, 'Biographies of Liberation: Testimonials to Labour in Socialist Hungary' in S. Kruks, R. Rapp and M.B. Young (eds.), *Promissory Notes. Women in the Transition to Socialism* (New York, 1989), pp. 306–22; M. Lampland, 'Unthinkable Subjects: Women and Labour in Socialist Hungary', *East European Quarterly*, 23 (4), 1990, pp. 389–98.

19 'Men at Work', p. 20.

20 S.L. Woodward, 'The Rights of Women: Ideology, Policy and Social Change in Yugoslavia' in S.L. Wolchik and A.G. Meyer (eds.), *Women, State and Party in Eastern Europe* (Durham, NC, 1985), p. 245.

21 Pittaway, 'Retreat from Collective Protest'.

22 F. Pine, 'Uneven burdens: Women in rural Poland' in A. Phizacklea, H. Pilkington and S. Rai (eds.), *Women in the Face of Change: The Soviet Union, Eastern Europe and China* (London, 1992), pp. 57–75.

23 M.B. Olujić, 'Economic and Demographic Change in Contemporary Yugoslavia: Persistence of Traditional Gender Ideology', *East European Quarterly*, 23 (4), 1990, p. 482.

24 'Handmaidens of Communism', p. 32.

25 PRO FO 371/8622, 'How a workman lives in Prague', p. 4.
26 'Decree No. 84', *News From Behind the Iron Curtain*, 1 (8), 1952, pp. 19–20.
27 PRO FO 371/77249, 'Czechoslovakia: Weekly Information Summary, 19ᵗʰ–25ᵗʰ October 1949', p. 2.
28 'Poland', *News From Behind the Iron Curtain*, 1 (8), 1952, p. 22.
29 'Peasant Rebellion Reported', p. 17.
30 'Albania', *News From Behind the Iron Curtain*, 1 (1), 1952, p. 33.
31 'Bulgaria', *News From Behind the Iron Curtain*, 1 (8), 1952, p. 19.
32 B. Kerewsky-Halpern, 'An Anthropologist in the Village' in J.B. Allcock and A. Young (eds.), *Black Lambs and Grey Falcons: Women Travelling in the Balkans* (New York, 2000), p. 193.
33 'Gary J. Handler' in A. Handler and S.V. Meschel (eds.), *Red Star, Blue Star: The Lives and Times of Jewish Students in Communist Hungary (1948–1956)* (Boulder, CO, 1997), p. 157.
34 Kerewsky-Halpern, 'An Anthropologist in the Village', p. 193.
35 F. Gáspár and K. Szabó (eds.), *Források Budapest Történetehez. V. kötet 1950–1954* (Budapest, 1985), pp. 75–6.
36 Crowley, 'Warsaw Interiors', p. 182.
37 Pittaway, 'Industrial Workers, Socialist Industrialization and the State', pp. 300–1.
38 'Letters from Poland', *News From Behind the Iron Curtain*, 1 (1), 1952, p. 35.
39 OSA RFE Magyar Gy.6, Item No. 08371/52, p. 2.
40 Petrescu, 'Workers and Peasant-Workers in a Working Class "Paradise" ', p. 4.
41 Pittaway, 'The Reproduction of Hierarchy', p. 764.
42 M. Pittaway, 'Stalinism, Working-Class Housing and Individual Autonomy: the Case of Private House-building in Hungary's Mining Areas, 1950–54' in Reid and Crowley (eds.), *Style and Socialism*, pp. 149–64.
43 'Letters from Poland', p. 36.
44 'The Czechoslovak Diet', *News From Behind the Iron Curtain*, 2 (10), 1953, p. 18.
45 W.L. Hixson, *Parting the Curtain: Propaganda, Culture and the Cold War, 1945–1961* (Basingstoke, 1998), chapters 2–3.
46 Pittaway, 'Industrial Workers, Socialist Industrialization and the State', p. 340.
47 'The Czechoslovak Currency Reform', p. 23.

48 Quoted in Lilly, *Power and Persuasion*, p. 89.
49 PRO FO 371/71265, 'Czechoslovakia: Weekly Information Summary, 14th–20th December 1948', p. 2.
50 Pittaway, 'The Reproduction of Hierarchy', pp. 742–3.
51 Lilly, *Power and Persuasion*, p. 141.
52 I. Márkus, 'Egyszerő Feljegyzések 1947–ből' in Márkus, *Az Ismeretlen Főszereplő*, p. 109.
53 PRO FO 371/71265, 'Czechoslovakia: Weekly Information Summary, 17th–23rd September 1948', p. 1.
54 'Not for Socialist Ears', *News From Behind the Iron Curtain*, 2 (1), 1953, p. 43.
55 'Political Education in Communist Europe', p. 23.
56 K.A. Lebow, 'Public works, private lives: youth brigades in Nowa Huta in the 1950s', *Contemporary European History*, 10 (2), 2001, pp. 199–219.
57 S. Horváth, 'A késdobáló és a jampecek. Szubkultúrák Sztálinvárosban, *Korall*, 1 (1), 2000, pp. 119–36.
58 Pittaway, 'Stalinism, Working-Class Housing and Individual Autonomy'.
59 B. Luthar and V. Zei, 'Shopping Across the Border: Yugoslav Shopping Expeditions to Trieste' (manuscripts, Ljubljana, 2003), p. 9.
60 Quoted in György, 'The Mirror of Everyday Life', p. 20.
61 *Esti Budapest*, 7 January 1953.
62 Quoted in Patterson, 'The New Class', p. 147.
63 Crowley, 'Warsaw's Shops', p. 41.
64 M. Pittaway, 'Work, Socialist Consumerism and Political Stabilization: Hungary, 1953–1960' (manuscripts, Southport, 1998).
65 Patterson, 'The New Class', pp. 130–1.
66 'A Kommunizmus építőinek kongresszusa': Részlet az SZKP XII. Kongresszusának anyagaiból (Budapest, 1961), pp. 224–5.
67 Crowley, 'Warsaw Interiors', p. 193.
68 J. Kósa, 'Budapest during the Kádár Era, 1957–1988' in A. Gerő and J. Poór (eds.), *Budapest: A History from its Beginnings to 1998*, trans. J. Zinner, C.D. Eby and N. Arató (Boulder, CO, 1997), p. 263.
69 Creed, *Domesticating Revolution*, p. 136.
70 Allcock, *Explaining Yugoslavia*, p. 137.
71 *Munka*, April 1954, p. 49.

72 Creed, *Domesticating Revolution*, pp. 200–2.

73 D. Crowley, 'Making the Socialist Home in Post-war Eastern Europe' in M. Pittaway (ed.), *Globalization and Europe* (Milton Keynes, 2003), pp. 249–95.

74 Crowley, 'Warsaw Interiors', p. 196.

75 Szántó, *Életmód, Művelődés, Szabadidő*, pp. 78–80.

76 Patterson, 'The New Class', p. 98.

77 Olujić, 'Economic and Demographic Change in Contemporary Yugoslavia'.

78 B. Einhorn, *Cinderella Goes to Market: Citizenship, Gender and Women's Movements in East Central Europe* (London, 1993), p. 264.

79 Heitlinger, *Women and State Socialism*, p. 141.

80 D. Crowley and S.E. Reid. 'Style and Socialism: Modernity and Material Culture in Post-War Eastern Europe' in Reid and Crowley (eds.), *Style and Socialism*, pp. 1–3.

81 Pittaway, 'Work, Socialist Consumerism and Political Stabilization'.

82 M. Neuburger, 'Veils, *Shalvari*, and Matters of Dress: Unravelling the Fabric of Women's Lives in Communist Bulgaria' in Reid and Crowley (eds.), *Style and Socialism*, pp. 180–1.

83 M. Pittaway, ' "They are already no longer peasants, but they still have not become workers": Making a stable working class in the Zalaegerszeg Clothes Factory' (manuscripts, Budapest, 1996), p. 8.

84 T.W. Ryback, *Rock Around the Bloc: A History of Rock Music in Eastern Europe and the Soviet Union* (New York, 1990), pp. 56–7.

85 A. Puddington, *Broadcasting Freedom: the Cold War Triumph of Radio Free Europe and Radio Liberty* (Lexington, 2000), pp. 137–41.

86 T. Elek, 'Where Is Youth Headed?' in W. Juhász (ed.), *Hungarian Social Science Reader 1945–1963* (New York, 1965), pp. 296–7.

87 MOL M-KS-288f.21/1958/22ö.e., pp. 229–31.

88 Fuszara, 'Abortion and the Formation of the Public Sphere in Poland', p. 242.

89 Heitlinger, *Women and State Socialism*, p. 187.

90 Kligman, *The Politics of Duplicity*, pp. 52–67.

91 Heitlinger, *Women and State Socialism*, p. 181.

92 Haney, *Inventing the Needy*, p. 104.

[93] 'Handmaidens of Communism', p. 32.
[94] Pittaway, 'Industrial Workers, Socialist Industrialisation and the State', p. 276.
[95] Haney, *Inventing the Needy*, p. 103.
[96] Lampland, 'Biographies of Liberation'.
[97] R. Schwanke, 'Frauenemanzipation in Albanien', *East European Quarterly*, 2 (1), 1968, p. 63n.
[98] P. Ramet, 'Women, Work and Self-Management in Yugoslavia', *East European Quarterly*, 17 (4), 1983, p. 463.
[99] Creed, *Domesticating Revolution*, pp. 200–2.
[100] Sampson, 'The Informal Sector in Eastern Europe', pp. 61–2.
[101] Quoted in J.W. Cole and J.A. Nydon, 'Class, Gender and Fertility: Contradictions of Social Life in Contemporary Romania', *East European Quarterly*, 23 (4), 1990, p. 473.
[102] Kemény, 'A nem regisztrált gazdaság Magyarországon', pp. 222–3.
[103] I.R. Gábor and P. Galasi, 'A "kiegészítő tevékenységek" társadalmi összefüggései' in H. Vass (ed.), *Válság és Megújulás: Gazdaság, társadalom és politika Magyarországon. Az MSZMP 25 éve* (Budapest, 1982), p. 201.
[104] Pittaway, 'Workers, Industrial Conflict and the State', pp. 45–56.
[105] W.G. Lockwood, 'Social Status and Cultural Change in a Bosnian Moslem Village', *East European Quarterly*, 9 (2), 1975, p. 130.
[106] Patterson, 'The New Class', pp. 10–11.
[107] Luthar and Zei, 'Shopping Across the Border', pp. 22–7.
[108] F. Halmos *Illő Alázattal* (Budapest, 1978), p. 131.

Chapter 6

[1] Politikatörténeti és Szakszervezeti Levéltár (Archive of Political History and Trade Unions), A Volt Szakszervezetek Központi Levéltár anyaga (Papers of the Former Central Archive of the Trade Unions, hereafter SZKL), Zala Szakszervezetek Megyei Tanácsa (Council of Zala County Trade Unions, hereafter Zala SZMT), /41d./1950, *Nagykanzsa, 1950 augusztus 11.*
[2] Quoted in F. Fejtö, *A History of the People's Democracies: Eastern Europe since Stalin*, trans. D. Weissbort (Harmondsworth, 1974), p. 12.
[3] Quoted in G. Stokes (ed.), *From Stalinism to Pluralism: A Documentary History of Eastern Europe since 1945* (New York, 1991), p. 96.

4 Quoted in M.K. Dziewanowski, *The Communist Party of Poland: An Outline of History* (Cambridge, MA, 1976), 2nd edition, p. 276.

5 Quoted in King, *History of the Romanian Communist Party*, p. 121.

6 Komárom-Esztergom Megyei Levéltár, Magyar Szocialista Munkáspárt Komárom-Esztergom Megyei Bizottság iratai (Komárom-Esztergom County Archive, Papers of the Archive of the Komárom-Esztergom County Committee of the Hungarian Socialist Workers' Party, hereafter KEML MSZMP KMBA ir.) 32f.4/1949/1ö.e.

7 Quoted in Z. Suda, *Zealots and Rebels: A History of the Ruling Communist Party of Czechoslovakia* (Stanford, CA, 1980), p. 255.

8 Quoted in Fejtö, *A History of the People's Democracies*, p. 76.

9 M.J.A. Standish, 'Enver Hoxha's Role in the Development of Socialist Albanian Myths' in S. Schwandner Sievers and B.J. Fischer (eds.), *Albanian Identities: Myth and History* (London, 2002), p. 121.

10 Crampton, *A Short History of Modern Bulgaria*, pp. 186–91; P.F. Sugar, 'East European Nationalisms in the 20th Century' in P.F. Sugar, *East European Nationalisms, Politics and Religion* (Aldershot, 1999), p. 359.

11 Quoted in Dziewanowski, *The Communist Party of Poland*, p. 283.

12 J. Kenédi, *Kis Állambiztonsági Olvasókönyv: október 23 – március 15 – június 16 a Kádár-korszakban* (Budapest, 1996).

13 F. Bondy, 'The Government vs. the Workers', reprinted in B. Lomax (ed.), *Hungarian Workers' Councils in 1956*, trans. B. Lomax and J. Schöpflin (Boulder, CO, 1990), p. 523.

14 Quoted in I. Romsics, *Hungary in the Twentieth Century*, trans. T. Wilkinson (Budapest, 2000), p. 333.

15 Quoted in P.A. Toma, 'The Czechoslovak Question under Communism', *East European Quarterly*, 3 (1), 1969, p. 18.

16 B.W. Jancar, *Czechoslovakia and the Absolute Monopoly of Power: A Study of Political Power in a Communist System* (New York, 1971), pp. 212–13.

17 Wachtel, *Making a Nation, Breaking a Nation*, pp. 173–4.

18 Rusinow, *The Yugoslav Experiment*, pp. 148–56.

19 'Structure of Security in Poland', *News From Behind the Iron Curtain*, 1 (1), 1952, p. 14.

20 Columbia University Libraries Rare Book and Manuscript

Library, Bakhmeteff Archive, Hungarian Refugees Project, Box 10, Interview No. 203, p. 28.

[21] 'The Czechoslovak Currency Reform', p. 23.

[22] 'Anti-State Activities Probed', *News From Behind the Iron Curtain*, 1 (1), 1952, p. 15.

[23] Lewis, *The Polish Volcano*, p. 32.

[24] S. Rácz, 'The Workers' Councils Gave their Stamp to the Entire Revolution' in Lomax (ed.), *Hungarian Workers' Councils in 1956*, p. 409.

[25] Lewis, *The Polish Volcano*, pp. 140–1.

[26] K. Frigyes (ed.), *Sortüzek 1956* (Lakitelek, 1993).

[27] Litván et al., *The Hungarian Revolution*, p. 77.

[28] Budapest Oral History Archive, 449, pp. 27–8.

[29] Pittaway, 'Workers, Industrial Conflict and the State', p. 23.

[30] I. Lovas and K. Anderson, 'State Terrorism in Hungary: the Case of Friendly Repression', *Telos*, 54, 1982–3, pp. 77–86.

[31] Paczkowski, *Lengyelország Története*, pp. 207–11.

[32] Myant, *The Czechoslovak Economy*, p. 75.

[33] Deletant, *Communist Terror in Romania*, p. 261.

[34] Litván et al., *The Hungarian Revolution*, pp. 89–90.

[35] G. Kiszely, *Állambiztonság 1956–1990* (Budapest, 2001), p. 194.

[36] Deletant, *Communist Terror in Romania*, p. 288.

[37] Deletant, *Ceauşescu and the Securitate*, pp. 93–4.

[38] M. Simečka, *The Restoration of Order: The Normalization of Czechoslovakia 1969–1979*, trans. A.G. Brain (London, 1984), p. 87.

[39] M. Pittaway, 'Control and Consent in Eastern Europe's Workers' States: Some Reflections on Totalitarianism, Social Organization and Social Control' (manuscripts, Milton Keynes, 2000), p. 5.

[40] M. Djilas, *Tito: the Story from Inside*, trans. V. Kojic and R. Hayes (London, 1981), p. 112.

[41] King, *History of the Romanian Communist Party*, pp. 72–3; M. Pittaway, 'Workers in Hungary' (manuscripts, Milton Keynes, 2003), p. 15.

[42] I. Szenes, *A Kommunista Párt Újjászervezése Magyarországon 1956–1957* (Budapest, 1976), p. 195.

[43] King, *History of the Romanian Communist Party*, p. 80.

[44] Dziewanowski, *The Communist Party of Poland*, p. 325.

[45] Denitch, *The Legitimation of a Revolution*, p. 94.

[46] D.N. Nelson, 'The Politics of Romanian Trade Unions' in A. Pravda

and B.A. Ruble (eds.), *Trade Unions in Communist States* (Boston, 1986), p. 120.

47 E.Z. Tóth, 'Változó Identitások Munkásnők Élettörténeti Elbeszéléseiben' in J.M. Rainer and É. Standeiszky (eds.), *1956-os Intézet Évkönyv 2002* (Budapest, 2002), pp. 76–89.

48 Quoted in P. Raina, 'Intellectuals and the Party in Bulgaria' in J.P. Shapiro and P.J. Potichnyi (eds.), *Change and Adaptation in Soviet and East European Politics* (New York, 1976), pp. 193–4.

49 Ryback, *Rock Around the Bloc*, pp. 69–70.

50 L. Kürti, *Youth and the State in Hungary: Capitalism, Communism and Class* (London, 2002), pp. 146–7.

51 Ryback, *Rock Around the Bloc*, p. 92.

52 Pittaway, 'Workers, Industrial Conflict and the State', p. 23.

53 Quoted in J. Kubik, *The Power of Symbols against the Symbols of Power: The Rise of Solidarity and the Fall of Socialism in Poland* (University Park, PA, 1994), p. 113.

54 P.F. Sugar, 'Religion, Nationalism and Politics in East-Central Europe' in Sugar, *East European Nationalisms*, p. 12.

55 F. Friedman, 'The Bosnian Muslims: The Making of a Yugoslav Nation' in Bokovoy, Irvine and Lilly (eds.), *State–Society Relations in Yugoslavia*, pp. 274–6.

56 Kiszely, *Állambiztonság*, pp. 97–143.

57 Deletant, *Ceauşescu and the Securitate*, pp. 212–16.

58 J. Bugajszki and M. Pollack, *East European Fault Lines: Dissent, Opposition, and Social Activism* (Boulder, CO, 1989), p. 149.

59 P. Michel, *Politics and Religion in Eastern Europe: Catholicism in Hungary, Poland and Czechoslovakia*, trans. A. Braley (Cambridge, 1991), p. 125.

60 Kubik, *The Power of Symbols against the Symbols of Power*, pp. 108–17.

61 Kenédi, *Kis Állambiztonsági Olvasókönyv*.

62 Toma, 'The Czechoslovak Question under Communism', pp. 20–2.

63 Tanner, *Croatia*, pp. 190–1.

64 N. Malcom, *Kosovo: A Short History* (London, 1998), p. 325.

65 Csizmadia, *A Magyar Demokratikus Ellenzék*, pp. 17–37.

66 Paczkowski, *Fél Évszázad*, pp. 241–2.

67 Rusinow, *The Yugoslav Experiment*, pp. 217–18.

68 Quoted in Williams, *The Prague Spring and its Aftermath*, p. 16.

Chapter 7

1 Williams, *The Prague Spring and its Aftermath*, pp. 121–31.
2 Quoted in Skilling, *Czechoslovakia's Interrupted Revolution*, p. 769.
3 Williams, *The Prague Spring and its Aftermath*, pp. 234–5.
4 Simečka, *The Restoration of Order*, p. 60.
5 Quoted in J.N. Stevens, *Czechoslovakia at the Crossroads: The Economic Dilemmas of Communism in Post-war Czechoslovakia* (Boulder, CO, 1985), p. 189.
6 Quoted in P. Bren, 'Weekend Getaways: The Chata, the Tramp, and the Politics of Private Life in Post-1968 Czechoslovakia' in Crowley and Reid (eds.), *Socialist Spaces*, p. 123.
7 V. Havel, 'The Power of the Powerless' in J. Vladislav (ed.), *Václav Havel: Living in Truth* (London, 1986), p. 54.
8 Csizmadia, *A Magyar Demokratikus Ellenzék*, pp. 38–83.
9 Quoted in S. László-Bencsik, *Történelem alulnézetben* (Budapest, 1975), p. 203.
10 Quoted in F. Halmos, *Illő Alázattal* (Budapest, 1978), p. 120.
11 Pittaway, 'Workers, Industrial Conflict and the State in Hungary', pp. 51–2.
12 R. Laba, *The Roots of Solidarity: A Political Sociology of Poland's Working-Class Democratization* (Princeton, NJ, 1991), p. 82.
13 Paczkowski, *Fél Évszázad*, p. 262.
14 Laba, *The Roots of Solidarity*, pp. 92–3.
15 K.J. Lepak, *Prelude to Solidarity: Poland and the Politics of the Gierek Regime* (New York, 1988), pp. 50–3.
16 V.C. Chrypiński, 'Political Change under Gierek' in Bromke and Strong (eds.), *Gierek's Poland*, p. 40.
17 Quoted in Lepak, *Prelude to Solidarity*, p. 70.
18 Quoted in R. Taras, *Poland: Socialist State, Rebellious Nation* (Boulder, 1986), p. 62.
19 Kubik, *The Power of Symbols against the Symbols of Power*, pp. 31–74.
20 D. Bingen, 'The Catholic Church as a Political Actor' in J. Bielasiak and M.D. Simon (eds.), *Polish Politics: Edge of the Abyss* (New York, 1984), p. 214.
21 Landau and Tomaszewski, *The Polish Economy*, pp. 291–3.
22 King, *History of the Romanian Communist Party*, pp. 143–4.
23 Quoted in Deletant, *Ceaușescu and the Securitate*, p. 119.
24 Quoted in Verdery, *National Ideology under Socialism*, p. 117.

25 Quoted in A.U. Gabanyi, 'Nicolae Ceauşescu and his Personality Cult' in A.U. Gabanyi, *The Ceauşescu Cult: Propaganda and Power Policy in Communist Romania* (Bucharest, 2000), p. 18.

26 A.U. Gabanyi, 'Ceauşescu's Birthday' in ibid., p. 27.

27 T. Gilberg, *Modernization in Romania since World War II* (New York, 1975), p. 151.

28 Deletant, *Ceauşescu and the Securitate*, p. 70.

29 Hunya, 'Ceauşescu-korszak gazdasága', p. 61.

30 Quoted in Standish, 'Enver Hoxha's Role in the Development of Socialist Albanian Myths', p. 122.

31 Quoted in Vickers, *Albania*, p. 200.

32 M. Neuburgerm, 'Veils, *Shalvari* and Matters of Dress: Unravelling the Fabric of Women's Lives in Communist Bulgaria' in Reid and Crowley (eds.), *Style and Socialism*, p. 182.

33 A. Pantev, 'The Historic Road of the Third Bulgarian State' in I. Zloch-Christy (ed.), *Bulgaria in a Time of Change: Economic and Political Dimensions* (Aldershot, 1996), p. 18.

34 Tanner, *Croatia*, pp. 191–5.

35 Quoted in Lampe, *Yugoslavia as History*, p. 308.

36 Quoted in Rusinow, *The Yugoslav Experiment*, p. 311.

37 Lampe, *Yugoslavia as History*, p. 313.

38 Rusinow, *The Yugoslav Experiment*, p. 317.

39 S.L. Woodward, *Balkan Tragedy: Chaos and Disillusion after the Cold War* (Washington DC, 1995), p. 40.

40 L. Csaba, *Eastern Europe in the World Economy*, trans. L. Csaba and E. Dessewffy (Cambridge, 1990), pp. 367–70.

41 R. Brenner, 'The Economics of Global Turbulence: A Special Report on the World Economy, 1950–98', *New Left Review*, 229, 1998, pp. 136–8.

42 Stevens, *Czechoslovakia at the Crossroads*, p. 252.

43 G. Kolankiewicz, 'Poland, 1980: the Working Class under "Anomic Socialism"' in Triska and Gati (eds.), *Blue Collar Workers in Eastern Europe*, p. 143.

44 D.M. Kemme, 'The Polish Crisis: An Economic Overview' in Bielasiak and Simon (eds.), *Polish Politics*, p. 37.

45 Hunya, 'Ceauşescu-korszak gazdasága', pp. 63–9.

46 Lampe, *Yugoslavia as History*, p. 325.

47 G. Földes, *Az Eladósodás Politikatörténete 1957–1986* (Budapest, 1995), pp. 77–142.

[48] Swain, *Hungary*, pp. 199–219.
[49] M. Vale (ed.), *Poland – the State of the Republic: Reports by the Experience and Future Discussion Group (DiP) Warsaw* (London, 1981), p. 28.
[50] Kolankiewicz, 'Poland, 1980', pp. 142–3.
[51] Myant, *Poland: A Crisis for Socialism*, pp. 91–2.
[52] Petrescu, 'Workers and Peasant-Workers in a Working Class "Paradise" ', pp. 8–10.
[53] Pittaway, 'Workers, Industrial Conflict and the State in Hungary', p. 53.
[54] Lepak, *Prelude to Solidarity*, pp. 167–71.
[55] Ryback, *Rock around the Bloc*, pp. 145–8.
[56] Keane, *Václav Havel*, pp. 243–8.
[57] Bugajski and Pollack, *East European Fault Lines*, p. 126.
[58] Csizmadia, *A Magyar Demokratikus Ellenzék*, pp. 98–216.
[59] Deletant, *Ceauşescu and the Securitate*, pp. 236–42.
[60] Bugajski and Pollack, *East European Fault Lines*, p. 139.
[61] Kubik, *The Power of Symbols against the Symbols of Power*, pp. 129–52.
[62] Lepak, *Prelude to Solidarity*, p. 195.
[63] Laba, *The Roots of Solidarity*, pp. 99–125.
[64] T. Garton Ash, *The Polish Revolution: Solidarity* (London, 1983), pp. 41–72.
[65] J. Staniszkis, *Poland's Self-Limiting Revolution*, ed. J.T. Gross (Princeton, NJ, 1984).

Chapter 8

[1] For a similar analysis see K. Verdery, 'What Was Socialism, and Why Did it Fall?' in V. Tismaneanu (ed.), *The Revolutions of 1989* (London, 1999), pp. 63–85.
[2] Brenner, 'The Economics of Global Turbulence', pp. 178–81.
[3] Hunya, 'Ceauşescu-korszak gazdasága', pp. 69–72.
[4] D.M. Nuti, 'The Polish Crisis: Economic Factors and Constraints' in J. Drewnowski (ed.), *Crisis in the East European Economy: the Spread of the Polish Disease* (London, 1982), pp. 59–60.
[5] *Poland: Stagnation, Collapse or Growth? A Report by an Independent Group of Economists in Poland* (London, 1988).
[6] Lampe, *Yugoslavia as History*, pp. 325–7.
[7] Stevens, *Czechoslovakia at the Crossroads*, pp. 299–301.

8 Crampton, *A Short History of Modern Bulgaria*, p. 197.
9 Bren, 'Weekend Getaways', pp. 134–6.
10 Quoted in Stevens, *Czechoslovakia at the Crossroads*, p. 287.
11 Quoted in A. Seleny, 'Constructing the Discourse of Trans-formation: Hungary, 1979–1982', *East European Politics and Societies*, 8 (3), 1994, p. 458.
12 Swain, *Hungary*, pp. 131–44.
13 Pittaway, 'Workers, Industrial Conflict and the State', p. 54.
14 Crampton, *A Short History of Modern Bulgaria*, pp. 197–9.
15 G. Sanford, *Military Rule in Poland: The Rebuilding of Communist Power, 1981–1983* (London, 1986), p. 139.
16 Nuti, 'The Polish Crisis', p. 61.
17 Paczkowski, *Fél Évszázad*, pp. 359–60.
18 *Poland: Stagnation, Collapse or Growth?*
19 Woodward, *Balkan Tragedy*, pp. 51–3.
20 Hunya, 'Ceauşescu-korszak gazdasága', pp. 74–82.
21 A.U. Gabanyi, 'The Ceauşescu Era – An Era of Restrictions' in Gabanyi, *The Ceauşescu Cult*, pp. 369–78.
22 K. Verdery, 'The "Etatization" of Time in Ceauşescu's Romania' in K. Verdery, *What Was Socialism and What Comes Next?* (Princeton, NJ, 1996), p. 56.
23 Kligman, *The Politics of Duplicity*, p. 146.
24 Petrescu, 'Workers and Peasant-Workers in a Working Class "Paradise" ', p. 14.
25 Gabanyi, 'The Ceauşescu Era – An Era of Restrictions', p. 377.
26 Petrescu, 'Workers and Peasant-Workers in a Working Class "Paradise" ', p. 11.
27 B. Magaš, *The Destruction of Yugoslavia: Tracking the Break-up 1980–92* (London, 1993), p. 98.
28 Allcock, *Explaining Yugoslavia*, p. 97.
29 Magaš, *The Destruction of Yugoslavia*, p. 116.
30 Quoted in Sanford, *Military Rule in Poland*, p. 269.
31 J. Wedel, *The Private Poland* (New York, 1986).
32 M. Burawoy and J. Lukács, *The Radiant Past: Ideology and Reality in Hungary's Road to Capitalism* (Chicago, 1992), pp. 111–42.
33 Quoted in L. Kürti, ' "Red Csepel": Working Youth in a Socialist Firm', *East European Quarterly*, 23 (4), 1990, p. 448.
34 A. Tóth, 'Semmi sem dőlt el, és mégis minden eldőlt: a szaksz-ervezetek a kerekasztalnál' in A. Bozóki (ed.), *A Rendszerváltás*

Forgatókönyve: Kerekasztal-tárgyalások 1985-ben – Alkotmányos Forradalom: Tanulmányok (Budapest, 2000), p. 309.

35 P.H. O'Neill, *Revolution from Within: the Hungarian Socialist Workers' Party and the Collapse of Communism* (Cheltenham, 1998), p. 89.

36 B. Wheaton and Z. Kavan, *The Velvet Revolution: Czechoslovakia, 1988–1991* (Boulder, CO, 1992), pp. 24–5.

37 R. Daskalov, 'A Democracy Born in Pain: Bulgarian Politics, 1989–1997' in J.D. Bell (ed.), *Bulgaria in Transition: Politics, Economics and Culture After Communism* (Boulder CO, 1998), p. 10.

38 S.P. Ramet, *Social Currents in Eastern Europe: the Sources and Meaning of the Great Transformation* (Durham, 1991), pp. 257–65.

39 Quoted in N.J. Miller, 'Reconstituting Serbia: 1945–1991' in Bokovoy, Irvine and Lilly (eds.), *State–Society Relations in Yugoslavia*, p. 299.

40 Malcom, *Kosovo*, p. 335.

41 Quoted in Magaš, *The Destruction of Yugoslavia*, p. 49.

42 Tanner, *Croatia*, pp. 208–9.

43 Paczkowski, *Fél Évszázad*, pp. 343–51.

44 Bugajski and Pollack, *East European Fault Lines*, pp. 126–7.

45 Csizmadia, *A Magyar Demokratikus Ellenzék*, pp. 217–317.

46 J. Rupnik (ed.), 'Totalitarianism Revisited' in J. Keane (ed.), *Civil Society and the State: New European Perspectives* (London, 1988), pp. 263–89.

47 T. Garton Ash, 'Does Central Europe Exist?' in Garton Ash, *The Uses of Adversity*, pp. 161–91.

48 Tanner, *Croatia*, p. 209.

49 Wheaton and Kavan, *The Velvet Revolution*, p. 25.

50 J. Figa, 'Socializing the State: Civil Society and Democratization from Below in Slovenia' in Bokovoy, Irvine and Lilly (eds.), *State–Society Relations in Yugoslavia*, pp. 163–82.

51 Kenney, *Carnival*, pp. 157–75.

52 Ramet, *Social Currents in Eastern Europe*, pp. 223–5.

53 Csizmadia, *A Magyar Demokratikus Ellenzék*, pp. 333–8.

54 R.L. Tőkes, *Hungary's Negotiated Revolution: Economic Reform, Social Change and Political Succession* (Cambridge, 1996), pp. 272–95.

55 M. Pittaway, 'Hungary' in S. White, J. Batt and P.G. Lewis (eds.),

Developments in Central and East European Politics 3 (Basingstoke, 2003), p. 59.

[56] O'Neill, *Revolution from Within*, pp. 71–114.

[57] A. Bozóki, 'A kerekasztal-tárgyalások és a rendszerváltozás' in Bozóki (ed.), *A Rendszerváltás Forgatókönyve*, pp. 21–53.

[58] R. Thomas, *Serbia under Milošević: Politics in the 1990s* (London, 1999), pp. 36–42.

[59] Quoted in L.J. Cohen, ' "Serpent in the Bosom": Slobodan Milošević and Serbian Nationalism' in Bokovoy, Irvine and Lilly (eds.), *State–Society Relations in Yugoslavia*, p. 321.

[60] A. LeBor, *Milosevic: A Biography* (London, 2003), pp. 78–82.

[61] T. Mastnak, 'From Social Movements to National Sovereignty' in Benderly and Kraft (eds.), *Independent Slovenia*, pp. 93–111.

[62] Woodward, *Balkan Tragedy*, pp. 102–3.

[63] J.F. Brown, *Surge to Freedom: The End of Communist Rule in Eastern Europe* (Durham, NC, 1991), pp. 82–8.

[64] G. Sanford, 'The Polish Road to Democratisation: from Political Impasse to the "Controlled Abdication" of Communist Power' in G. Sanford (ed.), *Democratization in Poland, 1988–90: Polish Voices* (Basingstoke, 1992), pp. 1–21.

[65] M. Fulbrook, *Anatomy of a Dictatorship: Inside the GDR 1949–1989* (Oxford, 1995), pp. 241–65.

[66] Daskalov, 'A Democracy Born in Pain', pp. 9–10.

[67] Ramet, *Social Currents in Eastern Europe*, pp. 262–4.

[68] Wheaton and Kavan, *The Velvet Revolution*, p. 25.

[69] U.A. Gabanyi, 'Disgraced Romanian leader calls for changes' in Gabanyi, *The Ceauşescu Cult*, p. 260.

Chapter 9

[1] F. Fukuyama, *The End of History and the Last Man* (New York, 1992).

[2] M. Glenny, *The Rebirth of History: Eastern Europe in the Age of Democracy* (Harmondsworth, 1990).

[3] Woodward, *Balkan Tragedy*, p. 115.

[4] Mastnak, 'From Social Movements to National Sovereignty'.

[5] Tanner, *Croatia*, pp. 221–9.

[6] Lampe, *Yugoslavia as History*, p. 337.

[7] Tanner, *Croatia*, p. 230.

[8] Thomas, *Serbia under Milošević*, pp. 52–86.

[9] Quoted in T. Judah, *The Serbs: History, Myth & the Destruction of Yugoslavia* (New Haven, 1997), p. 175.

[10] D.M. Perry, 'The Republic of Macedonia: finding its way' in K. Dawisha and B. Parrott (eds.), *Politics, Power and the Struggle for Democracy in South-East Europe* (Cambridge, 1997), pp. 226–81.

[11] Lampe, *Yugoslavia as History*, p. 368.

[12] S.L. Burg, 'Bosnia Herzegovina: a case of failed democratization' in Dawisha and Parrott (eds.), *Politics, Power and the Struggle for Democracy in South-East Europe*, p. 127.

[13] N. Malcom, *Bosnia: A Short History* (London, 1996), p. 222.

[14] Thomas, *Serbia under Milošević*, pp. 163–209.

[15] Tanner, *Croatia*, p. 294.

[16] Malcom, *Bosnia*, p. 264.

[17] T. Gallagher, *Romania after Ceauşescu: The Politics of Intolerance* (Edinburgh, 1995), pp. 87–90.

[18] Wheaton and Kavan, *The Velvet Revolution*, p. 168.

[19] D.M. Olson, 'Democratization and political participation: the experience of the Czech Republic' in K. Dawisha and B. Parrott (eds.), *The Consolidation of Democracy in East-Central Europe* (Cambridge, 1997), p. 176.

[20] S.L. Wolchik, 'Democratization and political participation in Slovakia' in Dawisha and Parrott (eds.), *The Consolidation of Democracy in East-Central Europe*, p. 234.

[21] Tanner, *Croatia*, p. 298.

[22] I. Vejvoda, 'Democratic Despotism: Federal Republic of Yugoslavia and Croatia' in G. Pridham and T. Gallagher (eds.), *Experimenting with Democracy: Regime Change in the Balkans* (London, 2000), pp. 224–9.

[23] T. Gallagher, 'Nationalism and Romanian Political Culture in the 1990s' in D. Light and D. Phinnemore (eds.), *Post-Communist Romania: Coming to Terms with Transition* (Basingstoke, 2001), pp. 107–9.

[24] Gallagher, *Romania after Ceauşescu*, pp. 194–210.

[25] J.D. Bell, 'Democratization and political participation in "postcommunist Bulgaria"' in Dawisha and Parrott (eds.), *Politics, Power and the Struggle for Democracy in South-East Europe*, pp. 353–77.

[26] J. Pettifer, 'Albania: the democratic deficit in the post-communist period' in Pridham and Gallagher (eds.), *Experimenting with Democracy*, pp. 238–41.

27 B. Fowkes, *The Post-Communist Era: Change and Continuity in Eastern Europe* (Basingstoke, 1999), pp. 29–36.
28 V. Tismaneanu, 'Romanian exceptionalism? Democracy, ethnocracy and uncertain pluralism in post-Ceauşescu Romania' in Dawisha and Parrott (eds.), *Politics, Power and the Struggle for Democracy in South-East Europe*, p. 421.
29 Gallagher, *Romania after Ceauşescu*, pp. 99–143.
30 P. Siani-Davies, 'The Revolution after the Revolution' in Light and Phinnemore (eds.), *Post-Communist Romania*, pp. 15–34.
31 J. Borneman, *Settling Accounts: Violence, Justice and Accountability in Postsocialist Europe* (Princeton, NJ, 1997), pp. 152–3.
32 N. Swain, 'The Smallholders versus the Green Barons: Class Relations in the Restructuring of Hungarian Agriculture' (University of Liverpool, Centre for Central and East European Studies, Rural Transition Series, Working Paper no. 8, Liverpool, 1993).
33 Borneman, *Settling Accounts*, p. 153.
34 K. Verdery, *The Vanishing Hectare: Property and Value in Postsocialist Transylvania* (Ithaca, NY, 2003), pp. 84–93.
35 J. McDonald, 'Transition to Utopia: A Reinterpretation of Economics, Ideas, and Politics in Hungary', *East European Politics and Societies*, 7 (2), 1993, pp. 203–39.
36 M. Belka, 'Lessons from the Polish transition' in G. Blazyca and R. Rapacki (eds.), *Poland into the New Millennium* (Cheltenham, 2001), p. 14.
37 P. Gowan, 'Neo-Liberal Theory and Practice for Eastern Europe', *New Left Review*, 213, 1995, p. 18.
38 Tismaneanu, 'Romanian exceptionalism?', p. 425.
39 M.L. Wyzan, 'Bulgarian Economic Policy and Performance, 1991–1997' in Bell (ed.), *Bulgaria in Transition*, p. 97.
40 I. Csaba and A. Semjén, 'Welfare institutions and the transition: in search of efficiency and equity' in L. Halpern and C. Wyplosz (eds.), *Hungary: Towards a Market Economy* (Cambridge, 1998), p. 301.
41 K. Mizsei (ed.), *Privatizáció Kelet-Európában: Alternatívák, Érdekek, Törvények* (Budapest, 1991).
42 L. Árva and B. Dicházi, *Globalizáció és külföldi tőkeberuházások Magyarországon* (Budapest, 1998), pp. 97–121.

[43] G. Eyal, I. Szelényi and E. Townsley, *Making Capitalism Without Capitalists: The New Ruling Elites in Eastern Europe* (London, 1998).

[44] D.A. Kideckel, 'The unmaking of an East-Central European Working Class' in C.M. Hann (ed.), *Postsocialism: Ideals, Ideologies and Practices in Eurasia* (London, 2002), p. 124.

[45] M. Pittaway, 'Dealing with Dictatorship: Socialism and the Sites of Memory in Contemporary Hungary' in C. Emsley (ed.), *War, Culture and Memory* (Milton Keynes, 2003).

[46] J. Wrobel, 'Young, Westernized, Moderate: The Polish Left after Communism' in C. Bukowski and B. Racz (eds.), *The Return of the Left in Post-communist States: Current Trends and Future Prospects* (Cheltenham, 1999), pp. 98–9.

[47] Pittaway, 'Hungary', pp. 66–7.

[48] A. Andreev, 'The political changes and political parties' in Zloch-Christy (ed.), *Bulgaria in a Time of Change*, p. 33.

[49] Olson, 'Democratization and political participation: the experience of the Czech Republic'.

[50] Pittaway, 'Hungary', p. 68.

[51] Wyzan, 'Bulgarian Economic Policy and Performance, 1991–1997', pp. 110–11.

[52] Pittaway, 'Hungary', pp. 69–71.

[53] F. Millard, 'Poland' in White, Batt and Lewis (eds.), *Developments in Central and East European Politics 3*, pp. 31–3.

[54] Wyzan, 'Bulgarian Economic Policy and Performance, 1991–1997', p. 113.

[55] M. Vickers and J. Pettifer, *Albania: From Anarchy to Balkan Identity* (London, 1997), pp. 227–46.

Suggestions for further reading

The list given below is far from a comprehensive bibliography. It is instead a selection of some of the most important studies published in the field, and is representative of both the strengths and weaknesses of the literature that is currently available. I have restricted myself to listing only English-language sources.

GENERAL

General regional surveys

Berend, I.T., *Central and Eastern Europe 1944–1993: Detour from the Periphery to the Periphery* (Cambridge, 1996).

Crampton, R.J., *Eastern Europe in the Twentieth Century and After* (London, 1997), 2nd edition.

Fejtö, F., *A History of the People's Democracies: Eastern Europe since Stalin*, trans. D. Weissbort (Harmondsworth, 1974).

Stokes, G. (ed.), *From Stalinism to Pluralism: A Documentary History of Eastern Europe since 1945* (New York, 1991).

Swain, G. and Swain, N., *Eastern Europe since 1945* (Basingstoke, 2003), 3rd edition.

Country surveys

Crampton, R.J., *A Short History of Modern Bulgaria* (Cambridge, 1987).

Deletant, D., *Ceauşescu and the Securitate: Coercion and Dissent in Romania, 1965–1989* (London, 1995).

Deletant, D., *Communist Terror in Romania: Gheorghiu-Dej and the Police State 1948–1965* (London, 1999).

Dowling, M., *Czechoslovakia* (London, 2002).

Lampe, J.R., *Yugoslavia as History: Twice There Was A Country* (Cambridge, 1996).

Paczkowski, A., *The Spring Will Be Ours: Poland and the Poles from Occupation to Freedom*, trans. J. Cave (University Park, PA, 2003).

Romsics, I., *Hungary in the Twentieth Century*, trans. T. Wilkinson (Budapest, 2000).

Swain, N., *Hungary: the Rise and Fall of Feasible Socialism* (London, 1992).

Vickers, M., *The Albanians: A Modern History* (London, 1999).

INTRODUCTION: THE OTHER EUROPE

Berend, I.T., *Decades of Crisis: Central and Eastern Europe before World War II* (Berkeley, CA, 1998).

Davies, N., *Europe: A History* (London, 1997).

Glenny, M., *The Balkans, 1804–1999. Nationalism, War and the Great Powers* (London, 1999).

Johnson, L.R., *Central Europe: Enemies, Neighbors, Friends* (New York, 2001), 2nd edition.

Mazower, M., *The Balkans* (London, 2000).

Neumann, I.B., *Uses of the Other: The East in European Identity Formation* (Manchester, 1999).

Okey, R., *Eastern Europe 1740–1985: Feudalism to Communism* (London, 1986), 2nd edition.

Todorova, M., *Imagining the Balkans* (New York, 1997).

Ugrešič, D., *The Culture of Lies: Antipolitical Essays*, trans. C. Hawkesworth (London, 1998).

Woolf, L., *Inventing Eastern Europe: The Map of Civilization on the Mind of the Enlightenment* (Stanford, CA, 1994).

CHAPTER 1: CRISIS, WAR AND OCCUPATION

Abrams, B.F., 'The Second World War and the East European Revolution', *East European Politics and Societies*, 16 (3), 2002.

Aly, G., *Final Solution: Nazi Population Policy and the Murder of the European Jews*, trans. B. Cooper and A. Brown (London, 1999).

Aly, G. and Heim, S. *Architects of Annihilation: Auschwitz and the Logic of Destruction*, trans. A.G. Blunden (London, 2002).

Banac, I. (ed.), *The Effects of World War I: The Class War after the Great War: The Rise of Communist Parties in East Central Europe, 1918–1921* (Boulder, CO, 1983).

Braham, R.L., *The Politics of Genocide: The Holocaust in Hungary* (Detroit, 2000).

Bryant, C., 'Either Czech or German: Fixing Nationality in Bohemia and Moravia, 1939–1946', *Slavic Review*, 61 (4), 2002.

Cesarani, D. (ed.), *Genocide and Rescue: The Holocaust in Hungary 1944* (Oxford, 1997).

Connelly, J., 'Nazis and Slavs: From Racial Theory to Racist Practice', *Central European History*, 32 (1), 1999.

Djilas, A., *The Contested Country: Yugoslav Unity and Communist Revolution 1919–1953* (Cambridge, MA, 1991).

Dreisziger, N. (ed.), *Hungary in the Age of Total War (1938–1948)* (Boulder, CO, 1998).

Eby, C.B., *Hungary at War: Citizens and Soldiers in World War II* (University Park, PA, 1998).

Gross, J.T., *Polish Society under German Occupation: The Generalgovernement, 1939–1944* (Princeton, NJ, 1979).

Gross, J.T., *Revolution from Abroad: The Soviet Conquest of Poland's Western Ukraine and Western Belorussia* (Princeton, NJ, 1988).

Jelinek, Y., *The Parish Republic: Hlinka's Slovak People's Party 1939–1945* (Boulder, CO, 1976).

Kaiser, D.E., *Economic Diplomacy and the Origins of the Second World War: Germany, Britain, France and Eastern Europe, 1930–1939* (Princeton, NJ, 1980).

Király, B.K. and Dreisziger, N.F. (eds.), *East Central European Society in World War I* (Boulder, CO, 1985).

Larsen, S.U., Hagtvet, B. and Myklebust, J.P. (eds.), *Who Were the Fascists? Social Roots of European Fascism* (Bergen, 1980).

Livezeanu, I., *Cultural Politics in Greater Romania: Regionalism, Nation Building and Ethnic Struggle* (Ithaca, NY, 1995).

Mastny, V., *The Czechs under Nazi Rule: The Failure of National Resistance, 1939–1942* (New York, 1971).

Naimark, N., *Fires of Hatred: Ethnic Cleansing in Twentieth-Century Europe* (Cambridge, MA, 2001).

Tanner, M., *Croatia: A Nation Forged in War* (New Haven, 1997).

Tismaneanu, V. and Pavel, D., 'Romania's Mystical Revolutionaries: The Generation of Angst and Adventure Revisited, *East European Politics and Societies*, 8 (3), 1994.

CHAPTER 2: BUILDING SOCIALISM

Abrams, B., 'The Politics of Retribution: The Trial of Jozef Tiso', *East European Politics and Societies*, 10 (2), 1996.

Bloomfield, J., *Passive Revolution: Politics and the Czechoslovak Working Class, 1945–1948* (London, 1979).

Blumi, I., 'The Politics of Culture and Power: the Roots of Hoxha's Postwar State', *East European Quarterly*, 31 (3), 1997.

Bokovoy, M.K., *Peasants and Communists: Politics and Ideology in the Yugoslav Countryside 1941–1953* (Pittsburgh, PA, 1998).

Connelly, J., *Captive University: The Sovietization of East German, Czech and Polish Higher Education, 1945–1956* (Chapel Hill, NC, 2000).

Coutovidis, J. and Reynolds, J., *Poland 1939–1947* (Leicester, 1986).

Deák, I., Gross, J.T. and Judt, T. (eds.), *The Politics of Retribution in Europe: World War II and its Aftermath* (Princeton, NJ, 2000).

Gati, C., *Hungary and the Soviet Bloc* (Durham, NC, 1986).

Hodos, G.H., *Show Trials: Stalinist Purges in Eastern Europe, 1948–1954* (New York, 1987).

Kemp-Welch, A. (ed.), *Stalinism in Poland, 1944–1956: Selected Papers from the Fifth World Congress of Central and Eastern European Studies, Warsaw, 1995* (Basingstoke, 1999).

Kenney, P., *Rebuilding Poland: Workers and Communists, 1945–1950* (Ithaca, NY, 1997).

Lilly, C.S., *Power and Persuasion: Ideology and Rhetoric in Communist Yugoslavia 1944–1953* (Boulder, CO, 2001).

Myant, M., *Socialism and Democracy in Czechoslovakia 1945–1948* (Cambridge, 1981).

Naimark, N. and Gibianski, L. (eds.), *The Establishment of Communist Regimes in Eastern Europe* (Boulder, CO, 1997).

Pelikán, J. (ed.), *The Czechoslovak Political Trials, 1950–1954: The Suppressed Report of the Dubček Government's Commission of Inquiry, 1968* (London, 1971).

Pittaway, M., 'The Social Limits of State Control: Time, the Industrial Wage Relation and Social Identity in Stalinist Hungary, 1948–1953, *Journal of Historical Sociology*, 12 (3), 1999.

Ther, P. and Siljak, A. (eds.), *Redrawing Nations: Ethnic Cleansing in East Central Europe, 1944–1949* (Lanham, 2001).

CHAPTER 3: CONSOLIDATING SOCIALISM

Denitch, B.D., *The Legitimation of a Revolution: the Yugoslav Case* (New Haven, 1976).

Granville, J., 'From the Archives of Warsaw and Budapest: A Comparison of the Events of 1956', *East European Politics and Societies*, 16 (2), 2002.

Lane, D. and Kolankiewicz, G. (eds.), *Social Groups in Polish Society* (London, 1973).

Lees, L.M., *Keeping Tito Afloat: the United States, Yugoslavia and the Cold War* (University Park, PA, 1997).

Litván, G. et al., *The Hungarian Revolution of 1956: Reform, Revolt and Repression 1953–1963* (Harlow, 1996).

Lomax, B., *Hungary 1956* (London, 1976).

Myant, M., *The Czechoslovak Economy: The Battle for Economic Reform* (Cambridge, 1988).

Péteri, G. (ed.), *Intellectual Life and the First Crisis of State Socialism in East Central Europe* (Trondheim, 2001).

Shawcross, W., *Dubcek: Dubcek and Czechoslovakia 1918–1990* (London, 1990).

Skilling, H.G., *Czechoslovakia's Interrupted Revolution* (Princeton, NJ, 1976).

Suri, J., *Power and Protest: Global Revolution and the Rise of Détente* (Cambridge, MA, 2003).

Verdery, K., *National Ideology under Socialism: Identity and Cultural Politics in Ceauşescu's Romania* (Berkeley, 1991).

Verona, S., *Military Occupation and Diplomacy: Soviet Troops in Romania, 1944–1958* (Duke, NC, 1992).

Williams, K., *The Prague Spring and its Aftermath: Czechoslovak Politics 1968–1970* (Cambridge, 1997).

Woodward, S.L., *Socialist Unemployment: The Political Economy of Yugoslavia, 1945–1991* (Princeton, NJ, 1995).

CHAPTER 4: A SOCIETY BASED ON PRODUCTIVE LABOUR

Burawoy, M. and Lukács, J., *The Radiant Past: Ideology and Reality in Hungary's Road to Capitalism* (Chicago, 1992).

Cartwright, A.L., *The Return of the Peasant: Land Reform in Post-Communist Romania* (London, 2001).

Creed, G.W., *Domesticating Revolution: From Socialist Reform to Ambivalent Transition in a Bulgarian Village* (University Park, PA, 1998).

Kideckel, D.A., 'The Social Organization of Production on a Romanian Cooperative Farm', *Dialectical Anthropology*, 1 (2), 1976.

Kideckel, D.A., *The Solitude of Collectivism: Romanian Villagers to the Revolution and Beyond* (Ithaca, NY, 1993).

Kürti, L., ' "Red Csepel": Working Youth in a Socialist Firm', *East European Quarterly*, 23 (4), 1990.

Lampland, M., 'Unthinkable Subjects: Women and Labor in Socialist Hungary', *East European Quarterly*, 23 (4), 1990.

Lampland, M., *The Object of Labor: Commodification in Socialist Hungary* (Chicago, 1995).

Lebow, K.A., 'Public works, private lives: youth brigades in Nowa Huta in the 1950s', *Contemporary European History*, 10 (2), 2001.

Pittaway, M., 'The Reproduction of Hierarchy: Skill, Working-Class Culture and the State in Early Socialist Hungary', *The Journal of Modern History*, 74 (4), 2002.

Svašek, M., 'Contacts: Social Dynamics in the Czechoslovak State-Socialist Art World', *Contemporary European History*, 11 (1), 2002.

Swain, N., *Collective Farms Which Work?* (Cambridge, 1985).

Swain, N., 'A framework for comparing social change in the post-socialist countryside', *East European Countryside*, 4, 1998.

Triska, J.F. and Gati, C. (eds.), *Blue Collar Workers in Eastern Europe* (London, 1981).

CHAPTER 5: REMAKING THE PRIVATE SPHERE

Crowley, D. and Reid, S.E. (eds.), *Socialist Spaces: Sites of Everyday Life in the Eastern Bloc* (Oxford, 2002).

Einhorn, B., *Cinderella Goes to Market: Citizenship, Gender and Women's Movements in East Central Europe* (London, 1993).

Funk, N. and Mueller, M. (eds.), *Gender Politics and Post-Communism: Reflections from Eastern Europe and the Former Soviet Union* (London, 1993).

Haney, L., *Inventing the Needy: Gender and the Politics of Welfare in Hungary* (Berkeley, CA, 2002).

Heitlinger, A., *Women and State Socialism: Sex Inequality in the Soviet Union and Czechoslovakia* (London, 1979).

Kenney, P., 'The Gender of Resistance in Communist Poland', *American Historical Review*, 104 (2), 1999.

Kligman, G., *The Politics of Duplicity: Controlling Reproduction in Ceausescu's Romania* (Berkeley, CA, 1998).

Lockwood, W.G., 'Social Status and Cultural Change in a Bosnian Moslem Village', *East European Quarterly*, 9 (2), 1975.

Olujić, M.B., 'Economic and Demographic Change in Contemporary Yugoslavia: Persistence of Traditional Gender Ideology', *East European Quarterly*, 23 (4), 1990.

Reid, S.E. and Crowley, D. (eds.), *Style and Socialism: Modernity and Material Culture in Postwar Eastern Europe* (Oxford, 2000).

Ryback, T.W., *Rock Around the Bloc: A History of Rock Music in Eastern Europe and the Soviet Union* (New York, 1990).

Sampson, S., 'The Informal Sector in Eastern Europe', *Telos*, 66, 1986.

Wedel, J., *The Private Poland* (New York, 1986).

Wolchik, S.L. and Meyer, A.G. (eds.), *Women, State and Party in Eastern Europe* (Durham, NC, 1985).

CHAPTER 6: THE SOCIALIST PUBLIC SPHERE AND ITS LIMITS

Bugajszki, J. and Pollack, M., *East European Fault Lines: Dissent, Opposition, and Social Activism* (Boulder, CO, 1989).

Jancar, B.W., *Czechoslovakia and the Absolute Monopoly of Power: A Study of Political Power in a Communist System* (New York, 1971).

Kubik, J., *The Power of Symbols against the Symbols of Power: The Rise of Solidarity and the Fall of Socialism in Poland* (University Park, PA, 1994).

Kürti, L., *Youth and the State in Hungary: Capitalism, Communism and Class* (London, 2002).

Lovas, I. and Anderson, K., 'State Terrorism in Hungary: the Case of Friendly Repression', *Telos*, 54, 1982–3.

Michel, P., *Politics and Religion in Eastern Europe: Catholicism in Hungary, Poland and Czechoslovakia*, trans. A. Braley (Cambridge, 1991).

Pravda, A. and Ruble, B.A. (eds.), *Trade Unions in Communist States* (Boston, 1986).

Schwandner Sievers, S. and Fischer, B.J. (eds.), *Albanian Identities: Myth and History* (London, 2002).

Shapiro, J.P. and Potichnyi, P.J. (eds.), *Change and Adaptation in Soviet and East European Politics* (New York, 1976).
Sugar, P.F., *East European Nationalisms, Politics and Religion* (Aldershot, 1999).
Toma, P.A., 'The Czechoslovak Question under Communism', *East European Quarterly*, 3 (1), 1969.

CHAPTER 7: SOCIALISM IN DECAY

Bielasiak, J. and Simon, M.D. (eds.), *Polish Politics: Edge of the Abyss* (New York, 1984).
Gabanyi, A.U., *The Ceauşescu Cult: Propaganda and Power Policy in Communist Romania* (Bucharest, 2000).
Garton Ash, T., *The Polish Revolution: Solidarity* (London, 1983).
Keane, J., *Václav Havel: A Political Tragedy in Six Acts* (London, 2000).
Laba, R., *The Roots of Solidarity: A Political Sociology of Poland's Working-Class Democratization* (Princeton, NJ, 1991).
Lepak, K.J., *Prelude to Solidarity: Poland and the Politics of the Gierek Regime* (New York, 1988).
Myant, M., *Poland: A Crisis for Socialism* (London, 1982).
Simečka, M., *The Restoration of Order: The Normalization of Czechoslovakia 1969–1979*, trans. A.G. Brain (London, 1984).
Staniszkis, J., *Poland's Self-Limiting Revolution*, ed. J.T. Gross (Princeton, NJ, 1984).
Stevens, J.N., *Czechoslovakia at the Crossroads: The Economic Dilemmas of Communism in Postwar Czechoslovakia* (Boulder, CO, 1985).
Vale, M. (ed.), *Poland – the State of the Republic: Reports by the Experience and Future Discussion Group (DiP) Warsaw* (London, 1981).
Vladislav, J. (ed.), *Václav Havel: Living in Truth* (London, 1986).

CHAPTER 8: THE COLLAPSE

Garton Ash, T., *The Uses of Adversity: Essays on the Fate of Central Europe* (London, 1991), 2nd edition.
Keane, J. (ed.), *Civil Society and the State: New European Perspectives* (London, 1988).
Kenney, P., *Carnival: Central Europe, 1989* (Princeton, NJ, 2002).

Magaš, B., *The Destruction of Yugoslavia: Tracking the Break-up 1980–92* (London, 1993).

O'Neill, P.H., *Revolution from Within: the Hungarian Socialist Workers' Party and the Collapse of Communism* (Cheltenham, 1998).

Ramet, S.P., *Social Currents in Eastern Europe: the Sources and Meaning of the Great Transformation* (Durham, 1991).

Sanford, G., *Military Rule in Poland: The Rebuilding of Communist Power, 1981–1983* (London, 1986).

Sanford, G. (ed.), *Democratization in Poland, 1988–90: Polish Voices* (Basingstoke, 1992).

Tismaneanu, V. (ed.), *The Revolutions of 1989* (London, 1999).

Tőkes, R.L., *Hungary's Negotiated Revolution: Economic Reform, Social Change and Political Succession* (Cambridge, 1996).

Wheaton, B. and Kavan, Z., *The Velvet Revolution: Czechoslovakia, 1988–1991* (Boulder, CO, 1992).

Woodward, S.L., *Balkan Tragedy: Chaos and Disillusion after the Cold War* (Washington DC, 1995).

CHAPTER 9: AFTER SOCIALISM

Bell, J.D. (ed.), *Bulgaria in Transition: Politics, Economics and Culture After Communism* (Boulder CO, 1998).

Blazyca, G. and Rapacki, R. (eds.), *Poland into the New Millennium* (Cheltenham, 2001).

Bukowski, C. and Racz, B. (eds.), *The Return of the Left in Post-communist States: Current Trends and Future Prospects* (Cheltenham, 1999).

Dawisha, K. and Parrott, B. (eds.), *The Consolidation of Democracy in East-Central Europe* (Cambridge, 1997).

Dawisha, K. and Parrott, B. (eds.), *Politics, Power and the Struggle for Democracy in South-East Europe* (Cambridge, 1997).

Eyal, G., Szelényi, I. and Townsley, E., *Making Capitalism Without Capitalists: The New Ruling Elites in Eastern Europe* (London, 1998).

Gallagher, T., *Romania after Ceauşescu: The Politics of Intolerance* (Edinburgh, 1995).

Halpern, L. and Wyplosz, C. (eds.), *Hungary: Towards a Market Economy* (Cambridge, 1998).

Hann, C.M. (ed.), *Postsocialism: Ideals, Ideologies and Practices in Eurasia* (London, 2002).

Judah, T., *The Serbs: History, Myth & the Destruction of Yugoslavia* (New Haven, 1997).

Light, D. and Phinnemore, D. (eds.), *Post-Communist Romania: Coming to Terms with Transition* (Basingstoke, 2001).

Thomas, R., *Serbia under Milošević: Politics in the 1990s* (London, 1999).

Verdery, K., *What Was Socialism and What Comes Next?* (Princeton, NJ, 1996).

Verdery, K., *The Vanishing Hectare: Property and Value in Postsocialist Transylvania* (Ithaca, NY, 2003).

Vickers, M. and Pettifer, J., *Albania: From Anarchy to Balkan Identity* (London, 1997).

Index

WITHDRAWN